KNOCKOUT

KNOCKOUT

—

MIA KANG

ABRAMS PRESS, NEW YORK

Library of Congress Control Number: 2020932370

ISBN: 978-1-4197-4332-0
eISBN: 978-1-64700-016-5

Printed and bound in the United States
10 9 8 7 6 5 4 3 2 1

Disclaimer: This is a work of nonfiction. The events and experiences detailed herein are all true and have been faithfully rendered as the author remembers them to the best of her ability. Some names and identities have been changed to protect the privacy of those individuals. All dialogue is as close to an approximation as possible to actual conversations that took place, to the best of the author's recollection.

ABRAMS The Art of Books
195 Broadway, New York, NY 10007
abramsbooks.com

CONTENTS

PROLOGUE

—

Here we go again, I thought.

When my agent, Deborah, called me one morning in 2016 to let me know that the lifestyle brand Guess was asking me to return for their next campaign, at first I was ecstatic. My career was at an all-time high and I had worked all over the world, but I was just breaking into the American market. And America was tough, man. We're talking the highest level of competition I had seen in my fifteen years as a model. I had shot for *Sports Illustrated*'s swimsuit model search a few months earlier, and this was another amazing opportunity. There was one caveat: I needed to lose weight.

"Whatever you did for *SI*, you need to do it again, because they don't think you're in your best shape right now," she said, hesitantly. She knew how bad that sounded.

To shrink down as much as I possibly could for *SI*, I had put myself through a ten-day liquid-only diet. Ten days. All liquids. Absolutely no solid food. It was extreme, and I hated every minute of it. But in my world, that was normal. I had been asked to starve and lose weight more times than I could remember, but this campaign had much more pressure attached to it. I was also twenty-seven years old, which for the modeling world was past my expiration date. This time, thinking about putting my body on an intense starvation regimen made my stomach drop with apprehension.

What's the worst part of starving yourself? Take your pick: Hunger that's so intense you can't sleep at night? The chain-smoking to curb your appetite and keep your hands and mouth busy? The anxiety that consumes you as you live in fear of being fired and sent home from the shoot for being too large? The paranoia that everyone on set is talking about you? The embarrassment and insecurity that plagues you when clients criticize your body, telling you that you are too big? The whirlwind of emotions you have when you don't fit into the sample-size clothes laid out in your dressing room? The stress that comes after the job is done, wondering if you're ever going to work with that client—or anyone—again? The body dysmorphia when you look at images of yourself and see a whale, even though you are far from it? The worry that you will never be thin enough, and your modeling agency will send you packing? It's a relentless cycle of anxiety and crippling self-doubt.

So that fleeting feeling of happiness from booking a campaign was quickly overshadowed by the immense pressure of what was to come in preparing for it. I know it sounds crazy—after all, this was a huge worldwide campaign for an iconic American brand. I should have been grateful, right? Yet more and more, I had been feeling that all the crazy shit I put myself through to be as skinny as possible was just not worth it. But I didn't know what else to do. I hadn't yet gained the personal strength and the self-respect that I would later learn from Muay Thai. At this point, I was still fighting with myself rather than someone in a ring.

I could feel the tears well up.

My body was literally saying, *Fuck, I can't do this again*, and I started bawling on the phone.

I didn't say anything as I tried to catch my breath and stop crying. Deborah finally broke the silence. I think she was taken aback by my reaction, and the mother in her kicked in. "I'm so sorry. I hate delivering news like this. You know I think of you like a daughter. . . ." A moment later, she added, "I hate this part of my job." She started crying, too, and soon we were both sniffling into our phones.

"I'll do it. I'll do it. I've had enough, but I'll do it," I said. And then I added, "But, after this, I am done."

It was true. I couldn't do it anymore. The pressure to look "my best" (i.e., as skinny as possible) had worn me down, and after modeling for more than half of my life, the extreme dieting was taking its toll on my physical and mental health. I was unhealthily thin already, but in the warped world I lived in, I didn't know that my weight was abnormal or that the stress I was putting on myself was dangerous. I only knew that I was miserable.

Whatever I did, it never seemed to be enough. I was never pretty enough, never thin enough, never good enough.

And here I was again, being asked to take another hit to the body.

I dropped the weight and got through the shoot, but I needed to get away. I needed to escape the pressure cooker I was in, or . . . I didn't know what I'd do. On the outside, I had a modeling career that other models would kill for. But on the inside, I was living with crippling anxiety and depression.

So I went to Thailand for a ten-day vacation, which was about as far away as I could get from the crazy merry-go-round of the fashion world. Little did I know that my whole life was about to change, and I certainly didn't know that it would happen in the sweaty ring of a remote Muay Thai gym.

1. YOU ARE NOT YOUR PAST

———

I NEVER ASPIRED TO BE A MODEL. Growing up in Hong Kong in the nineties, I never thought I would grace the pages of *Vogue* or walk the catwalks in the clothes of coveted designers. Because back then I was overweight. Back then, my biggest aspiration was to get through a school day without being bullied, teased, and ridiculed for my weight. Every day, for years.

Those years took place on a beautifully manicured enclave of Discovery Bay, about a twenty- to thirty-minute ferry ride from downtown Hong Kong, also known as Central. The road systems in Discovery Bay were such that cars were not permitted, and everyone rode around in golf carts. My street, Seabee Lane, ran along the western edge of the bay. My house was built into the hillside. It was three stories: On the top floor were the dining room and kitchen; downstairs opened to a large living room with a balcony that had a gorgeous view overlooking the beach and an inlet. Down another flight of stairs were our bedrooms.

My family was sort of an Asian version of *Modern Family*—my British dad had had two sons, Malcolm and Alistair, from a previous marriage to a Taiwanese woman named Morty. My mum, who is South Korean, had two daughters, Anouk and Gaby, with her previous husband. Before I was born, both families had been living in

Taiwan when their respective relationships ended. Fate would bring my parents together on the sidelines of the Taipei American School soccer field where Gaby and Malcolm played soccer together. They fell in love, and my siblings were soon informed that they were to be brothers and sisters, and the newly formed family of six moved to Hong Kong, where I was born in 1988. My oldest sister, Anouk, is ten years older than me, then Malcolm and Gaby, both seven years older, then Alistair, three years older. My brothers weren't around much, because they lived with their mum most of the time, but when we were together, we looked like a mixed bag of Asian and Caucasian lineage. A modern family in the truest form.

The gang playing dress-up at home. Left to right: Gaby, Alistair, me (in the pram), Malcolm, and Anouk. Hong Kong, 1989.

My dad—or, as I affectionately call him, Daddy or Padre—is of a different generation. He was born in the UK in 1944, where parenting was more strict, and he'd often talk about teachers who disciplined students with "the boot" or the cane. He wasn't that tough, but he was certainly stern with us, and he didn't try to act like a friend, as some fathers do; he was very much an authority figure, and he had absolutely no time or tolerance for bullshit (and he still doesn't). Growing up, I idolized him, and I still do. I know I'm biased, but he's the smartest and most impressive man I've ever come across. Tall, athletic, and handsome, he is also brilliant—he has a PhD, went to Oxford University, and studied theoretical physics. He's written books and contributed to the field, but he left academia behind (he taught at UCLA earlier in his career) and started his own freight-forwarding company, which, as CEO, he eventually took public. He is also worldly—he loves to go to new places and do new things, and he was certainly able do that with his company. My family got to benefit from his travel bug: He took us on great

My dad's graduation photo from Oxford University. Oxford, England, 1969.

Daddy in the Kalahari desert, Namibia, early 1990s.

adventures like white-water rafting in the Philippines, fishing in the Great Barrier Reef, sailing through the Windward Islands, going on safari in Botswana, and skiing in St. Moritz. He raised us to become citizens of the world, with a wanderlust to go everywhere. Every school vacation was spent trekking to some exciting locale and experiencing different cultures.

He traveled a lot for work, though, and the more successful his company became, the more he was on the road. When he *was* home, we all vied for his attention. If he was home for the weekend, my brothers would come and visit and we'd have a rare family night, usually with spaghetti on the menu. We'd sit at our huge, round marble dining table, and he'd ask about what we were learning in school. Needless to say, it was (and still is) hard to impress him. With an IQ that qualifies for Mensa, he'd always tell us that if we worked hard and used our brains, we could create opportunities that

Malcolm, Alistair, Daddy, and me. Namibia, Africa, early 1990s.

would help us succeed in life. To keep us on our toes, he'd quiz us with all kinds of brain teasers, each one more perplexing than the last. Like this one: "There are three light switches downstairs, and one light bulb upstairs. How can you figure out which light switch controls the light bulb by making only one trip upstairs?"

All of us would inevitably scan around the table with quizzical looks on our faces, trying to figure it out. I can honestly tell you that I never seemed to be able to beat my siblings to the answers, but I chalk that up to the fact that, at age four, I was too young to keep up.

Where I did shine (at least I'd like to *think* that I shined) was during family "joke time." My dad has an amazing sense of humor—it's that bone-dry British humor made famous by comedies like *Monty Python's Flying Circus*, *Black Adder*, and *Fawlty Towers*. Having a sharp wit, a talent for bantering back and forth, and the ability to laugh at life and at yourself—all very British traits—was really important to him. Since the puzzles weren't my strong suit, I'd tell jokes to see if I could get him to laugh. But at my age, they made absolutely no sense. I didn't actually *know* any jokes, so I made them up! I also found them so hilarious that I could barely get them out without collapsing in a fit of laughter.

My mum would laugh at my jokes, though. Stunning and intelligent like my dad, she worked off and on as an interpreter for the government and global companies. She was athletic, perpetually tanned, and proud of her naturally dark, curly hair (which is *rare* for an Asian woman). Tall and lean, she had model posture that added to her natural elegance. Her perfume of choice was Chanel No. 5, and she wore little makeup—she didn't need it—other than Chanel lipstick for a pop of color on her lips. Always dressed in an understated style, she never left home without her two staple pieces of jewelry: a gold Rolex that hung off her tiny left wrist, and a shimmering gold Cartier love bracelet on the right. I would often adoringly watch her get ready for a night out, taking mental notes for when I grew up.

While she had a classic and timeless look, my mum was a rebel at heart. She had grown up in South Korea, a country steeped in long-standing cultural restrictions and expectations. Arranged marriages had still been common, and her ticket out of one was becoming a stewardess for Northwest Airlines. She also studied English literature at university and became the first person from the Korean side of my family to live outside of Korea. She was opinionated and hot-blooded (as many of us Korean women are). She was never afraid to let you know when she was mad. On those occasions

My drop-dead-gorgeous mother and me on the
beach. Boracay, Philippines, 1989.

when my mum would lose it, I blamed myself. I believed I was a bad
kid. I thought I was the root of the problem. I didn't yet understand
that her upbringing left her struggling with a lot with demons, and
because of that, she found it hard to parent at times.

With time I've come to the realization that my mum had a lot
of issues she never addressed, so she took them out on us. I don't
know a lot of the details, but I wish she had shared them with me.

She is an amazing woman, but she had a tough childhood. As a
kid, I didn't fully grasp the concept (does anyone?) of a parent being
a person—having goals, dreams, regrets—outside of being a mum.
In Asian culture in particular, feelings or issues are swept under
the enormous proverbial rug. My mum ran away from Korea and
whatever she dealt with in her own childhood at a young age; while

she found herself a great life and family, it didn't help that she had kids, in my opinion, before she was ready. She was pregnant with my oldest sister when she was twenty-one. I think she resented us a little because she stayed in her various relationships not because she wanted to, but because of her children. There were a whole bunch of issues she tried to escape by drinking. Some people just feel like their stability or happiness depends on an external source—whether it's religion, a man, or a liquor bottle.

When she was being a mother, meaning that she wasn't drinking, she was the best. I loved the times she worked, because when she was interpreting for a conference or symposium, she would stay sober before the gig to prepare. When she was drinking, it was bad. It was like living with Dr. Jekyll and Mr. Hyde.

When I was around three or four, Anouk and Gaby would sometimes put me in my bitchin' red-and-white checkered stroller and take me to "the plaza," a cluster of shops, restaurants, and a couple of supermarkets on the other side of our little bay. For teenagers looking to waste some time, it was the only place to be. I was too young to remember much of it, except for sitting with them and their friends. There were boys and cigarettes—you know, typical teenagers hanging out. Only later did I realize that these walks were a ruse to get us out of the house when Mum was drinking. My sisters didn't want to be around her when she was in an angry or irrational alcohol-fueled mood. It was best to get out of her sight, so our options were either the plaza or behind the closed door of one of our bedrooms, where they'd distract me with games.

My mum often wanted us out of the house, too, not wanting the responsibility of parenting for a few hours while she drank. She liked to send us off to McDonald's for dinner. A brand-spanking-new location had just opened up in Discovery Bay—and I know that's hard to imagine with one on every block in the United States, but at the time, it was a *big deal*. She would give us three HK$20 notes, which could buy any combo meal with plenty of change to spare. My sisters would sit me in my stroller and we would walk down to the plaza. Usually, by the time we came back, Mum would be too drunk and preoccupied to notice us stealthily sliding right into bed.

On a few occasions, we weren't so fortunate. After one McDonald's trip, my sisters and I had come home, full from nuggets and fries, to our mother standing by the door, seething and swaying. As we walked into the house and I jumped out of my stroller, Mum started in on us.

"How dare you take money out of my wallet without asking!" she yelled, totally slurring her words. She was accusing us of stealing the money she had given us. Confused, Anouk spoke up: "But, Mom, you gave us that money. . . ."

She wasn't even hearing us. She warned, "All of you are so bad. I'm going to have you sent away to boarding school! They can deal with you, I've had enough."

We knew better than to anger her any further, so we stopped challenging her; we knew this issue wouldn't exist anymore come morning, when the fog of her drinking had cleared. Whether she blacked out from the drinking, or she just simply chose to ignore what she remembered the next day, her tantrums were never spoken about after those grim nights. There were never apologies nor any accountability for her behavior.

On another night in the thick of summer, the swirling red lights of a fire truck parked outside our house greeted us as we turned onto our street on our way back from the plaza.

"Hello?" Anouk carefully called out as we walked through our open front door. We were greeted by two firemen, who had responded to a call. My mum had started a small kitchen fire while drunkenly making instant noodles on the stove. By the time the firefighters showed up, she was passed out on the couch. We knew not to mention anything about the previous night's drama the next day.

Drinking, memory loss, abusive behavior—these weren't isolated incidents. My sisters were verbally abused, picked apart, and name-called, but they learned how to navigate our mother when she was drinking and protected me when they could. But there were times they couldn't, and so I got my share, too. There were a few times when my mum called me into the dining room and demanded that I stand on a chair as she smacked me on my bum with an old-school wooden carpet-beater stick. Often, I could never figure out why. When my mum didn't want to deal with me at all, she would make me go to the study. There I'd stay for hours. Usually, after crying myself to sleep on the couch, I would wake hours later and quietly sneak back downstairs to my bedroom.

Did I think this was bizarre behavior? At the time I didn't know any different. Your parents are your parents. You love them unconditionally. As I got older, I became more aware of the situation and I'd do whatever I could to try to stop her from drinking. At times I'd flat out ask my mum to choose between drinking and me. I'd pour her beers out into the sink, trying to reason with her, but I'd end up in tears, realizing it was all useless. When she wanted to drink, nothing—and no one—could stop her. Her alcohol use would ebb and flow throughout my childhood, and in turn, so did my relationship with my mum. On and off. Everything was dependent on her emotional state. When it was good it was good, and when she was sober, she had the capability of being a fantastic mother. Over the years, though, the emotional wounds inflicted by my mum became harder and harder to heal, mostly because of her lack of remorse or accountability. And because of this, our relationship would fracture as I grew older.

But I was still very young at this point, and for all the upset she brought, she was a constant in my young life. I was very attached to my mum as a child, especially since my dad was away so much (and when he wasn't out of town, he was out often, entertaining clients). I resented him for it at the time. I was a child and had no concept of work or how to provide for a family. He seemed unfamiliar to me; I felt like I never saw him, and the generational gap between us was big. When he'd come home from a business trip, he'd always make an effort and bring me a souvenir. My mum would tell me in Korean to "go give your dad a kiss."

"No, later," I'd reply, in Korean. It's like we had our own secret language; it made me feel really close to her.

I was resentful of him for leaving us alone, angry when he came back, and scared of him because he was unfamiliar to me after being away for so long. It was hard to have a connection with my dad when he was gone so often. With my mum, she was there all the time, in good and in bad. I would often sit with her, doodling or opening peanuts for her, keeping her company as she sat at the dining table drinking, always in the same seat. I loved drawing—it gave me a sense of calm and control no matter how chaotic things were, and it allowed me to fully retreat into my emotions and imagination.

One night—I must have been around four—I proudly held up a drawing to my dad, convinced he was going to shower me with praise about how good it was and how I had natural talent. Maybe he would compliment me on the fancy lettering I had carefully copied off of the Myers's rum bottle my mum had been drinking.

"Look what Mummy was drinking last night," I told him as he held the drawing in his hand.

I waited for his smile to beam down on me, but instead he turned to my mum, fuming. "Are you drinking again!?"

A part of me now thinks I intentionally stirred up tension between them. I wanted to make my dad understand that when my mum was drinking, I wasn't being taken care of properly. I couldn't explain the psychology of it back then, of course, but part of my tattling was in the hopes that my dad would intervene, showing that he cared. I wanted him to stay home. I wanted him to handle the situation. I wanted him to stop my mum from drinking. He tried, but I wanted him to do more. I wanted him to fix it, but I know now, no one but my mum could have fixed it.

For a very long time, my mum's behavior made me very angry. To complicate things, my dad also drank a lot, although he was more of a high-functioning social drinker. As a young child, encountering that crack in my parents' façade was heartbreaking and confusing.

In addition to (or even because of) the drinking, my parents fought a lot. Fights never became physical, but they were loud. I would lie awake scared all night as the walls would reverberate with all the yelling. They'd slam doors, shaking the entire house. Sometimes they'd drag me into their drama, as if I was old enough to even comprehend what was going on. I know they stuck together for us kids, but at the time I used to wish they would split up. When I was a bit older, I would actually beg my parents to do so. I would plead, "Just break up, please. I'd rather live with each of you separately, because the two of you together is an absolute shitstorm."

Since that wasn't going to happen, I started keeping to myself. I didn't want to make a fuss or be a nuisance. I just wanted to be invisible. By the time I was six, home became even more dysfunctional after my sisters and brothers left for school—my brothers went to boarding school in the UK, and my sisters went to Switzerland. All of them, gone. I had lost my protectors as well as any sort of family structure. All of a sudden, I had to grow up really fast. I went from being the baby of a big family to being an only child. For the first time, I truly felt what my house was *really* like. And at times it was hard to live there.

Sometimes when my mum was drinking, I would call my oldest sister, Anouk, in Switzerland. (Yes, long-distance. From the house landline; do those still exist?) I would tell her I was scared and I didn't know what to do.

Anouk would tell me, "It's okay. Go to your room and climb into bed. Go to sleep. Turn off the lights or get your teddy bears." And I would do just that. It helped to know I wasn't alone.

SCHOOL, UNFORTUNATELY, WASN'T MUCH BETTER. I had been overweight since I was a toddler, something that didn't register until primary school. Once I didn't have my older brothers and sisters to hide behind, the real bullying started, and it was up to me to survive. I felt isolated. As a refuge, I turned to my pet turtles. I had four: Leonardo, Donatello, Michelangelo, and Raphael. It was 1994 and the Teenage Mutant Ninja Turtles were a TV phenomenon all over the world. And I, like millions of other kids (and adults), was *obsessed*. They were fucking *cool*. Back then, I would sneak in an episode every day before school after my dad left for work. He didn't let us watch a lot of TV—he was always reminding us that brain activity is lower while watching TV than while sleeping. Although I was petrified of becoming brain-dead, when it came to TMNT, I could not resist. So of course I named my four turtles after them.

To me, they were *IT*. I'm a very all-or-nothing kind of person, and so back then I had to own every piece of TMNT merchandise. My brothers and sisters happily obliged. They bought me T-shirts, backpacks . . . you name it, I had it (yes, even those annoying shoes that light up every time you take a step). My siblings were pretty much my own personal superheroes at that time, and I idolized them—almost as much as I idolized TMNT.

With my sibling protectors gone, my turtles became my confidants. I talked to them, I fed them, and I even cleaned them with a toothbrush. (My mum said they smelled [they kinda did].) Every. Single. Day. I spent hours a day playing with them, pretending they were the real deal and that together, we'd fight evil forces and save the world.

One day after school, I ran home to play with my turtles (since I was overweight, I never *ran* anywhere, so I use the term loosely here). I headed straight for the kitchen, expecting to see my beloved pets waiting for me in their clear plastic tank that sat atop a white wooden stool. But when I got there, it was just the stool. No plastic container. No turtles. *Where were they?* I went back downstairs. Off the living room, there was a set of sliding glass doors that led to a balcony overlooking Discovery Bay. My mum was out there with her back to me, so I couldn't see what she was doing. I pulled open the glass door, which was so heavy I needed to put all my weight into it to make it budge. It made a screech as it slid open. It was then that I saw what she was doing. She had Donatello in her hand, and I watched her effortlessly toss him over the edge of the balcony.

"What are you doing?" I asked, confused.

"Setting them free," she slurred, unsteady on her feet.

The rest of the turtles had already met their maker, as she had thrown them into the trees below. I could tell from her distinct wobble that she was drunk. She told me she was doing them a favor by letting them go, but I knew what was happening. Because they stank, she wanted them out of the house. My turtles were gone, but that wasn't the worst part. She may have been drunk, but she knew what she was doing, and she knew how much it would hurt me. (For her part, she has denied that this ever happened.)

As horrific as that day was for me, this experience—and many others like it—made me who I am today. Although I now accept that growing up around addiction was part of my childhood, I'd be lying if I said the memories don't still, and won't forever, haunt me. I grew up in a madhouse. But I survived, and I like to think of the good that came out of it instead of the bad that I endured: I learned coping skills that served me well. I raised myself; I learned to protect myself and how to keep going. The old adage is true: What doesn't kill you makes you stronger. I also forged an incredible bond with my siblings, who protect and support me to this day. At the time, I couldn't see how out of control things truly were, and though I didn't know it then, these experiences were the building blocks for the person I would come to be.

MY CIRCUMSTANCES ALSO REALLY FUELED my imagination. Because I was alone a lot, I had to be my own entertainment, and I learned to love being on my own. I'd often daydream about what my future would look like. I dreamed of leaving home as an attractive, stylish woman in my twenties and moving to New York City to pursue an amazing career; I'd have my own apartment and an amazing boyfriend (maybe even my ultimate childhood crush, Backstreet Boy Nick Carter). I let my imagination take me away from my reality. It was my way of coping. It was my way of fighting for my own life, because even back then I realized that, at the end of the day, you're all you have.

That's not to say I didn't try to make friends. But I struggled because I had always felt different. I struggled with my mixed race. I struggled because I wasn't from a happy home like other kids. I struggled because I wasn't a tomboy, but I wasn't a girly girl either. I was too loud for the quiet kids and too quiet for the loud kids. I struggled to find kids who I could relate to. But I tried. I tried *so hard* that I resorted to the worst possible thing: lying. If there was a new toy, or accessory, or article of clothing all the kids had, I would lie and say I had it, too, even if I didn't. I'd lie about anything to fit in. At the time, David Beckham and Michael Owen were two of the biggest soccer stars, and every girl in my year fawned over them, each having her preference. I would say I would like one or the other, depending on which girl I was talking to and who they preferred. (Truth be told, I didn't particularly have the hots for either.) Not only would I lie to try to get some sort of attention and be admired, but I also felt the need to compensate so people would stop just seeing me as overweight. I'd lie and say things like my mum was a policewoman and could get people arrested, or that my grandparents lived in a house bigger than Buckingham Palace. (When I think about this now, it's absurd, but at the time it was a desperate attempt to simply fit in.) At an early age, I was uncomfortable in my own skin. I didn't know how to be myself. I was desperate to be accepted, or at least avoid getting picked on. I just wanted some sort of connection with people. I was looking for something I didn't have at home.

Still, I kept trying. At primary school—Discovery Bay International School (DBIS)—there was a bit of a cultural divide between the Asian kids and foreigners (Hong Kong is a former British colony and a financial hub, so there is a huge expat population). When I was around seven, the "cool" white kids were repurposing Gatorade bottles into water bottles—the old-school ones with a nipple top— while I drank Korean barley tea called *bori cha* that was packed for me in my lunchbox. The kids teased me for it, so I'd lie and say it was apple juice. My lunch—Korean rice and seaweed rolls called *kimbap*—looked different from the cool kids' lunches. Those kids would have Western sandwiches like peanut butter and jelly or ham and cheese with a side of potato chips. To them, my lunch was "weird"—a symbol that I was different from them. I wasn't Western; nor was I fully Asian. It was confusing being a third-culture kid: having parents from two different continents and being raised in a third country. I had no sense of where I was from or where I belonged. I felt like I didn't fit in anywhere.

Looking back at it now, I see that this unsettled feeling fueled my eating issues, and it didn't help matters once my siblings were out of the house. What little structure we did have in the household was gone. My dad started traveling more for work, and my mum had more freedom to do whatever she wanted to do. She was often busy with her own problems. I was left alone with our helper (while that is a luxury in the States, in Southeast Asia it is very common to have a housekeeper). We would go to the local supermarket called ParknShop, and I could get whatever I wanted. I was obsessed with

American food that I'd see in movies and on TV—pizza pockets, microwave pizzas, and canned ravioli. I ate whatever I wanted to eat. I would just ask my helper to make pasta and she would, no matter what time it was. I had no guidance on what to eat and what not to eat. I had no idea that I had to eat vegetables or that I needed protein. I had no concept of *nourishment*. I'd come home from school and I'd eat crap and some microwaved garbage, and nobody told me not to. (Certainly, our helper was not about to overstep by saying something.)

I didn't know it then, but I was also eating because I was filling a void. It made me happy. Well, what I considered "happy." However fleeting, each bite was a little boost of dopamine. Eating gave me emotional comfort—so much so that I became reliant on it. The more I ate, the more bursts of gratification. It gave me a sense of satiety lacking in my life; it filled a hole left open by a lack of friends or a stable home life. It was a vicious cycle that led me to gain more and more weight.

I knew I was overweight. My parents knew I was overweight. But my mum was casual about it. One day after school, I was standing in the kitchen with my mum and I asked her, "The kids at school called me fat . . . am I fat?"

"Oh, it's just baby fat, Mia. You will lose it as you get older," she replied.

"But what about this?" I asked, pointing to my six-year-old armpit chub between the upper chest and the arm. I noticed that the other girls at school didn't have it; neither did my mum. "How do I get rid of it?"

"Look at me, do I have it? No, because I'm an adult. You'll grow out of it, little Mia. It's just baby fat," she assured me.

Oh, good, I thought. I'll grow out of it someday. I can keep eating.

My dad, on the other hand, was on my ass about it nonfuckingstop—when he was home, that is. I already had an irrational fear that my parents didn't love me, and I often thought back

My mother and me. Hong Kong, 2001.

then that he loved me less because I was overweight. It didn't help that my parents were super lean and fit. My dad played squash, tennis, golf; he waterskied, hiked, ran . . . he did anything physical. He had even rowed in the famed Henley Royal Regatta. He was always very active. (He can still whup my ass in the gym and beat me on a run.) My whole family was athletic as fuck, except me.

My parents were so disciplined that no matter how much they drank, they were up at six A.M. to exercise. During the week, they'd jog up to the end of Seabee Lane, which took you to the foot of a large hill that had a steep set of bum-burning stairs all the way to the top. They liked to go "up the mountain" every day, rain or shine. No matter how hot. No matter how humid (and Hong Kong summers often come with ninety-plus-degree heat and more than 85 percent humidity).

On the weekends, they would go on even longer hikes, trekking from one part of Hong Kong to another. While many know

Hong Kong for its picturesque urban waterfront with towering apartment buildings and office skyscrapers, 90 percent of the islands still remain untouched by developers. There are a number of hiking trails crisscrossing the island, like the one that takes hikers from Discovery Bay to Silvermine Bay, or the MacLehose Trail or Dragon's Back. They would always make me go, but I dreaded it for a few reasons. First, I would get chafing on the inside of my thighs, because they inevitably rubbed together. I know that sounds like a stupid reason not to go for a beautiful hike, but anyone who has experienced a bad chafe would understand. (Whenever I complained about it, my dad would say, matter-of-factly, "It's because you need to lose weight.") Second, I would get tired. It was embarrassing that my own parents would have to periodically wait for me to catch up. Third, I'd get hungry. My parents couldn't understand why a young, vibrant child needed to take so many breaks. I wanted to stop for water and snacks all the time. Never once did I ever think how lucky I was to have such an amazing place to climb; I couldn't wait for it to be over.

While I gave them my best whines during these hikes, I realize now that my father was trying to instill in me a love for maintaining a healthy and active lifestyle. My dad held my siblings and me to a very high standard, and although his perfection was hard to live up to, he really just wanted the best for us. You need to love yourself while striving to be better. Self-love and self-improvement go hand in hand. I didn't understand this yet.

I held all my anxieties inside and kept eating. When I was six or seven, I was in a PE class, playing a game called "stuck in the mud." We were running around in a covered tiled patio that was off the playground because it was raining. I was "stuck in the mud," and I was standing still, arms and legs wide like a starfish, when I spotted them from the corner of my eye. A few potato chips on the floor leftover from break time. I fucking loved chips (still do). Without even blinking, I bent down and pretended to adjust my shoe, and then like a real fucking weirdo, I stuffed a chip in my mouth. Oh, let me just double knot this shoe . . . and I ate another one.

A kid in class saw right through my act and asked, "Hey, did you just eat chips off the *floor*?!" I froze, like a clichéd deer in the headlights, but I managed to answer, mouth full of chip pieces: "No, I don't know what you're talking about. . . ."

In that moment I realized my relationship with food was out of control.

2. THE LOVE NOTE

—

"... WELL, YOU'RE *FAT*!"

Boom. That was how a fight with my schoolmate Andrea ended. I don't even remember what the fight was about. I was in my fourth year at primary school, and we had been waiting for class to begin when we started trading childish barbs, as eight-year-olds do. Then she shocked me by blurting out that hurtful one-liner. I was thunderstruck, hurt by her bluntness. My mouth agape, my mind went blank. I couldn't think of a zinger comeback. It hurt too much. I held in the pain all day, but I cried to my mum after I got home. "Everyone thinks I'm fat!" (Leave it to me to be dramatic, driving up the ante by changing one person's opinion to the entire school's.)

She reassured me again, as she had a dozen times by this point. "It's just baby fat. Don't worry about it. You'll grow out of it." My parents instilled in me the belief that any moment is a small, singular frame of the bigger movie that makes up your life. No matter how painful or uncomfortable the moment was, it was temporary. Their advice was to just get through school—it's only a fraction of a person's life. Their thinking rang in my ears throughout my childhood, buoying me during shitty times. If I could just let go of those hurtful moments and get through school, I would be okay. But fuck, it wasn't easy. Sometimes it felt like mission impossible.

As I got myself through primary school, my main source of reassurance and encouragement was my bedroom wall that was plastered with posters of my favorite celebs and models. Tyra Banks's first *Sports Illustrated* cover, where she wears the polka-dot bikini, was up there in a coveted position. Tyra would stare back at me, letting me know that someday I was going to be beautiful and successful, and life was going to be fine. But as I got older and was still heavy, I started asking questions. *When will I lose this weight? Will it be tomorrow? Next month?* The childish fantasy of growing up to be just like Tyra, Britney, or Mel C (Sporty Spice, of course) kept me going. (If only I could have told the adolescent me who was going through all this hurt and pain that she was going to have a successful career someday, that she was going to kick ass in Muay Thai, that everything really was going to be okay, I would have saved her so much anguish.)

Things got more complicated as I grew older. When I was about eight, I hit that tender age when you start to feel *those* feelings—you know, those butterflies in your tummy that you're not quite sure what to do with. Everything I knew about the opposite sex at this point I learned from what I what I saw on TV or what I heard in the girls' school bathroom. I started liking boys—one boy in particular, the new kid in school. His name was Alistair, but everyone called him Ali. He had just arrived from the UK and was an instant hit with the girls, with his blond hair and soccer moves. Some kids (the "popular girls") convinced me that it was a good idea to write this boy a love note, so I did. I wasn't scared—the concept of rejection didn't exist in my adolescent mind. I wrote my proclamation of love in super-tiny handwriting on a torn piece of paper. It read: "I think about you every second of every minute of every hour of every day." (Lol, I know, a young Shakespeare.) I folded the paper once, twice, and over again to make a tiny little square. I drew a few girly hearts on it to echo my affections.

I knew I had to muster the courage to pass it to him, but I'd always had a bit of fearlessness in me, and it came in handy at a time like this. From across the playground, I watched him open it, unfolding and unfolding. It seemed like a lifetime of unfolding. The pang of anxiety I had was somewhat assuaged by the thought that he'd read it, walk over, put his arms around me, dip me, and give me a huge kiss, just like in some kind of teen rom-com. I was not so lucky. Instead, when he opened it, he burst out laughing, and then he showed the note to all the other boys crowded around him, peering over his shoulder, dying at what it said. I think he was embarrassed that someone like *me* had a crush on *him*. (Like, ew, *she* likes me?) I watched the same girls who had convinced me to write the note snicker in unison. I really liked Ali, and it was the first time I felt that punch-in-the-gut kind of rejection and heartbreak. It was also the first time I realized it was outrageous, and apparently hilarious, that a fat girl like me could ever be with the most popular boy in school. What was I thinking? That's just not the way the world works. I think those girls knew that, and they played into this understood natural order of things for their own amusement—and I was humiliated. I should just accept that I was a loner and I didn't fit in anywhere.

Not getting anywhere with the popular crowd, I tried to fit in with the kids on a lower rung of the social ladder, the "unpopular" kids. They had something that I didn't—one another. They had friends they could confide in, united as outsiders braving cold adolescence together. For some reason, I didn't connect with them either, and in primary school I never did manage to find friends whom I could rely on, talk to, or joke with.

I was on my own. I learned to cope on my own. How did I do this? I avoided attention and tried to blend in wherever and whenever I could. The humiliation, name calling, and being picked on were just too much, and rather than try to fit in, I figured it was better for me to go unnoticed. Live under the radar. Stay in the shadows. Of course, food was another coping mechanism. I ate when I was alone, and I was alone all the time. Eating helped me fill that void.

These coping mechanisms weren't the best way to deal with my issues by any means, but they did get me through school. Looking back on this, I now know that being a victim of something bad doesn't mean having to remain a victim for life. While I didn't have any control over the bullying, I had control over how I reacted to it. But that is a lesson it takes time to learn.

At the age of ten, I started secondary school. Because my birthday falls in December, I was nearly a year younger than most of the kids, who were eleven. Island School was much larger than DBIS, with more than a thousand kids from various primary schools. It was very international, too; with more than thirty nationalities represented, it was like a mini-UN. I thought a new environment would result in a clean slate for me and life would get a little easier. I was hopeful because the new school meant a whole new crop of kids—kids who didn't know me. Maybe I'd make new friends, and maybe I wouldn't be bullied. Maybe I'd even be *cool*!

I was naive to be so hopeful, though. After all, bullies exist everywhere, don't they? And, as I soon found out, this school had the same environment I was used to, except on a much larger scale.

In fact it was even more cliquey, creating a wider divide between the popular and unpopular kids. I am not sure if this was the case at other multiculturally diverse schools, but at Island School, the "in" crowd consisted mostly of Caucasian kids who had big personalities and a packed social calendar. Grades and studying just weren't as important for them as for the Asian kids. This cultural divide was vast, more palpable than at primary school, and added yet another layer between me and the cool kids. Being of mixed race, I felt like I didn't fit into either culture. I was smart and got good grades, but I wasn't a pure bookworm. I had interest in both social circles and both cultures, but I didn't blend into either. As a result I kept to myself, went about my business with my head down, and tried to ignore the noise. And yet, as hard as I tried to be invisible, I was still picked on. Every day, walking into any classroom meant a high probability of a nasty comment, name calling, or worse: being the victim of a prank.

Or the victim of cyberbullying—although back then it didn't have a name yet. In 2000, the Internet exploded, and kids took to it like ducks to water, using it all the time. We were on it for school, we were on it for games, and we were on it for socializing. Xanga was the site du jour (this was even pre-Myspace . . . remember Myspace?). As a precursor to Facebook and more sophisticated blogs, Xanga helped users design their pages and create posts with different fonts, colors, and pictures. It even had the horrible features of ranking your friends and giving "eProps" (the equivalent of a "like"). Despite how slow it was during the dinosaur era of dial-up connection, we became hooked. There were no guidelines, rulebooks, or etiquette for how to behave back then—for better or worse, we were all winging it, behind the mask of a screen.

After school, everyone would hop on AOL Instant Messenger (AIM) or MSN Instant Messenger and chat. It was in this virtual space where boys would ask girls out and girls would gossip about other girls. It was where jokes were told, test answers were given, and rumors were spread. It was also where kids would post silly quizzes for other students to answer. The once-indispensable class note—what used to get sent around with coy, one-handed pass-offs to the classmate behind you—was now also virtual. There would be quirky questions like "If you could pick one celebrity to marry, who would it be?!" Stupid shit like that. Then you would have to fill it out and forward it on to five people, or there would be terrible consequences, like your computer would get a virus, your crush wouldn't like you back, or you would have bad luck for a year.

One day after school, I was sitting on my dad's big, soft leather wheely chair behind his desk in the study, messing around on his ultra-clunky IBM computer. I found myself on a classmate's page, reading through a quiz she had just posted. I stopped at this question: "If you had a knife, what would you do with it?" My eyes froze at the answer.

"KILL MIA."

Um . . . what?

I read it a second and then a third time to make sure I was reading it right.

I was. And I knew who wrote it. Lisa—a brassy, tomboyish, mixed-ethnic girl (like me) who was also not "in" with the popular crowd (like me), but she had her own little crew. My existence apparently offended her *that* much. Mortified, shocked, and overwhelmed, I ran down to my room, locked myself in, and cried. In my rush to get away, I left the page open on my dad's computer. My dad saw the quiz and reported it to the school. The next thing I knew, Lisa was suspended. However, even after she had been called out as the culprit, I still believed that I was the problem. I thought I was being punished for not fitting in, and I considered it a social price that I not only must pay for being fat, but would probably have to pay for the rest of my life. No one accepted me, and they ridiculed me for that. I blamed myself back then, but I now know better. I don't think all bullies are bad people. (Hear me out.) We all have trauma that we go through, and some of us just react to it differently; some people don't know what to do with their pain and anger. Some people take it out on themselves, and some take out on other people. I had no concept of this as a child, but in hindsight, Lisa must have had some issues going on and she needed a punching bag, which was me. It wasn't about me, really.

Even with Lisa's suspension, the bullying didn't let up. I couldn't always see it at first. Two boys in my class—Allen and Yoav—were popular, good-looking, smart, athletic, and best friends. I am not sure when or how it started, but they began being really nice to me—to be honest, I was surprised at anything directed toward me other than laughter or asking for homework answers. They started by giving me little compliments and smiles here and there. Before the start of class or in the halls they'd take turns coming up to me to say something nice, such as "Wow, you look great today," or "I think you're really pretty, are you going to the dance on Friday?" Then the other would break in with "What are you doing? I was gonna ask her that!"

At eleven, I was definitely not used to any sort of positive attention from the opposite sex, so I'd get shy around them. Inside, though, I would be beaming, feeling like the belle of the ball. *Allen likes me? Wait, Yoav likes me, too? They both like me? And they are fighting over me? No way.* They would get me all in a lather until they would break character and crack themselves up. I was so gullible, they managed to pull this prank off a couple of times before I wised up. *Oh, I get it now. It was all a joke. I'm a joke.* They got a kick out of watching me get excited, and I didn't disappoint.

The realization broke my heart. *Why me? Am I a bad person? Am I doing something that's not cool?* I would ask myself these questions over and over, but I knew deep down it was because I was fat. Fundamentally, I was just different. Despite my efforts, I didn't check all the acceptable social boxes.

It would torment me so much that I even asked my parents—no, begged them—several times to let me be homeschooled.

"PLEEEEASSE, I can't go back there. I can't deal with it anymore," I would cry.

"Absolutely not," they would answer every time. "Just get through it. This is just a tiny blip in your life, and it will be over before you know it. In twenty years, you will look back and barely remember school."

It wasn't what a kid wanted to hear, but that was how my parents rolled. Deal with it. Life's tough. I couldn't possibly have understood it back then, but they were one hundred percent right. Even though school was torture, I was able to observe the arcane hierarchy in the school microcosm. I learned who I could trust and who I couldn't. I mastered how to navigate certain social situations, and at times how to move undetected to avoid bullies. If I had been homeschooled, I would have avoided so much heartache, but I never would have learned the lessons that I now know made me a much stronger, tougher, and more resilient person. Just because things get uncomfortable does not mean that you give up; sticking through something that's hard and facing challenges head-on is exactly what causes us to grow.

I also honed some Darwin-worthy survival skills, as I went to great lengths to perfect my powers of invisibility. Even the simple task of getting my ass to and from school became an undertaking of spy-like reconnaissance. To get there in the morning, I took a bus to a ferry that took me to the mainland, and yet another bus to the school grounds. This routine always killed me because I didn't just have to deal with the dread and embarrassment of walking on and sitting by myself once, but rather three times before school had even started every day. I mapped out in my head a battle-hardened plan for getting home: "Okay, the school bell rings at 3:10 P.M. If I run and get the early bus that leaves at 3:15, I can make the 3:30 ferry. Most of the other kids take the later bus and the 3:50 ferry, so if I miss the early bus I'll stay after school and read or draw in my sketchbooks to kill time and take a taxi for the 4:10 ferry. . . ." Even with trying to ease my anxiety by fortifying myself with a game plan, the routine caused an incredible amount of stress. I came up with reasons to avoid it altogether, saving my money to take a taxi so I didn't have to take a bus at all. There are few things worse than that mortifying, heart-freefalling-to-your-stomach feeling when you walk onto a bus or into a classroom and feel the surly stares zooming in on you. Nearly every day, I'd try and get on the bus as early as possible to nab a seat in the front so I didn't have to walk down the entire aisle; when the other kids got on, I'd bury my face in a book so I didn't have to make eye contact.

Sometimes the attention was unavoidable. Every group of kids had co-opted a place where they hung out during breaks. The cool kids had claimed the playground by the nurse's office, right near one of the basketball courts. Once I was on my way to the nurse's office but I didn't want to walk past them and draw any kind of attention to myself, so I decided to walk through the court to circumvent them as much as possible. Sounds good in theory, right? Well. I made a run for it and was almost to the other side when DONK, a basketball bumped me right on the head. A howl of laughter came from all directions as kids witnessed the hit. My plan could not have gone any worse if I fucking tried.

Speaking of basketball, that brings me to the bane of my pre-teen existence: Sports. Running. Exercise. Ugh. Twice a month our class would go on a three-kilometer (about a two-mile) run called "second pagoda." The school was nestled in the hills of the Mid-Levels district, and in those hills was a hiking trail that led to two pagodas. Halfway through, you'd reach one pagoda. When you reached the second pagoda, you could turn back. I. Fucking. Hated. This. From the ages of nine to thirteen, this was the most dreaded and humiliating thing I had to do. Why? Because everyone would have to wait for every last student to finish the run, which meant everybody would be waiting for me as I eventually waddled across the finish line, about thirty-five minutes after the start. Every time, I would try to think of any and every possible way to cheat the system. Just like I had figured out a way to travel to and from school unseen, I tried to wrangle myself out of this embarrassing situation. Unfortunately, I failed disastrously, often comically, at every attempt. I'd pray for rain so we could do something indoors like dodgeball, where I'd intentionally throw myself at a ball and get hit so I could sit out for the rest of the class.

I tried *everything* to get out of it. One time, I grabbed some dirt from the side of the road, rubbed it all over my knees, and went back to the starting point, saying that I fell and hurt myself. That didn't fool anyone. I continued to rack my brain for ideas, scheming to beat the system. Hmmm, could I take a shortcut and turn around before I got to the second pagoda, after the last kid ran past me? No one would see me do it. The times were recorded, of course, but I would at least better my time. That way, all the kids who had finished wouldn't have to wait as long for me, cutting my embarrassment by half.

The system was one step ahead of me, though, as the school decided to place a student at the second pagoda who would mark the hand of each runner with a pen to indicate that the full trail had been completed, closing that cardio-avoiding loophole. Aha! What if I found the same marker they used, hid it in my shorts, and marked my own hand when no one was around? Before I could try that stunt, they closed that loophole, too—the marker color changed with every run, so I never knew what color they'd use.

I had one more scheme in my pocket: I asked my mum to write a sick note. Of course, she answered with the typical motherly answer: "No. Do the run. It's good for you." I had no way out. I had to run—well, I wouldn't even call it running, rather a painfully slow waddle—all the way to the second pagoda.

When we all gathered at the starting line, the super-athletic kids would line up right in the first row. I would be wayyyy in the back, untying my own shoelaces or some other last-minute attempt to get out of the run. But no luck: The teacher would yell, "Go!" and there'd be the click of a stopwatch as I pathetically hurled my body forward with very minimal effort.

I was usually not even close to the first pagoda when all the sporty kids would pass me on the trail, already on their way back from the second pagoda. And they would laugh as they whizzed by. I was humiliated, on top of feeling like I was dying. You know when you pull a heavy wheeled suitcase? That is how it feels when you are really overweight; your own weight is too heavy for you. The other kids, the ones who sped past me, looked so light, almost as if they were flying. I felt like I was dragging the weight of my own body, and I remember feeling the weight and realizing there was something wrong.

MY DOCTOR COULD SEE SOMETHING WAS WRONG, TOO. I had gained more weight by the time I went to see him when I was thirteen. He tried his best not to be overly harsh, while making it clear it was time to start thinking about getting that number down. "You know, a lot of health issues can be caused by obesity, like diabetes, heart problems, high blood pressure. . . ." He continued, but I am not sure what else he said. His mouth moved, words spilling out, but I couldn't hear him. I was in shock. I don't know if it was because the news came from an authority figure like a doctor, but having him tell me that I needed to lose weight finally opened my eyes to the reality of my situation. My dad was right; Andrea was right; everybody in school was right. And I was the child of an academic, so the need for data and facts was part of my DNA. Here, the doctor gave me a stark diagnosis based on a set of undeniable facts. Everything had been subjective up until this point—I could rationalize all of my parents' comments and classmates' jabs away. The doctor's verdict, however, was an objective fact, black-and-white. The fantasy I had kept up throughout my childhood—boo'ed Nick Carter from the Backstreet Boys and being beautiful, living in New York City—shattered. My life wasn't going to be what I wanted it to be if I continued down this path.

It's one thing to be overweight, but it's another to be overweight in Asian society. The Asian beauty standard is so specific—super petite, small frame, no muscle definition, little curves, and pure white skin. There's something very submissive about the look. The word "slim" was everywhere in advertising and media. Ads for weight-loss pills, powders, creams, and clinics were splattered across billboards and magazine pages. There was no escaping it, so being larger than average in that environment made me feel that much more enormous, especially at the time when I was progressing from Hello Kitty underwear to training bras. I was always the largest size in Asian sizing. I had to shop at Western stores like Marks & Spencer that carried a wider range of sizes I could fit into—zero, two, four, six, eight, ten—just like in the United States. I felt that I had a place. I had a size. There were sizes bigger than me, and there were sizes smaller. It just made me feel a little bit more normal. I bought everything in these Western stores, because psychologically it made me feel like I wasn't the biggest, most gigantic fucking thing in the country.

Even with these warning signs—the bullying, the larger sizes, and finally, my doctor's stark advice—it still hadn't really sunk in. I had been a fairly confident kid with a sense of humor (remember joke nights?), and my brothers and sisters had helped me to become pretty fearless (I wrote a boy a fucking love note at the age of eight, for God's sake). But the self-hate started to creep in. Those hormones that were kicking in at this time didn't help. The childlike, carefree mindset slipped away; I started to brutally compare myself with others, and insecurity grew.

Do you know when it *truly* sunk in? It was when I saw a picture of myself. My sister Anouk had been home from Switzerland and wanted to take photos of me. She was always doing fun stuff like that, paying attention to me, making me feel special. I carefully selected the outfit for my shoot: a spaghetti-strap top and gray sweatpants, a look obviously inspired by Sporty Spice. When the film was developed (Gen Z, you're probably wondering what *film* is, lol), I was so shocked at how big I looked. I mean, I knew I was big, but not *that* big! It was the heaviest I'd ever seen myself. I thought, *Oh my God, this is what I look like?*

Then a million other thoughts ran through my head: *How did I get this way? Am I just going to keep getting bigger? Is this what I am going to look like for the rest of my life?* It was not the picture I had in my head of how I was going to look as I grew up. There was no good angle to hide the pudginess—that pouch of fat by the armpit, the stomach fat, the double chin. I think it was safe to say that Nick

An image from the goofy photo shoot with my sister Anouk, when I realized just how overweight I was. Hong Kong, 2002.

Carter would not look at me twice. I wanted to destroy those pictures. I wanted to run and hide. But they also made me determined to get rid of the fat. I remember grabbing my belly rolls, knowing how it caused me so much misery, wishing I could just get a knife and cut it all off. And that was the day that I made a promise to myself. *Now everything changes.*

Looking back on it, I see that this epiphany was exactly what I needed to get motivated. Well, that and stepping on the scale. And as a matter of self-discipline, my parents were always weighing themselves. In fact, they were pretty militant about it. When they'd come back from their morning run, they'd step on the scale, and they'd yell out their numbers to each other while I got ready for school. It was always in the range of 50–53 kilos for my mum, and my dad hovered around 80 kilos. Those numbers would go up and down, depending on whether they were eating and drinking a lot, and how much they were exercising. As innocuous as this ritual sounds, hearing these numbers set these weird standards in my head. So weighing myself for the first time is burned in my memory forever: I stepped on my parents' scale in their bathroom, and it was one of those old-school ones with the needle and an analog dial. I had taken off my clothes, save my undies, and I stepped on the scale, one leg at a time. The red needle bounced back and forth until it finally settled on a black line: 72 kilos. Almost as much as my dad. Fuck.

Wow. I stared at that number until I finally admitted to myself that I was overweight, and I was not healthy. This wasn't baby fat; this wasn't something I was going to grow out of. I needed to do something about this. But where would I start? I didn't know how to fix it. I just knew it had to do with eating less food. That's what my dad was always on my case about, and that's what my parents did when they were watching their weight. So I started there.

There was a tuck shop (a shop that sold snacks, drinks, and lunch) in school that had a few hot options for lunch. My favorites were chicken curry and rice, Singapore noodles, and mapo tofu with minced pork. Every day there was a different menu. We had two breaks in the day (a short break and a long break), in addition to lunch. Snacks for those breaks consisted of siu mai dumplings, a cup of noodles, sausage rolls, fries, pizza, chips, and candy. Normally I would just buy crap every single break. What else was I going to do to fill the time? I just sat by myself or walked around and ate, pretending I had somewhere to go.

So I started there. I was never really a breakfast person, but I did like those snack breaks. *Okay. No buying food every break*, I said to myself. This became step #1 on the road to a new me.

Next, I tried to figure out what to eat by observing what other kids were eating. Given my limited social circle, my first subject was a Greek/Australian classmate named Lauren. She had a larger-than-life personality and was always very friendly with me; she also had been struggling with her preteen weight. I noticed that she brought in her own food—homemade pasta prepared with butter and black pepper. "I'm trying to be healthier," she said when I asked her about it. "I don't buy tuck shop food."

I thought to myself, *Hmmm. Maybe that's it. No more buying lunch at the tuck shop, either.* My step #2. I started taking my own lunch to school; I figured a small packed lunch would keep me out of the tuck shop. I brought in exactly the same thing that Lauren brought in: pasta with butter and black pepper. I didn't know anything about how to be healthy; nor did I realize that pasta was probably not the best option when trying to lose weight, given I had zero activity in my life. But I didn't know any better. I had no idea. *I was a child.* I just saw what she was eating, took her reasoning at face value, and then copied her *exactly*.

The funny thing is that I didn't even like butter (and still don't). So when I brought my lunch to school that first day, I didn't even finish it, because I couldn't stomach it. I had a couple of bites before I put the Tupperware lid back on and placed it back into my bag. For the rest of the afternoon, I felt lighter. When I weighed myself the next morning (I had my own scale in my room), I had lost a kilo. *Aha! Here we go. I'm on to something. Not eating means the number on the scale goes down. Got it.* I started to skip lunch altogether (step #3).

I started a routine: wake up, skip breakfast, go to school, and drink only liquids throughout the day. The school had vending machines that sold sugar-free lemon tea boxes, Diet Cokes, and other drinks. If I was really hungry, I would drink a little carton of fat-free chocolate milk. At lunchtime, I would go to the library instead of following other students to the tuck shop. I would build a little fort with beanbags in the corner and take a nap, where I could forget the hunger pangs for a bit, and it also made the day go faster.

I didn't have as much time to think about food, and the more time passed, the sooner I would finally be skinny. I had no conception that taking a slower, more measured path would mean more sustainable and healthier weight loss—I just wanted to lose as much weight as I possibly could, as fast as I could.

When I would get home, around 4:30, I'd ask my helper to make me either a bowl of steamed broccoli or boiled potatoes, and I'd throw a little Maggi sauce on for taste. I still hadn't done any research, and I'm not sure why I picked those two things outside of the fact that I enjoyed eating them, but that was my sustenance for the day. This is what happens when an uninformed thirteen-year-old creates her own diet. As I barely ate, I watched the numbers on the scale go down.

Awesome. Now let's try to go the whole day without eating anything. That's how it progressed. I would often try to see how long I could hold out before eating—the longest I went was four days without any solid food. Yup, you read that right. (As a food-loving adult well into my eating disorder recovery, I now recoil in shock and horror at the extremes I took to lose weight.) All of it was willpower at work, and this is going to sound fucked up, but I was proud of myself at the time—that I had the control and the desire to will something into being. But of course, in time I came to see how wildly misdirected my willpower was.

Willpower combined with my skill for being invisible helped me down the unnatural and dangerous path into an eating disorder. I was able to blend in, sneak around unnoticed, stay hidden among the crowd. If I had had friends and had been more social, I wouldn't have been able to get away with it. People would have noticed my not eating. They would have also smelled my "hunger breath," caused by ketosis, a condition that occurs when the body starts breaking down its own fat. They would have also seen that I had no energy. But I didn't have anything I needed to expend much energy on. I was the quiet, good girl who didn't draw any attention to herself.

And so the act of starving myself went unnoticed. My siblings were out of the house, my dad traveled a lot, and my mum was taking a lot of trips to Korea, so regular family dinners had become a thing of the past. I was left on my own with our helper, who didn't say anything about my sudden change in eating habits. If either or both of my parents were home, they'd usually let me skip out on dinner when I told them I had a project to work on or a test to study for; they loved my studiousness. If my dad had just gotten home from a trip, sometimes they'd insist that I join them for dinner. When I did, I ate what they ate—mostly steamed fresh fish, steamed red or brown rice, and steamed vegetables—but I picked and pushed food around my plate until enough time had passed and I could excuse myself, saying I needed to get back to my schoolwork. I was being conscientious; nothing to be alarmed about. Nothing to see here. To them, I was just a really good girl who studied all the time. My parents also liked the "self-control" I was showing, that my life didn't revolve around what delicious thing I was going to eat next.

All this scheming and hiding worked; I kept losing weight. I was also constantly cranky—and tired. Without my giving it any food, my body had no fuel. I was just *hangry*. All the time. I think it slowly changed me as a person. I became angry and dark. Anyone who's experienced that sort of hunger can testify to how it alters your mood, mostly because of low blood sugar. But I didn't know that. I genuinely didn't know what I was doing to my body, to my metabolism. And nobody was really there to tell me that it was wrong. Not just wrong, but dangerous. Even if anyone had said something, I don't think that would have stopped me.

My mum was the first to notice my crankiness, but she blamed it on hormones. (When you are thirteen, everything gets blamed on hormones, which, ironically, made me even angrier.) When my parents finally noticed the weight loss, they chalked it up to my newfound discipline of not eating everything in sight. They didn't know I wasn't eating at all during the day, so they didn't know there was reason to be concerned. In fact, they were happy to see me not shoving every piece of food into my piehole.

From the moment I decided to try to lose weight, I recorded my progress. I was always making study schedules and to-do lists for school, so I used the same method to track my food intake and weight. It was a good way to hold myself accountable; any failure on my part would be logged in black and white. I would write in my fluffy notebook, covered in light blue faux fur (it was the early 2000s, after all, when everything was pastel, fluffy, and glittery). This is where, every day, in the center of the lined page, I would weigh myself and write down the number of kilos first thing every morning. (You are at your lightest when you first wake up, which is one thing I learned from my parents' obsession with their own weight.) As you flipped through the pages, the numbers would decrease: 72, 72, 71, 71, 71, 70, 70, 69. I was losing about a kilo every couple of days. It was hugely satisfying to see the number drop every day, so I was vigilant about recording it, and I'd often flip through the book to make sure it was real. I became obsessed.

In just four months I had lost a third of my weight, plunging down more than 20 kilos to 48 kilos (107 pounds). *Whoa.* So I decided to up the stakes. *Let's see if I can get that number down into the double digits. Maybe then Nick Carter wouldn't be too much of a distant dream after all.*

3. A NUMBER ON THE SCALE

———

I THOUGHT I WAS IN TROUBLE. I was in chemistry class, sitting in the far back corner of the room, busy solving a series of problems that our teacher, Mrs. Hopkins, had given us. As I looked up in thought, I was startled to see her walking my way. I panicked. You know when you question your whole life in about twenty seconds? Well, that's what I did. Did I not do well on last week's test? That couldn't be it. She was my housemistress, which meant that she had a supervisory role at the school. Maybe she knew something I didn't know? Was I not doing well in another subject? Highly unlikely, except maybe PE. Was I having problems with other students? It couldn't be that, because I barely interacted with them. In a burst of optimism, I thought maybe I'd done really well on some homework. Maybe she was coming to tell me I was excelling academically— every Asian kid's dream.

When she reached me, she leaned over, rested her hands on the desk, and hesitated before speaking. Mrs. Hopkins was not a woman of hesitation, so I knew this was a serious and sensitive matter. Finally, she whispered to me, careful that no one else could hear, "Are you eating all of your meals?"

Taken aback, I blurted out, "Yes . . . except for breakfast." I have no idea why I said that. I just panicked and said something that I thought sounded normal. It wasn't even close to being true, though.

There was a long pause—an uncomfortably long pause. She looked at me as if she was sizing me up, trying to see if I was lying. I didn't flinch and gave her my best poker face.

She finally answered. "Hmmm. Okay. Well, remember to eat breakfast—it's the most important meal of the day."

And then, saying nothing else, she turned on her heels and walked away. A rush of heat ran through me. My heart raced. My mind was on repeat: *OMG OMG OMG OMG OMG! What just happened?* I always had good relationships with my teachers—I sort of lived for their approval, so it felt unnatural to lie to her. I knew that it couldn't possibly lead to anything good, but to be honest, there was also a rush of excitement. Part of me was thrilled that somebody had noticed all the hard work I had been doing. And if I am *really* honest, the adrenaline that rushed all through my body gave me a satisfying high. So I thought, *Maybe if I lose more weight, more people will say that, and I'll get to experience this feeling over and over again.* At the same time, though, I felt a little tinge of panic.

I tried to make sense of it all: This was the first time my secret felt exposed. I knew what I was doing wasn't normal. I started wondering, *Am I drawing too much attention to myself? Did she believe me or not? Am I going to get called into the headmaster's office? Or worse, am I going to be forced to see the school counselor? God, I hope not, because that would potentially halt all the progress I have made, and I am not done yet. If that happens, I'm going to seem even more uncool than I already am. But wait, does this mean I am thin?* It was a conflicting set of new and uncharted emotions that would only get more complicated.

It was equal parts scary, confusing, and exciting, and that was just the start. One day in PE, we were headed to swim class in the school's outdoor pool. Now hear this: I actually liked to swim. In fact, I had been swimming since I could walk. Anouk, who was an amazing swimmer, taught me well, and I was surprisingly pretty good.

We had all gone into the changing rooms to put on our navy blue and maroon one-piece swimsuits. We scooped up our goggles, swimming caps, and ear plugs, placed towels in the crooks of our arms, and lined up against the wall of the hallway, ready to walk in single file to the school swimming pool. Like a drill sergeant, the teacher went down the line inspecting each of us, making sure we were paying attention and had everything we needed in hand. I had been in the back of the line, with my head down to avoid eye contact with anyone. When she got to me, she stopped.

"Wow, Mia, your suit is so loose. It's falling off you," she said in a surprised tone. She continued, "Get a new one, or you can't go swimming next time, 'kay?" Then, turning her attention to the rest of the class, she shouted, "All right, everyone, follow me," and led us to the pool.

I was embarrassed this time around because, unlike with Mrs. Hopkins, this happened in front of the whole class. I could feel everyone's eyes on me. A few of the kids even echoed the teacher's comments, saying that they had also noticed how big the suit was on me. I felt that familiar heat of excited panic rush through my body. *I wonder if Mrs. Hopkins said something to her. Is she going to tell on me? Am I in trouble? Will all the teachers start talking and put two and two together? If people find out about my diet, then I'll have to stop, and I don't want to stop.* These thoughts again conflicted with others: *If I need to get a new suit, that must mean all my efforts are working. I'm getting results.*

Even my navy blue school uniform skirt had gotten too big. I had rolled the waist down, once, twice, then three times, but eventually I had to buy a new skirt. I went from a 34 to a 23 (going from a US size 10 down to a 4) but still didn't think I was thin. After all, it's not like the scale ever reads, "Congratulations! You're finally skinny!" My thirteen-year-old brain didn't know how to process any of these feelings. I knew that I liked the attention, yet I felt that I needed to hide my method from everyone, which I knew also meant that I was doing something "wrong." I had a "secret." I understood eating regularly was normal, so not eating was bad. But I truly thought I was on a crash diet, and once I was skinny, I could resume life as usual. At this point, I didn't know that my habits were signs of a disorder. All I knew was that I wanted to lose as much weight as I could, as if that would be the answer to everything.

ON WEDNESDAYS AFTER SCHOOL, I took a modern dance class. I liked dance just as much as I liked swimming; I think it was because it didn't feel like exercise. After all, who doesn't like to put music on and dance around? (Admit it! You did this, too—every teen dances around their bedroom, fantasizing about performing onstage in front of millions of adoring fans.) It also got my dad off my back about doing some sort of exercise, so it really was a win-win.

My dance uniform was a black stretchy unitard that had a slightly flared cut in the legs and a halter top. As I lost more and more weight, I would adjust my unitard by tying a knot at the neck of the halter to make the whole thing tighter. But in time that wasn't enough, so I cut out a chunk of the neck strap and got my helper to sew it back together.

This DIY fix must have looked bizarre—bizarre enough to get the attention of my teacher, Melissa. A beautiful Australian blonde, she was a professional dancer with a cool big-sister kind of vibe. We all had girl crushes on her, and after class we'd circle around her, mesmerized, as she told us about her backup dancing gigs for various pop stars, or about the newest guy she was dating.

One day before class Melissa said to me, in her cool and casual Australian accent, "That leotard's hanging off you, girl. You should really get a new one." Now cool Melissa noticed, too. What a feat.

At the end of class, she pulled me and a girl called Meme (pronounced "may-may") aside and told us to stay behind. As everyone was changing their shoes to go home, she asked the two of us, "Have you ever thought about modeling?"

Silence.

Silence.

More silence.

I looked at Meme and waited for her to answer, not sure why I was involved here. She was of mixed race—her father was from New Zealand and her mother was Polynesian—and she was so beautiful, charming, and confident. Surely Melissa was talking to her, not me. I was probably just there as moral support for Meme. But all Meme did was look back at me.

Wait . . . is she talking to both of us? Am I supposed to say something right now? Did she say "model"? Like in a magazine and on a runway?!

Maybe she means something else. Nope, I'm pretty sure that is what she meant.

OMG there has been silence for way too long. This is getting awkward. MIA, SAY SOMETHING.

"Ummm . . ." I stammered, before Meme took the reins.

Meme, wide-eyed with excitement, pushed her hair behind her ears and said, "No, I've never modeled before."

I stayed silent.

Melissa explained, "Well, I have a friend who owns a modeling agency, and I think you should both go in to see her—if your parents say it's okay, that is."

OKAY, IT'S CONFIRMED. SHE IS DEFINITELY TALKING TO BOTH OF US. But Meme is gorgeous and skinny and definitely should model. Does this mean I am those things as well?! A big portion of my bedroom walls were adorned with ripped-out magazine pages of models of the time, like Kate Moss, Naomi Campbell, and the aforementioned Tyra Banks, but it never ever occurred to me that I could be a model.

I was only thirteen, so once I got my brain back into normal working order, I had so many questions (like *what's an agency?*). But they would have to wait. Melissa handed us the agency's business card to give to our parents, which I handed to my mum as soon as I got home. She was hesitant at first, but after she talked to Meme's mum, who was super keen on the idea, they arranged to take us both in together. No one was familiar with the process, so this was just a "let's see what this is all about" meeting.

The next few days were a whirlwind: the agency was a boutique one, with a small office in Central, Hong Hong's business district, where all the action is. Their minimalist, all-white office was bright and chic, and we were seated at the waiting room's round table with two agents, Rebecca and Lisa, two *gwai-los*—Hong Kong slang for foreigners (it literally translates to "white ghost"). They snapped some Polaroids (yes, back then we used Polaroid cameras) of us one by one. I had no clue how to pose, so I watched Meme as she hammed it up and "smized" for the camera. When it was my turn, I just stood there as if I was sitting for a passport photo. *Oh wow, am I even capable of this?*

Rebecca and Lisa then explained how representation works: I'd sign a contract with them, and they'd submit photos for castings and jobs. But I needed to build up a "portfolio," or a "book," which is a selection of the best photos used to show clients what I can do. Any jobs booked would have a 20 percent commission taken out. My mum used an agency for her translating work, so she understood the fees; there was no real downside, except for making sure I didn't miss any school. It would be a good way for me to make some money.

I have to hand it to my parents here. That evening they sat me down and we had a serious conversation. They explained that this would be something that I'd do in my free time only. My dad laid down the law: "The deal is that this doesn't interfere with school and your grades are not to be affected in any way. In fact, I want your grades to go up, if anything. I'll let you do it so long as you're responsible and mature about it."

If I did this, I would have to keep up the A grades (with a C in PE, but whatever). I would have no free time. I could potentially become the kind of girl that girls like me taped up on bedroom walls and envied. Yeah, I fucking wanted to try to do this.

A couple of days later, I booked my first job, an editorial for *BC Magazine,* a sort of *Time Out* for Hong Kong. It was that fast. Poof, as if a fairy had waved her magic wand over me. I was a model.

Well, let's not get ahead of ourselves. I still needed to learn *how* to model. On that first shoot, I just sat on a stool in front of the camera. I mean just that—I sat there. I didn't move; I didn't pose. I actually didn't even sit up straight. Thank God, Lisa—a woman from the agency who was also an established photographer—happened to be assigned to the shoot. A friendly face made the day a bit less terrifying. She was gentle, coaching me with her kind, motherly voice: "Chin up . . . chin down . . . now tilt your head to the left . . . Okay, turn your shoulders away from me. . . ." As scared as I was, it was thrilling. I also found a new respect for models—it took me a long time to understand the complexities of lighting, angles, and posing. There is so much more to it than just being aesthetically pleasing.

I was curious about the agency, what it did and who it represented, so I went online and checked out its website. There they had listed all the models they repped, and each model had a dedicated page with various headshots and measurements. I recognized many of them from magazines, billboards, and even music videos. A few weeks later, I had my own page, too. It was hard to take in. To be included in this amazing group of top Hong Kong models was surreal. There was Celina Jade, a beautiful, super-popular schoolmate who had already made a name for herself as a model and Cantopop singer, and Maggie Q, who's now a famous actress as well. There

One of my first shoots, at thirteen years old.
Just sitting there not having a clue about how to
actually model. Hong Kong, 2003.

was Cara G., Gaile, Rosemary V., all top models. There was Sam W., and Tara R., too, girls from other schools who were also booking jobs. See the pattern? In Hong Kong, models were generally referred to by their first name and the initial of their last name. I was Mia K. *I* had a nickname.

Do you know what I noticed as I checked out these girls? There was a page for the fully Asian girls, Caucasian girls, and Eurasian girls. But a lot of them looked like me—they were of a mixed race. In school, I had always felt different because of my English-Korean background, but now I no longer I felt like an outsider. I belonged to a group. Because we were of a mixed race, we were considered "exotic" looking, and in demand. We were all "products" of a market controlled by supply and demand, just like everything else. It's terrible to put a price tag on people's looks, but this was the new reality I was suddenly swept up in. I was to become part of this small group that was highly valued. My being mixed was cool. Being different was *desirable*. And being thin was a requirement to stay in the group.

I started spending a lot of time after school on the website, clicking on the models' profiles—way more time than I'd like to admit. In fact, it sounds creepy, veering to stalkerish, now that I type this, but at the time, I was just a nerd who wanted to know everything about this new world that I had entered. I expanded my research, going outside my agency to check out other modeling agency websites. They were a treasure trove of information for a girl who was decidedly becoming obsessed with her weight. They all listed the same information listed about their models, each having their own page with their portfolio and stats about hair color, eye color, and height, bust, waist, hip, and shoe measurements. I'd come home from school, get on my mum's or dad's computer, and look up different models. I went through each girl's page, scrutinizing every picture, analyzing their bodies, and creating an image for myself of what models are "supposed" to look like. I studied their arms and how they had no extra meat on them at all. I looked at the thigh gaps, visible hip bones and ribs, protruding collarbones, the angular cheek- and jawbones, and elongated necks. I took note of who was smaller and thinner. *Oh, her hips are thirty-five inches, and hers are thirty-four inches. Whoa, her hips are thirty-three—that's tiny.* (I was a thirty-five hip.) Then I would go to castings and continue to torment myself there, sizing up the models in person. *She's bigger than me. That one over there, she is smaller.* I'd see a girl who had thirty-six-inch hips. *Okay,* I would think, *I don't want thirty-six.* I know this all sounds crazy. Do you know how fucking small thirty-six inches is?! This was when it turned for me: It was no longer just about weight. I became obsessed with measurements, specifically waist and hip measurements. My height and bust, well, I couldn't do much about that. I was shorter than a lot of models, a bit of a disadvantage, but I was still growing at thirteen. However, I did have *some* control over my waist and hips.

When I look back now, one of the most surprising realizations is just how fast and easily I put pressure on myself. I invented a dangerous numbers game in my head. The agents never said any-thing or put any kind of pressure on me to lose weight, at least at that age, but it didn't take me long to figure out the unspoken law that there was a major correlation between the thinner a girl was and the number of jobs she booked. So, if I wanted to book the jobs, I had to be the skinniest, right? And I wanted to book those jobs, because they were proof that I *was* the skinniest. And thus, the cycle began.

MY FIRST BIG CASTING OPPORTUNITY was for a huge, global denim brand. I couldn't believe I was even considered, but they wanted a Eurasian girl and picked several of us to cast. I was so excited, but with that came a new feeling: doubt. I had wanted it so much that I began to pick myself apart, telling myself why I'd never get the job. I wasn't the tallest, or the skinniest, or the prettiest. I had neither the confidence nor the experience. It was the start of many insecurities I would develop about my body as a model.

One day after school, I went in my school uniform to the brand's corporate office, where Celina Jade was already taking test shots in a pair of perfectly fitted jeans. I watched her carefully as she tried on different jeans and posed as if it was second nature. I was charmed by her movements and her gestures as she worked the camera. I was mesmerized. Now that I think about it, my star-ing at her from a wheely chair on the other end of the room must have been creepy, but at the time, I was too busy studying her so I could mimic her poses to realize it. All of it seemed so unreal. *What the fuck is actually happening? I'm here. With her. I'm in the same room with Celina Jade. No way. People like her are my competition? There is no way in hell that I even have a chance at this job. She's so much prettier and more experienced, and I don't even know how to take a fucking picture.*

I managed to get through the test shots and, after I found out that Celina also lived in Discovery Bay, we took the ferry home together. I seized the moment as an opportunity to pick her brain about modeling. I tried hard to act cool and nonchalant as I asked her how she balanced both school and work.

"For me, it's not an option. I help support my family, so I want to book as many jobs as I can. Out of every ten castings, I get maybe one job, so you gotta just keep going to the castings, keep trying, keep putting yourself out there. I learned to balance the work while keeping my grades up."

I took everything she said to heart. This was a whole new life for me, and I didn't want to mess it up. *Wow, she can do it all. I want to do it all.*

When I got home, I interrogated my mother immediately. "Mum, did they call? Did I get it?! Did I get it?!" I was as impatient as a kid on Christmas morning.

To stop me from begging, my mum called the agency. "Hi there, Mia is anxious to know if she got the job. Do you know anything yet?"

"Not yet," Lisa chuckled into the phone. "Tell Mia to be patient. Castings take a few days at least to get confirmed. And just so you know, we'll only call you if she gets the job. We won't call if she doesn't get it."

This didn't stop me from pestering my mum to keep calling.

Oh my God, the anticipation is just too much. How am I going to survive? Will it be like this all the time?

Two *long* days passed, and I nearly lost my mind every single time the house phone rang, but I finally got the call. I got the job! Me! No fucking way. I could not believe it. I was really proud of myself. I didn't stop to consider whether or not I had actually *done* anything to be proud of. In my increasingly twisted way of thinking, I felt like all the "work" of starving myself was paying off. And my reward? I was paid more money than I'd ever seen in my thirteen-year-old life.

One glitch: I had to take off two days from school. As with any and all school-related matters, my dad was involved. When he came home from work that day, he and my mum sat me down for a "conversation."

My dad started. "Mia, I'm sure this is all so thrilling for you. If things keep going the way they are, you're going to make good money. But I want you to save. You'll need to learn the value of money, so that means you'll start paying for your own stuff. Haircuts, clothes, any extra stuff you want—you are now financially in charge. If you want to earn money, you must learn to save and to spend responsibly."

"Yes, Daddy. Got it!" I couldn't contain my excitement; I would have said yes to anything my dad asked me at that moment.

The next thing I knew, I was oiled up in a triangle bikini top and tight jeans for a steamy summer denim campaign shoot. My counterpart was a Japanese male model, Yuya, whom I was familiar with from all my "research" online. (By this time I had stalked the entire model population via all of Hong Kong's agency websites.) We met each other while in hair and makeup, and we chitchatted. He was much older than me, in his mid- to late-twenties. He was astonished by how young I was, but I later found out that this was far from uncommon in the industry. It was nice to get to know him a bit—it made me feel a bit less nervous. It also made it a little less awkward on set, as we were told to dance and get very close to each other. I felt like Britney Spears in her music video "I'm a Slave 4 U," flinging my hair from side to side while I danced. Little did I know practicing in front of my bedroom mirror would come in handy! We didn't kiss, but the implication was there for sure. (I'd never made out with a guy before, so this was the most intimate moment I'd ever had!) At the time I didn't question anything that was happening, like how inappropriate the age difference was; I was just excited and loving the experience. But take a look around you; so many fashion ads are sexualizing young females. I remember him saying, "Dude, I'm not going to kiss you. You're so fucking young." *Okay, good, because I wouldn't even know how to.* I was just trying to get through the day without anyone noticing I had no actual idea what I was doing. Let's be real: I was still so green.

EVERYTHING ABOUT ME WAS THE SAME except that number on the scale, but that seemed to have determined my whole life. Modeling agencies weren't the only ones taking notice. I was shocked at how people started treating me so differently because of my weight. All of a sudden, boys—the same ones who had made my life hell—now wanted to talk to me. I was the same girl, just without twenty-odd extra kilos on her. At the same time, I had been teased for so long that I found it hard to believe a boy could even like me. It was all very confusing.

I didn't trust them, or anyone—not after all the years of feeling excluded and embarrassed about who I was. I had made a mental note about how it was all so bizarre, but at the same time, I was so hungry for approval and friends that I was very forgiving. I was excited by the attention, and I felt—for the first time in my life—*accepted*.

One morning, I was sitting in registration (sort of like homeroom in the United States) and writing in my school diary before classes started. A girl at my table noticed a few Polaroids I had kept from the shoot sticking out of the diary's sleeve. In those days before digitalization, photographers would take Polaroids to test the lighting. I'd always ask if I could take them home as a souvenir.

"Hey, what are those?" she asked.

I struggled to give an answer, "Oh . . . it's . . . uh . . . pictures from my modeling shoot."

"Can I see?" she asked.

I hesitated.

"Sure," I finally responded, and handed her the small stack of shots. As she looked through them, a small group of other classmates swarmed around us, also checking out the photos as they got passed around. They bombarded me with questions: "So you're

Thirteen years old, on set for my first big
campaign shoot for a popular denim brand. Hong
Kong, 2003.

modeling now?" "What was it like?" "Did you get paid?" "What was
this for?" Another chimed in, "Did you get to keep the clothes?" (No,
I didn't. Unfortunately, keeping swag is generally an urban legend.)
These were the same kids who didn't give me the time of day before,
mind you. Don't get me wrong. I liked the attention; it made me
think that I *should* be proud. I may not have been a star athlete or
top of the class, but I'd found something that was uniquely mine.

LATER, AS WE WERE ALL HEADING to our first class of the
day, Allen came up to me quietly and asked to see the photos, too.
"Okay," I said, sheepishly handing them over. After going through

them, he said to me, "You look amazing." It wasn't so much what he said, but the way he said it that gave me butterflies. That, my friends, was the beginning of our sweet relationship. (Back then, it didn't take much. It was that time in life when dating is so new that if you are caught talking to someone of the opposite sex, the rumor mill has you practically engaged.)

I chose to forget what Allen had done. I was willing to overlook his prior behavior because I liked him, plain and simple. And when I got to know him, he was a completely different boy from the one who'd pranked me months earlier. Cool, cute, and popular, he was Chinese and had a lot of family in New York, so he was really Americanized (we used the term "ABC," American-born Chinese). He was kind of from both worlds, like me, and he hung out with everyone, both the Western kids and the Asian kids. He was also a true dork: He was in the top math class and did Kumon (an after-school program that taught individualized math). He also had a little glow-up of his own: when he first got to the Island School, he was chubby, wore glasses, and had out-of-control hair. But then he grew six inches, got contacts, and discovered hair gel. I realized that he just did dumb shit to show off in front of his friends, like all kids do. One on one, he was sincere and seemed different from the rest of the boys. He was just *good*.

We'd started our romance by passing notes during class. He'd buy me a lemon tea during our breaks, and we would chat after school and late at night on MSN. Then Allen upped his game: He asked me to a party. He was almost a year older than me, and he was friends with kids in the year above us (a fact that upped his coolness factor by ten), and one was throwing the party. Even though it was all very innocent, just a group of kids hanging out in someone's living room, I told my mum I was going to the movies. Some people were drinking, but I was not. Not really. We shared a bottle of Smirnoff Ice, one of those bottled vodka mixed drinks. A couple of sips were enough for me to get giggly, and enough for Allen's face to turn bright red with "Asian flush." We were flirting, getting closer, and I even dared to sit on his lap.

He asked me, "Can I kiss you?"

Let me stop here for a second: I had *dreamed* of this day. After the trauma of the love note fiasco, I never ever thought I would have a boyfriend or even a first kiss. I had fantasized about first kisses, gawped as I watched Disney movies, and practiced French kissing on the back of my hand (I hate to admit it, but on my stuffed animals, too). I imagined my first kiss would be accompanied by fireworks exploding and romantic music. Okay, back to our story.

I responded, "I won't kiss you unless you're my boyfriend."

"Well then, do you want to be my girlfriend?"

"Yes," I answered, and then we kissed like two inexperienced teens. I was so nervous. *God, am I doing it right? OMG, this feels amazing. Is he enjoying this?* As our noses crushed each other, we figured out the angles and the tongue movements—it was everything I'd ever imagined. Yes, even fireworks.

Sappy, right? I still get goose bumps when I think about that moment.

Come Monday, we sat next to each other in registration, met up between classes, and made plans for after school. All the butterflies fluttered in my stomach each time I saw him, and it felt amazing. And he was so proud to show me off; I felt so accepted and loved. Allen was a positive influence on me—I am not sure I would be here today without him. And believe me, I put him through the wringer with my eating and body issues. But in this moment, none of those difficulties had come to pass yet. And when they eventually did, he got me, and he tried to understand what I was going through. He was my first. My first everything. And when I say everything, I mean *everything*: I lost my virginity with him. I was thirteen, he was fourteen, and although some people may think that's too young, it didn't feel that way to me.

A few months later, when the denim ad came out, it was *everywhere*. It was on the sides of buses, on billboards, on the huge jumbotron screen in Hong Kong's Times Square. The posters were plastered in every one of their stores. It was surreal.

Only then did it hit me how my life had changed. And it hit me even more when others realized it.

Suddenly I was a model. Suddenly people were paying me money to take my photo. It's a difficult thing for an adolescent to process, especially one who is not used to any sort of attention. All of this happened at warp speed, too, since the weight loss was so rapid. I tried to keep a level head about it and have a nonchalant attitude toward it all. But society was rewarding me for being thin and unhealthy. It was showing me a flip side of how superficial people were, and how much looks could change someone's entire perception of a person. I was getting all of the attention because of a number on a scale, and the lower it got, the more positive feedback I received. Same girl. Different weight. It messed with my head, and I started playing an even more dangerous game with food—not that I knew how precarious it was at the time. But the stakes were higher now; I was getting paid to be skinny. I don't know if my eating issues would have spiraled out of control if I hadn't modeled, but it certainly didn't help. For sure, modeling added fuel to the already burning fire.

The insidious nature of eating disorders is that they can develop into other disorders, which is, sadly, an all-too-common cycle for girls (and boys as well). They are extremely complicated, and there is no one reason why or how they start. And there can be more than one disorder at work—anorexia, bulimia, body dysmorphia—all overlapping with one another to a greater or lesser degree. Most people take the disease into adulthood and suffer from it for the rest of their lives. Studies show twenty million American women will be affected by an eating disorder at some point in their lifetime; ten million men are affected.[1] (One in two hundred American women suffers from anorexia alone.)

Regardless of gender, the disorder is caused by a complex combination of genetic, emotional, psychological, and societal factors.[2] And the main reason for my not eating was to give myself a sense of control over my life when I felt like had none. For me, anorexia brought with it a subtle and invasive disorder of body dysmorphia. Everybody has something they don't like about their appearance, a perceived flaw, whether it's their nose, thighs, love handles, or jawline. And it's common to see a photo where we feel like we look fat (then to see it five years later and think, *What was I thinking? God, if I could only look like that again!*). Well, my self-perception became so distorted that it was like looking into a funhouse mirror—I would see fat where there was none and imperfections that just were not there. I'd wrap measuring tape around my thighs to prove to myself I wasn't the monster I saw in the mirror. If I tucked my pelvis and my thighs touched, I knew I had more to lose. I would scrutinize my body, grab any flesh I could possibly get between two fingers, and tell myself I could lose more, that this meat had to go.

I thought I would get to a certain "skinny" weight and then I'd finally be happy. I thought at some point I'd hit the "resume" button and be able to eat again. I thought I was just on an extreme crash diet with an end date, even though I didn't know when that day would come. So starving had become the norm. I wasn't losing much more weight, as my metabolism became so slow it was basically at a standstill, so I needed to starve all the time to maintain the number on the scale. I was uninformed, so I had no idea that yo-yo dieting and bingeing were just around the corner. I'd eat and see how my body clung to every single calorie, gram of sugar, and ounce

1 Jenna Fletcher, "Types of Eating Disorder: Do I Have One?," Medical News Today, September 5, 2019, https://www.medicalnewstoday.com/articles/326266.php.

2 "Eating Disorders: Why Do They Happen?," ULifeline, accessed March 24, 2020, http://www.ulifeline.org/articles/400-eating-disorders-why-do-they-happen.

of fat. If my weight went up, the guilt would be overwhelming, and I had no choice but to starve again.

My body got to the point where it couldn't take any more loss. It needed food. When this happened, I ran through a mental checklist of achievements. *I have become a model, I've done a big campaign, I have a boyfriend and a social life—I think I've made it. Hmmm, maybe I can stop dieting. Because fuck, I'm hungry.* I had been fantasizing about food and having cravings for months. *Fuck it, let's go. Diet over.* My brain started to say, *You've earned some food. Treat yourself. Reward yourself for all the hard work.*

One day that voice got louder and louder. It wanted Pringles—pizza-flavored Pringles, to be precise. So, after school, when my mum picked me up from the ferry, I asked her, "Can we stop at 7-Eleven?" Sounding surprised, she asked, "What do you want to get?"

"Pizza-flavored Pringles."

She drove me to the store, and I walked through the sliding doors on a mission: I headed straight to the chips section. I hadn't been there in a while, and the snack shelves were overstuffed with bags of forbidden chips and treats gleaming in all of their colorful plastic glory. One package promised more deliciousness than the others. I picked up the Pringles, then went through every shelf in every aisle, pulling one snack after another off the shelf and into my arms until I couldn't carry anything else. The months and months of starvation took over and I couldn't control myself. I don't remember all of what I picked up, except the Pringles, a Kinder Bueno chocolate bar, and some other incredibly junky snacks that I dumped as a load on the register counter, impatient to get home and devour all of it.

When I got back in the car, Mum asked, "You're really going to eat all that?"

"Yup."

And I did. I went to my bedroom, sat on my sheepskin rug, and watched myself in the mirror while I ate all of it. The visual element of seeing myself eat was so satisfying—it was like I was eating twice. It felt so good. The pleasure chemical of dopamine flooded my brain, simulating pure bliss. I was thin and I was eating whatever I wanted! For about a minute. Then suddenly that incredible feeling of joy turned into an overwhelming sensation of disgust.

A tsunami-size wave of guilt came flooding over me, washing away all of that satisfaction. That's when I heard it. An unfamiliar voice started speaking to me. *I can't believe you ate all that. You are such a fat piece of shit. You are getting fat all over again.* Sitting on the floor, looking into the mirror, I suddenly saw nothing but a fat girl looking back at me. It was as if I had gained all that weight back. It felt like all the food I just ate was instantly being absorbed by my thighs, stomach, arms. *This needs to come out of me. I need to feel lighter again. I can't live with myself.* I named that voice the Binge Monster. It started showing up again and again to torment me when I was hungry or goad me in a moment of weakness. I don't know why, but I envisioned it as a big purple furry ogre who lived in my head. "Go ahead, eat that . . . you can't get fat from one meal." Its voice drowned out every other voice of reason, and the second the food touched my lips, it would start laughing, knowing that the guilt would find me and torment me.

Allen saw that monster in me. We would often hang out at his house after school, and one day he ordered a pizza. The extra-large Pizza Hut pizza arrived, filling the room with the lip-smacking smells of melted cheese and hot pepperoni. Having not eaten anything proper in days, I should have been happy to put something in my stomach, but instead I became enraged that he ordered it, that he would dare to bring such temptation around me.

"Why would you do this? Why would you put a pizza in front of me!?" I cried as he laid it on the coffee table in the living room.

"What?" he asked, clueless. "What are you talking about?"

"I don't want pizza. Get it away from me!" I yelled.

"Okay, so don't have any," he replied, trying to calm me as he took a slice for himself and started playing a game on his computer.

I sat on the sofa with my arms crossed defiantly for as long as I could, but the smell was intoxicating and I cracked. "I'm so hungry, so fucking hungry," I mumbled.

"So eat the food, Mia. If you're so hungry, *eat*." He was being patient with me. Any other boy would have probably thought I was crazy.

I asked him, "You don't think I'm fat? I can eat the pizza, right?"

He assured me that I looked beautiful.

"Fine, I'll eat the fucking pizza."

And I did. I ate the whole fucking thing, except for Allen's lone slice. An entire XL pizza.

Afterward, wracked with guilt, I paced around the apartment, holding my stomach. It felt so uncomfortably full I wanted to take it all back, to go back in time to stop myself from gorging on the pizza. I sat on the sofa and cried, going back and forth between tormenting myself and tormenting Allen. "Why did you let me eat the whole pizza? Who eats a whole pizza!? I shouldn't even be eating fucking pizza." In my head, a loop began to play: *I have to go throw up. I am so fat. I am so fucking fat. I can't live with myself. I need Allen to tell me I'm not fat.*

THIS WAS NOT THE FIRST TIME I put Allen through such theatrics. He saw me through a lot. He must have known something was wrong, but as a fifteen-year-old boy, he didn't understand it or know how to help me. No teenager would. Having two sisters, Allen knew that girls typically watch their weight, and he most likely thought that since I was a model, I had to be even more diligent. I never knew when a job would pop up, and I took advantage of them when they did (except during exams). But I don't think he had a clue as to how fucked-up I was getting about food. I just became that annoying girlfriend who was constantly asking her boyfriend to appease her panicked psyche. He was too young and uninformed to think anything was wrong. Even if he did know what was going on, would I have stopped? I don't think so. My problem was bigger than Allen, bigger than I even understood at the time. The disease was consuming me, and I didn't even know it.

I started exhibiting other traits of anorexia at this time, like the weird fascination with watching other people eat, as if I were eating through them. Allen would be a frequent proxy, depending on what I craved each week. Once I went through a toasted bagel, cream cheese, and smoked salmon phase, but I would never dare eat it myself. So I would get up extra early to make Allen the delicious sandwich that I wanted to eat, wrap it up, and go on my bus-ferry-bus commute holding this fucking thing. When I got to school, I would hand it to him and watch him eat it, asking him over and over again if it was good. He probably thought I was just being a sweet, thoughtful girlfriend. I'd like to think so, too, but I know better—it was a weird ritual that reflected my deteriorating relationship with food. And it was about to get even worse.

One day after school, I came home to my mum doing a very un-Mum-like thing—she was cooking Korean instant noodles called shin ramyun. Though she was a health nut, she'd occasionally indulge in half a pack of these processed noodles as a treat.

OMG, I want some.

"Can I have a little bit of that?" I asked.

"Sure, I'll make you some. Sit down."

I sat down at our small table in the kitchen with my mum, and while we ate, we talked about the day. It was weird—we didn't do this very often (if at all), so it was nice to share this rare moment of normalcy with her. I was happy, sitting there with her. She ate her food slowly and savored every bite. I, on the other hand, wolfed it down as if I hadn't eaten in days (because I probably hadn't). I slurped all the soup, too. As I sat there, that now-familiar surge of guilt came rushing in. The feeling felt worse this time, as it if were burning through me. I thought maybe I could talk to my mum about the shit that was going on in my head. *She can help me. After all, she is my mother. She just ate the same thing—does she feel the same thing I do? She also watches her weight . . . maybe she has gone through the same things I'm going through right now?* This seemed as a good a time as any; I had her attention, for sure, and we were—dare I say it?—bonding. We had never talked about what I was going through, though. For all I knew, she just thought I looked good, having lost weight. She didn't seem concerned about how much I had lost; at this point I was just healthier than I had been, and she seemed happy about that. I didn't want to blurt anything out, so I tested the waters first.

"I don't feel good," I said. What I meant was, *I don't feel good about myself. I hate myself.*

She must have thought I meant that I felt nauseous. "Are you okay?"

"I really don't feel good. I feel like I want to throw up."

"If that's how you feel, then you should go and throw up."

Was she giving me permission to throw up? I got up from the table and went downstairs to my bathroom. *My mum said it was cool, so I guess it is okay.* I know now my talking to her was a cry for help. I wanted relief from the constant internal dialogue that was going on. I wanted to get rid of that giant purple monster.

The noodles were spicy, so what came up was particularly acrid. It burned my throat. *Oh God, did I get it all out?* I kept going and going until there was nothing left. As gross as it was, it was oddly and sadistically satisfying to watch every single bite I took come back up.

While I felt like I had just done something really gross, I also felt like I had just figured out how to cheat the system. I got to eat the food I wanted to eat without the calories. I didn't know it then, but I had crossed the line into another disorder, bulimia, and it quickly became a common occurrence.

My mum didn't know it, but I took her approval this one time as a signal to go full steam ahead. Once I did, it quickly became a pattern: I would go anywhere up to four days without solid foods, and then I'd stuff my face. Then I'd feel like shit, so shitty that I'd make myself throw up. I know now that it was such a natural progression from anorexia to bulimia because starving yourself is just not sustainable; you become so hungry that you binge. Your metabolism is shot, as the body starts storing everything that touches your lips because it is so deprived. The only way to avoid gaining a few pounds in a day is to throw it all up immediately after eating. I got the pleasure of consuming food but without keeping the calories. *Here is the answer. I've found the best of both worlds.* I was so wrong. I had absolutely no regard for health. I knew nothing about metabolism or my body or hormones. I had no idea that my body couldn't handle it and that I was messing up my entire digestive system. I was fucking it all up, and the repercussions would last a lifetime.

As I became more and more obsessed, I took to the Internet to get my hands on information about dieting, but instead found myself poring over "ana" and "mia" blogs—"ana" is short for "anorexia," and "mia" is short for "bulimia" (the irony). These blogs opened a whole new world that fed my growing addiction: It was an anorexic girl's dream to find the secret trove of blogs out there with girls sharing photos of their "progress." I scanned through hundreds of images of girls with razor-thin faces, protruding shoulders and hips, stick-thin legs. Skin and bones. All rake thin, they were looking for affirmation from other fellow sufferers. I would look at the pictures and enviously think, *I am not there yet. I'm just getting dieting tips.* I wanted to get there, though, and that thought in and of itself meant that I was already a full-blown anorexic.

It was on these blogs that I read about the importance of calories, but it was in a vacuum; there was no discussion about caloric intake in the broader context of nutrition. There was no talk of healthy fiber, fats, and protein. Armed with this limited knowledge, I started to calculate numbers and figures as I compulsively looked up how to minimize and burn calories. Every day I wrote down how many calories I ate in my book. I was meticulous about it, recording my food intake in charts and diagrams, like a mad scientist on the brink of a major breakthrough. I would record all the Diet Coke and sugar-free drinks I drank, not realizing that there was so much more to consider than just the number of calories.

As I went down this rabbit hole, I picked up other pieces of "advice," like dealing with yellowing teeth: "Make sure to brush your teeth after you throw up, but remember not to swallow any of the toothpaste because toothpaste has calories." Or this: "After throwing up food, drink more water and throw up again to make sure everything is out. Wash your hands quickly to avoid yellowing fingers." Each tip was more extreme than the last. Nowhere was a discussion of the precarious game we were all playing with our bodies, depleting them of necessary nutrients and causing serious dehydration.

I also continued to obsess over models, researching supermodels' measurements and weight. When I exhausted my research about every model in Hong Kong, I took it worldwide. I started looking up global supermodels I would see in magazines and on Fashion TV. I would obsess over the physical traits typical supermodels had—how their thighs don't touch when they walk, how their ribs are visible, how their wrist bones protrude. How much does Kate Moss weigh? Forty-five kilos (around one hundred pounds). How many kilos was Snejana Onopka? Gemma Ward? I could just Google all of it—at this point I had my own laptop that let me run loose on the Internet. To me, these numbers and stats were yardsticks of beauty. The lower the number, the more beautiful the woman. I really thought it was that simple. And unfortunately, the entertainment and fashion industries agreed. In the eighties and early nineties, the slightly fuller Amazonian women reigned—Heidi Klum, Tyra Banks, Elle Macpherson, Cindy Crawford, Helena Christensen—all beautiful and tall but healthy-looking women. But in the second half of the nineties and into the 2000s, the modeling industry expanded and the competition got tighter, and the skinnier you were, the more jobs you would book—the number on the scale gave you an advantage. With this increased supply of models and heightened competition, the ideal changed. The look was "heroin chic." Designers started finding new muses, and as beautiful as they were, they were extraordinarily skinny, and their look reset the standard of beauty for the time. When you'd flip through any fashion magazine, it would be page after page of protruding collar bones, shoulders, and hip bones; no boobs, no hips, no butt. It was a body type long idealized in Hong Kong. In Hollywood, celebrities like Paris Hilton, Lindsay Lohan, and Nicole Richie were setting a similar example with their super skinny frames (in low-rise jeans, no less—let's never bring back low-rise jeans, please!).

It was a body type my father idealized, and it was the body type my mum had. When I was younger, I would often hear him comment, in his British accent, "That woman has a huge arse." Or he'd mention how big someone's thighs were. I internalized all this cultural and familial idealization, which added to my already hypercritical view of my body. I analyzed every inch of it, compared and judged it against the standards I knew, and finally decided my thighs were my biggest flaw, too. After that, I became obsessed with maintaining a "thigh gap" and achieving that perfect little triangle of space between my legs. I'd even watch runway shows on TV and study the models strutting their stuff. I'd analyze their walks, their strides, their arm swings, their hip movements, but most of all, I'd pay attention to how big their thigh gap was.

I continued to record my shrinking measurements, calories, and daily food intake in my notebook. I wrote about the information and tips I had found online and pasted photos of my favorite models and celebrities onto the book's pages. Part diary, part scrapbook, part record log, this book held all my secrets, thoughts, and obsessions. It became my bible. My "thinspiration" book. This book was my best friend and my constant companion as I waded through the muck of my eating disorders.

I hid the book in my bedroom, tucked in a top cubby of my white built-in wardrobe. One day my mum found it—she always loved to go through our shit. When I came home from school that day, she followed me into my bedroom. I sat on my bed, she sat down next to me, and she said, "I found your book."

My heart sank. *FUCK.*

"You have a lot of self-control—very good," she added. *Um, what?* Was she fucking congratulating me? I was mystified. Didn't she see how obsessed I was becoming by recording every piece of food I ate? Did she not find it alarming that I had kept tabs on other models' weight and measurements? I look back on this moment now and wonder if it was because I didn't look like I had anorexia—you know, that look of emaciation, of only skin and bones. Eating disorders and disordered eating can occur in *everyone,* no matter your size—one does not have to look like they are on the verge of death to have a problem. I had grown increasingly aware that what I was doing wasn't right, so a small part of me was disappointed that my mum didn't ask concerned questions like "Are you okay?" My book didn't raise any alarm bells for her. My mum would not save me from myself. But even if she had said something, it would not have changed my behavior. No one can force someone out of an eating disorder, just as no one can force someone to overcome a drug addiction. You have to truly want to get better.

And I was not ready for that. I knew what I was doing, even though I may have denied it. In that moment, when I imagined being sent to rehab or a clinic, I thought all my progress would go to waste. I was not ready to be exposed.

As I continued to struggle with food, I also struggled with my blossoming social life, one which had not existed before. A new boyfriend, new friends, a blossoming career, a full social calendar—I didn't really understand it all. I was overwhelmed, and I started making poor decisions (in addition to the poor decision of not eating).

I was struggling emotionally. On the one hand, it felt amazing to finally be accepted, but on the flip side, I kept wondering what made me finally good enough. Was it because I had lost weight? Was it because I was a model? It all seemed too good, too soon.

And then I met Chelsea.

4. A SLIPPERY SLOPE

———

"DOES ANYONE DO *ANYTHING* FUN AROUND HERE?" boomed an unfamiliar voice in a posh British accent. It was a Monday in year nine, and I had been walking onto the playground during the day's first break when I saw a huddle of kids talking over in the corner (the same corner I used to avoid before my transformation). I threw my backpack down and walked over, my eyes stopping on a tall girl with stunning looks: long, layered, flaxen hair, ample breasts, and big brown eyes with the longest, thickest, curliest dark eyelashes I had ever seen. She was holding court over the popular kids in my year, introducing herself to everyone and getting acquainted. She was a transplant from the UK—the new girl in school.

"I'm from England, but I'm really Norwegian," she explained. She had a confidence I hadn't seen before. "Does anyone smoke?" she added. I could tell she was looking for more than just schoolyard fun by the mischievous way she asked the question. I was instantly drawn to her.

"I do," I replied. "Hi, I'm Mia." When I said I smoked, that was stretching the truth a bit—I had really only puffed a few cigarettes, and even then, I never really inhaled. But I wanted to impress her.

"Hi, I'm Chelsea."

"Sometimes we hang out and smoke at Pacific Place roof if you want to come. We're going today. . . ." PP roof was a beautiful rooftop park with cement benches and unobstructed views of the city. It was a popular spot for kids to hang out after school and on the weekends.

That day after school I went with Allen and a few other kids to PP roof. Chelsea was there already, elegantly puffing on a cigarette like Greta Garbo, elbow on her hip, hand loosely holding the cig as she pursed her lips, lifted her neck, and delicately inhaled and puffed smoke straight up into the air. As her lips released the cigarette, they made a unique kissing sound. She made it look so chic. *Wow, smoking looks beautiful.* I could tell she was trouble, but if trouble looked like that, I wanted in.

We sat down together among a group of kids and talked as we smoked. I filled her in on everyone at school—who gets up to what, who's dating whom, who likes whom, who was in a clique, who the hot guys were. I learned about her upbringing, where she lived, and why her family had moved to Hong Kong. I told her all about me. We got on like a fucking house on fire. Instant connection.

We talked and talked as people drifted off. We didn't want to go home. We wanted to keep talking, and we were the last of the kids to leave the park. We promised to hang out the next day at school.

And we did. Smoking cigarettes after school became a regular thing as we were quick to find out that, although she was from a different continent, we had so much in common. I had never really had a best friend before, and for her part, well, she was in a new country with no friends. It was a level playing field. For us though, it went beyond just hitting it off and sharing superficial commonalities; our family backgrounds were remarkably similar. She had also felt alcoholism in her household, with parents too mired in their own issues to focus attention on her. She also had two older brothers who lived away from home, so she was practically an only child, too. In each other, we had found someone we could talk to about our fucked-up families. We each understood what the other was going through. Mum drinking again? Yes. Mine too.

Parents fighting again? Yes. Mine too. No judgment, only empathy and understanding.

Having a new best friend may not sound like a big deal, but as my life went from zero to ninety miles per hour, it was. It was only a year earlier that I had tried to be as invisible as possible. I had seen my future, and it was as a loner quietly working in some office, living her life unnoticed (and definitely not dating a Backstreet Boy). But that was before losing weight. Before modeling. Before my life drastically changed. I was no longer invisible. I was on billboards and in magazines; I had friends; I had a boyfriend. Being on my own for so many years, I found all this attention overwhelming and confusing, and I started making decisions based on how much fun I could have rather than on what was good for me. Maybe it was because I had always been a good girl and had avoided drama—there had been so much of that in my household already—but now I had the opportunity to shed that shy-girl image and be a *normal* teenager. It was an opportunity I'd never thought I would have, and, of course, being a teenager meant being a little rebellious. I began looking for trouble, and I found it with Chelsea.

Our after-school smokes soon progressed to smoking in the girls' bathroom during break times and drinking at the public basketball courts where everyone hung out on Friday nights. We'd just talk—about boys, about school, about our parents and what was going on at home. I had my siblings, but they were thousands of miles away. I had Allen, but he didn't understand everything I was going through because he came from a relatively normal and loving household. Chelsea understood. She got it. Probably even more importantly, we both felt *safe* with each other, and that reality created something special between us. We had each other's backs. We became each other's support system as the two freaks from freaky households living in a world of normal people. We found ourselves hating to say goodbye, not wanting to leave and go back to our frequently chaotic homes. We couldn't wait to be with each other again.

We became so close.

One day—I don't remember who suggested it—we decided to skip school to spend the day together. This was not an easy accomplishment, as our school was so fucking strict—security cameras were placed over all of the school entrances and exits, lateness was not tolerated, and a parent's note was required for any missed days. Our escape was a production, to say the least. When we decided what day we were going to do it, we made a plan of action. First up were the notes from our parents. We decided to type out the notes, rather than write them, so we only had to get the signatures perfect. Then we practiced and practiced and practiced the signatures before we got them right.

Parents' notes, check.

Next, we needed IDs for booze. There was an international student center that printed IDs without asking for proof of age—don't ask me why; we didn't ask—but we had managed to get real student cards that said we were over eighteen. I had asked to make my age nineteen, but I changed it up because everyone else had cards that made them eighteen. (How many eighteen-year-olds can there be in Hong Kong?!)

IDs, check.

We also knew to bring a change of clothes in our backpacks. Our school uniforms would raise flags to law-abiding citizens, who could call the school and report us.

Extra set of clothes, check.

The morning of our escape, we dressed in our uniforms and left our houses at the usual time, but instead of heading off to school we met up at the nearby Hopewell Center. There, we found a public bathroom and changed out of our uniforms into our "normal" clothes. We crumpled up our uniforms, stuffed them into our bags, and headed off to the Wellcome supermarket for some refreshments. Successfully out of our uniforms and on the streets, we felt like we had busted out of prison. We felt a rush of independence, outsmarting the suckers stuck in school. We had the whole day to ourselves, with only one item on the agenda: to have the fucking time of our lives. First off, drinks. We were teenagers after all, so we used our IDs to buy a bottle of cheap gin and a Tetra Pak of apple juice. It was a weird combo, like us. I think we picked the two just because it was unheard of. We even gave our drink a name: the "MiChel"—a mashup of "Mia" and "Chelsea."

We walked to PP roof, which would normally be teeming with kids but was empty when we got there at ten A.M. We started drinking: a swig of gin, a swig of apple juice, then a cig in between, until we finished both bottles. One moment, we were laughing and stumbling around; the next, we felt like retching and could barely sit up straight.

"I feel sick," I said to Chelsea.

"Mmm, me too," she agreed, holding her stomach. Then, almost in unison, we started vomiting in the bushes. We somehow managed to hold it together enough to take a cab back to her house and pass out for the rest of the afternoon.

Why did we do this? Partially because we were fourteen. It was the rebellious nature of the teenage years. But, as our friendship grew, we pushed the boundaries of that rebellion. I hung out with her more and more and was with Allen less and less. And we didn't just drink, we drank *a lot*. The more we hung out, the more we'd drink. And we always drank until we got sick. It was like we could forget our angsty teen issues even if it was just for a few hours if we blacked out. Looking back on it now, it's plain to see what compelled us to these extremes. It was self-destruction. We were two hurting teenagers who felt we deserved to be punished, even if that punishment came by our own hand.

Soon we took our sneaking out to the next level. We started hanging out in Lan Kwai Fong, the nightlife hub of Hong Kong. We'd tell our parents we were going to see a movie, calculate down to the minute how much time we had until said movie let out and the closest ferry departed, then head off to a bar, the cheaper the better. It wasn't about having a good time; it was about getting fucked-up. One bar, Bulldogs, was a favorite for no other reason than it accepted our IDs without question. On one particular night, there was a group of Marines out on the town. They were *everywhere*—every club and bar in Lan Kwai Fong was filled with them. They were rowdy and ready to party, and probably hadn't seen a female in a minute. They hooted and hollered and tried to buy us drinks when we walked through the crowd to get to the bar. We could not have given a single fuck. That was not why we were there. In fact, we saw it as an annoying distraction that disrupted our little world. We walked right past them, straight to the bar, ordered four rum and cokes each, and started downing them. Inevitably, we'd have about half an hour's worth of fun before we had to throw up.

We'd throw up in the bathroom, then go back to the bar for another round. Somehow, we'd always manage to remember our curfew, and when it was time to go, we'd stumble out. Chelsea would hail a cab to take her home, and I'd hail another one, high heels in hand, in a race to get to the ferry. I had gotten really good at my calculations: I knew the exact time to leave in order to hail a cab and make the eleven P.M. ferry. I would try my best not to get sick in the cab, but if I did, I'd give the driver HK$100 (about $15 US) for his troubles and get out fast, ignoring the yelling in Cantonese as he drove away. The ferry ride was another twenty to thirty minutes. I'd buy a couple of waters and down them to try to sober up, knowing the ferry had a bathroom if I needed to throw up. My parents were usually asleep, so I'd be able to get home and slip into my bedroom unnoticed.

The next day, we'd call each other as soon as we woke up (at fourteen, what was a hangover?) and debrief about the previous night's escapades—what we could remember of them, anyway. *What was with that guy who tried to make you dance? Or that idiot who tried to buy you a drink? Haha, yeah, and you nearly got sick all over him. Did you throw up in the cab? Yes. Did you? YES. Hahahahaha. Did the driver get mad? Yup!*

Soon we were hitting repeat on this scenario *every weekend*: We'd come up with an alibi, arrive at a bar, drink way too much, get sick, somehow manage to get home, and crawl into bed like good girls before curfew. We both loved the thrill of doing shit we weren't supposed to do, made possible by our strategic and covert tactics. We operated on the thrill that our parents *could* find out. It was pretty much the same modus operandi I had with my eating issues. *I could get in a lot of trouble for this.* That was the thrill. *I am doing an irresponsible thing. I hope no one notices,* all the while kind of wishing someone did. It was as if we were daring someone to put a stop to our recklessness. But with both sets of parents otherwise engaged with their own issues, no one did.

So we pushed the boundaries further. We got such a rush from it all—being in bars, drinking, sneaking around—that saying goodbye and rushing for curfew sucked. How could we get more time together? Could we push the envelope even more? Could we stay out all night? Do what adults do? We envisioned dancing, laughing, and partying until the sun came up. WE WANTED A NONSTOP PARTY. Fuck the curfew! So that is what we did—we decided to stay out all night. I told my parents that I was sleeping over at Chelsea's house, and she did the same. Once on our own, we dressed the part: We put on low-rise jeans with our thongs sticking out (never a good look), crop tops, chunky heels, and dangly earrings. To house all my shit, I carried a miniature shoulder bag stuffed with a top to change into the next day so my alibi of sleeping over at a friend's house held up. My hair was highlighted blond and pin straight (it was the 2000s, and everyone had their hair chemically straightened to be flat, flat, flat). As we headed out, both of us thought, *Our parents would kill us if they found out.* So I double-checked our covers: "You sure your mum isn't going to call my mum?"

"Positive. My mum is out tonight," Chelsea replied.

And with that reassurance, we snuck off to Lan Kwai Fong. With our IDs (and in our outfits), we got into the clubs, where we drank and danced the night away.

At four A.M., as last call was announced, we got slapped with the reality (one I'm sure some of you are familiar with) that hits you when the lights come up in the club. Suddenly, the room that had previously had a soft, dreamy ambiance became a stark, disgustingly filthy place that smelled like stank beer. We checked ourselves out in a mirror and recoiled after seeing our makeup had run halfway down our sweaty faces during the night, and we weren't as cute as we thought we were. Yeah, it was time to get out. That glamorous vision of dancing the night away, grabbing breakfast somewhere, and making our way home basking in morning sunlight was not to be. Our romantic visions were dashed as the reality set in that clubs close, people get tired, hangovers kick in, the temperature drops, and ultimately . . . the party does end.

We hadn't thought far enough ahead to come up with a game plan for the morning. We couldn't go home. Not at this hour. So, we opted for the best park with an inviting bench. The park on top of the ferry pier was nicely groomed with long cement benches and was a seven-minute cab ride away. We headed over there and parked ourselves on two benches that overlooked the water. But soon it got chilly (our crop tops weren't exactly thermal), and we rubbed our arms, trying in vain to keep ourselves warm as we waited for the sun to come up. We couldn't really sleep on the cold hard slabs, so we just smoked joints till the sun came up. (Yes, we had gotten into that, too.) The cold wind made it hard to roll, and the hash, along with the alcohol that was in my system, made everything feel really fucking sideways.

Have you ever been out until sunrise? I always thought it would be some sort of life-changing experience, but it was actually pretty depressing. As light peeked over the horizon, we saw people starting to trickle out of their homes to go for a jog or do tai chi in the park, or make their way to work. There is nothing worse than watching people get up early and start their productive days while you're still up from the night before, feeling like death.

Needless to say, the novelty of staying out all night got old fast. It was a newbie mistake for sure, but if we were to continue to do this, Chelsea and I agreed, we needed to up our game and find a better place to wait out the sunrise. Allen, who didn't really have a curfew, would often hang out at 24/7 gaming centers. In Asia, gaming is huge, and these places were sprinkled all over Hong Kong. Bleary-eyed, sleep-deprived kids would park themselves at a station and stay up for days playing *Counterstrike* or *Defense of the Ancients* (DOTA) with friends. There were even restaurants in these places, so they never had to stop playing; they could just get sustenance delivered to their gaming station and survive for days.

Hmmm, maybe they are on to something here, we thought. So, on the nights that Chelsea and I wanted to stay out, we'd find out where Allen was, pay the cheap hourly rate, find empty chairs, move the keyboards aside, lay our heads down, and try to sleep until morning. I say "try" because the chairs were extremely hard, and the staff would wake us up every time they'd do their rounds. The air-conditioning was always on full blast, and with all the games' dramatic sound effects like explosions, gunfire, and battle screams, it was not so quiet, but at least we felt safe.

We started smoking more and more hash. In Hong Kong, there was barely any access to weed, so we'd smoke that instead. I had to buy it off triad affiliates (Hong Kong gang members). Part of me loved that I was flirting with danger. The old, quiet, "good" Mia was gone; this new Mia was brazen, restless, and becoming increasingly out of control.

We'd find quiet places to smoke—in a deserted park or in a forgotten alley—a hard thing to do, as Hong Kong is so heavily populated. One time, Chelsea and I were out with Alex and Karen, other schoolmates we had become friendly with, and we had slipped into a dark alley in Lan Kwai Fong to smoke before we met up with other kids from school to go drinking. Now, when I say alley, I mean an alley—a four- or five-feet-wide dingy back street behind buildings, filled with smelly trash bags, rats that scrambled underneath them, and dirty droplets of water dripping from air conditioners in windows above. I had been sitting on the ground rolling a joint in a hundred–Hong Kong–dollar bill in my lap; I was laser focused, trying to roll this joint for everyone in near darkness. I wasn't a seasoned stoner yet, so my rolling skills were amateur at best, but I felt the pressure to do it well and fast—everyone was dying to smoke. I kept dropping it and having to start over. I was nearly done when suddenly, someone yelled, "Hey!" from behind us. We all turned around in unison. It was a policeman, and he was standing right behind me. Before I could even register what was happening, Karen and Alex bolted. Chelsea looked at me and yelled, "RUN!" before scurrying off herself. I quickly scrunched up the note with all the hash and tobacco in my hand and ran. We booked it out of the alley and onto the main road of bars and clubs, down the hill, through the throngs of people on the street. The policeman chased after us, waving his hands in the air and yelling something, but we were out of earshot.

After a high-speed foot chase worthy of *Cops*, we lost him.

We stopped and caught our breath. We all looked at each other, huffing and puffing, and then we burst out laughing. But then I looked in my handbag and noticed my wallet (and my ID) wasn't there. I must have left it behind. *That's what he was waving in the air. Oh shit, my ID. Oh shit, my fake ID! Oh my God, my hash was hidden in my wallet. Fuck.*

The next day, the police rang my house phone. My mum answered the call, so she told me the police had my wallet. Oddly, she didn't ask me for any further clarification. I went to pick it up, worried what would happen once I got to the station. I resigned myself to the idea that I would be in trouble and had decided that I would accept whatever was coming my way. I would take responsibility. But after I signed in at the desk, they just handed me my wallet. No questions asked. Everything was there, money and cards, except the hash. But no one said anything. I got away with it. This close encounter was a whole new level of a thrill—*I nearly got caught*. My parents could have found out. I could have been in trouble with the police. But none of that happened. I felt fully alive. To me, this high was off the charts compared to my previous teen antics. We started to push that envelope even more. We graduated to shoplifting.

It's not like we needed anything—we all had money. It wasn't for the actual loot—lip gloss from drug stores, bras from Marks & Spencer, a cute top from a market stall—it was for the thrill of it. Running from the cops wasn't scary; in fact, it was exhilarating. The closer we got to getting caught, the bigger the rush. It was all or nothing with me, and at the time, it seemed like all we were doing was having some harmless fun. But, in reality, what we were doing was self-sabotaging and dangerous.

All this was a great distraction from my eating disorders. It was much better to be out causing trouble than sitting in my bedroom craving food and looking at images of stick-thin models. But those thoughts were still very much there. Chelsea suffered from them, too, so needless to say, we encouraged each other's worst tendencies. This became yet another secret for the two of us to share, another similarity that bound us to each other and separated us from the rest of the world. We would frequently have check-ins with each other:

"I want to be skinnier." *Me too!*

"I haven't eaten all day." *I haven't either.*

"I haven't eaten since yesterday." *Me neither.*

"I hate myself." *Me too.*

"Ever notice that when your stomach is rumbling but you have a cigarette, the rumbling stops?" *Yes, I have.*

It was just another way we clicked. I could tell her my worst demons, and she would love me unconditionally. We'd encourage each other to not eat for as long as possible. Then we'd drink, and because neither of us had anything in our stomachs to soak up the alcohol, it hit us harder.

Once, after our first break of the school day, Chelsea and I met up at our usual spot on the playground. We hugged, and I noticed Chelsea was wearing a Rastafarian-colored terry cloth wristband— green, yellow, and red. *How random,* I thought. *So unlike Chelsea.*

"What's that?" I asked.

"I just thought it was cool. I found it in my room. I like it," she replied. Then she asked me about my previous night. We had been dealing with a lot in our respective homes, and she knew I was having a particularly tough day.

"It sucked," I told her. "I got so frustrated with my mum and her drinking that I did something kind of weird. I cut myself." I held out my wrist. Hidden under a bunch of black rubber bracelets were several lines of red cuts across my wrist, all overlapping one another. I did it with a math compass. It was the first time I had done something like that, but I didn't hesitate with Chelsea. I knew she wouldn't judge me.

Let me stop for a moment. I hadn't ever cut myself before. But my home life was at its worst with my parents' fighting and my mum's drinking. I felt like shit every time I went home, because I didn't know what was going to happen. I felt trapped as I listened to them screaming through my locked bedroom door. I fucking hated the yelling, and the icy aftershocks of tension that came with it. My parents also loved to involve me in their fights as some kind of referee or jury. When my mum would sit upstairs and drink, I would avoid her by just staying behind the locked door of my bedroom, because she would start to do unpredictable shit, such as calling people to complain about my dad or what a troublesome daughter I was. I hated the house I lived in, and I hated my parents at the time. I just hated everything. And I hated my behavior being dismissed as just having teenage angst or everything being blamed on hormones—it only made me feel even more unseen and ignored. So this particular night, I sat in my room at my desk, wanting to feel something else. I cut myself, thinking that it would make me feel better and provide some sort of emotional release. It didn't. I was still in the same place, feeling the same emotions. And I needed to find something to cover up the ugly marks.

Chelsea grabbed my wrist in shock, pulled me closer to her, and lifted the band to show me what it was covering up: several red cuts, all about an inch long on her tanned forearm. She whispered, "*SAME!*"

Little did we know back then what it meant: that we were cutting to help with emotional pain that we couldn't settle inside ourselves. It was a physical cry for help. Chelsea was the only one who could comfort me and make me feel less crazy. Normal kids get to go back to homes that are safe, calm, and loving. We, on the other hand, had to brace ourselves to go home. We would give ourselves pep talks to prepare for the chaos that could be waiting.

There's no denying it: We loved each other. I had no secrets, no fears, no inhibitions, no boundaries with her, and that soon manifested physically in our relationship. We would kiss each other sometimes, and it felt totally comfortable. I thought she was the most beautiful girl in the world (I still do), and I wanted to protect her. Although we got up to some crazy and destructive shit together, I am thankful that our paths crossed, because without her and that safe place—no matter how temporary it was—I think I would have gone down a much more dangerous path.

It was confusing for us, and for Allen, too. He didn't fully understand the bubble that Chelsea and I lived in. It wasn't that he didn't like Chelsea; he just didn't like being made to feel like an outsider with his own girlfriend. He thought she was a bad influence, and he (quite fairly) didn't approve of the dangerous situations we put ourselves in. She had these wounds, and so did I; we brought them out of each other, but that also soothed each of us. He first knew me as Mia, the quiet fat girl, the Mia who didn't drink or go out all night to get fucked-up. He watched me change; he was up for me having fun but didn't like it when I was reckless. He was sensible and had a good head on his shoulders. As for Chelsea, she didn't always like that I gave him my time and affection; it took away from her time with me. It turned out to be a bit of a weird love triangle—well, that's how I felt anyway. I felt pulled between the two. Sometimes Allen won, and sometimes Chelsea won.

One of the (dozens of) times when Allen and I were on a break throughout our four-year romance, I was determined to make him

My two loves. Allen, me, and Chelsea in a sticker-photo booth. Hong Kong, 2004.

jealous—you know, that seething, can't-sleep, can't-eat green-eyed monster. But what would make Allen that jealous? Another boy. An older boy. And an older, bad boy. I knew just the one. *Matt.* He was a few years older, which, at that time, felt like twenty years. I liked that—it felt very adult to me. He was a charming motherfucker, and he could make anyone laugh. One year, he volunteered to play a drag queen in a school musical. He went all out—full-on drag makeup with fake eyelashes, latex corset, fishnets, platformed pleather stilettos—and he sang his little heart out. It was his sense of humor that made me ignore the red flags.

Heroin had become a big problem in Hong Kong around this time, and even our beautiful enclave of Discovery Bay wasn't spared. When I was little, my sister Gaby lost a best friend to heroin, and more recently, a boy in my school—Matt's friend—had died of an overdose. Matt had his own issues with the drug, and his friend's death was a wake-up call for him. As far as I knew, he was clean when I started dating him. I would not have gotten involved if I knew he had been using. But to be honest, I had no idea what a heroin addiction was and what it entailed.

Our getting together was done in typical teenager fashion: We saw each other out and flirted until we made out and exchanged numbers. The first few times we hung out were great. He just made me laugh, laugh, laugh the entire time we were together. But I began to notice some of those red flags, the first of which was when he started to ask for money. Looking back on it now, I see that my guard should have gone up, but it didn't. I was just so young.

"Hey, I feel really bad asking, but can I borrow two hundred [about twenty-five US] dollars?" he said hesitantly. "My parents don't trust me with money."

Hmmm, your parents not trusting you . . . another red flag.

"What for?" I asked.

"Well, it's for methadone. It keeps me off heroin."

"What?" I had no idea what he was talking about.

"Methadone. It's a heroin substitute. I take it so I don't go back on heroin. I wouldn't ask if I didn't need it."

I believed him. I fucking believed him. He was charming. He was an actor. He was an addict. I fell for his charade, worrying that he would have the desire to use again if I didn't give him the money. That's worthy of a PhD in manipulation if you ask me. I gave him the money, and I continued to do so because I thought I was helping him stay straight. Believe me, I cringe at this now. I wish I could have slapped that young version of me in the face, told her what was really going on, told her to run far, far away. At fourteen, I didn't understand the intricacies of addiction, particularly heroin addiction. All I knew was that I lived in a household with alcohol abuse, and it was a scary and uncontrollable environment.

We had been hanging out for a couple of weeks when one day after school, Matt and I were sitting by the pier waiting for the ferry that would take me home, and he turned to me and said, "I have something to tell you."

"What?" I asked, my voice tinged with worry.

"I'm using again."

I froze. I didn't even fully understand what he meant.

My blank stare back at him must have clued Matt in to the fact that I was in a state of total confusion. So he pulled up the sleeve of his red flannel shirt and showed me the bloodred marks on his arm. Track marks. *Fuck.* I didn't even know what the fuck track marks were. I sat there, frozen. I didn't ask or say anything.

"Oh my God, it feels so good getting that off my chest. Now you know. I am not hiding anything from you anymore," he said to me, relieved. I, on the other hand, was shocked. I thought, *Great, glad you feel better because I am LOSING MY SHIT. WHAT THE FUCK? What do I do with all this? Should I tell someone? Ask him to get help?* My mind raced with a thousand questions, but I knew that I was in way over my head. I couldn't speak. The bell for the ferry rang just in time, and I managed to stutter out a curt, "Bye, I'll call you later . . ." and run down to the turnstiles. I couldn't get out of there fast enough.

On that ferry ride home, I texted Chelsea, Alex, and Karen and asked what I should do. Everyone gave different advice: Break up with him, talk to him, help him. Their responses were just a mirror of my jumbled thoughts. And then, in the middle of all this, I received a message from Matt: TEXT ME WHEN YOU GET HOME SAFE. SO GLAD I'M NOT KEEPING A SECRET FROM YOU ANYMORE. MISS YOU ALREADY. X

All I could think was, *How did I get myself in this situation?* I was really just trying to make Allen jealous. This had gotten way too serious, too fast.

Like a typical teenager, I didn't know how to handle it, so I left it alone for the moment. I figured I would deal with it later. I knew it was a delicate situation, and I didn't want to do anything that would cause him to take any rash actions. I couldn't see it clearly at the time, but I had put his burden squarely on my shoulders. I was being selfless in a situation where I should have been selfish. From the moment he admitted to me that he was using, there was a rapid uptick in his using and equally rapid decline in our relationship.

I started to notice that money would go missing—HK$200 every time, to be exact. I put two and two together and realized, *Okay, now he isn't even bothering to ask me for money.* He was taking me for a ride. And yet I still didn't do anything, aside from keeping an eagle eye on my wallet. In fact, I still wanted to help him. One night, a group of us went to a club called Dreams that was a good spot that didn't question our IDs. Matt had gone to the bathroom, and when he came back, he whispered to me, "I just used—I feel sooo good."

I didn't know what to say. But I remembered my sister telling me that she wished she helped her friend more, so I wanted to help Matt before it was too late. There I was, a teenager who was no angel herself, feeling way out of her depth. I had no idea what to do, yet this person's health somehow felt like my responsibility.

His glassy eyes couldn't focus, and he was sluggish as he walked. I looked at him, though, with all the sympathy a naive girl could have, and told him, "You're gonna make it out of this addiction, and I'll do anything I can to help. You're going to get off of this. One in three people who try heroin come out of it alive. You're going to be that one."

I looked up into his hazy, half closed eyes as he took a super long drag off a Marlboro Red and I realized he wasn't even listening to me. He was high, and that was all that mattered to him. It was at that moment I knew I had to end it, but I didn't know how. I felt like someone's life was in my hands. He became insecure very quickly, and thus he began to cling to me. After school, he'd wait for me and try to play it off as him just being a sweet boyfriend. He became dependent on me emotionally, because I was the only one who knew his secret, and (I'm kicking myself as I write this) I tolerated it. If he had told anyone else, he would have been shunned or forced into rehab. Everyone else in his circle was on a zero-tolerance policy with him; his secret was only safe with me.

The interactions I had with him got increasingly worse and worse, just as *he* got increasingly worse and worse: thinner, paler, sunken eyes with dark bags. He was using more and more. The worse he got, the more scared I became to break it off.

And then he told me he loved me. And I was terrified.

We had been talking on the phone, and I was pacing in the study. I didn't want to be on the phone with him and was barely participating in the conversation. My mind was otherwise occupied, racing with excuses to end the call, and more importantly, to get out of this situation altogether, when I heard "I love you" from the other end of the line. I fell back onto the couch, covering my eyes in disbelief.

"Thank you?" I managed to respond. *Fuck, that sounded bad.* But seriously? We had known each other for a couple of weeks, *maybe* a month. He didn't love me. He just didn't want me to leave him. Everything that came out of his mouth was a lie. I had to get off the phone.

"I've got to go. I've really . . . I got to go. My mum is calling for me. . . ." I cringed as I hung up. *Fuck, fuck, fuck.*

I needed to end the relationship carefully. One evening, not long after Dreams, I was at home catching up on homework. I heard my phone buzz. I saw his name flash on my screen. I picked up.

"Hey, what are you doing right now?" he asked me. Then he added, "I came to Discovery Bay to see you. I need to see you. PLEASE."

I wished I'd never answered.

"Please come down. I am almost there. Just see me for thirty minutes?"

I didn't want to see him, but I didn't know what else to do, so I told my parents I was meeting a friend by the beach and went out and found him sitting in a stairwell behind the closed security guard station. No one was around. He looked like shit. He was sitting on a step, fiddling with a half-empty water bottle, one leg shaking from restlessness. I could tell he was all fucked-up, even under the soft light. I could see the sunken purplish circles that shadowed his eyes.

"Hey," I said, hesitantly. He nodded in response. I sat next to him on the step, but I held my knees to my chest as if to protect myself. I was so unbearably uncomfortable, but I made small talk for a bit. Then he turned to me and said, "Well, now that you know, I can do it in front of you. . . ."

Wait, what? What's he talking about? Before I could even process what he had said, off came his belt, and out came a spoon, a bag of powder, a lighter, and a needle. He was going to shoot up in front of me. I was partially in disbelief, partially in shock, and partially scared shitless. And honestly, partially fascinated. I was oddly curious about this thing that can ruin people's lives. Then I thought to myself, *Don't say anything, just wait for it to be over. You don't wanna make him angry or emotional.* I instinctively turned to this coping strategy I had learned from my childhood. When someone wants to get fucked-up, there is no stopping them. As a child I would remain quiet and tried to lay low. So here I did the same: I shut up and sat still.

I watched, keeping silent, as he narrated the entire process:

"I tie my belt around my arm to get a good vein, then I put the powder on the spoon and mix it with a small capful of water. Then I heat up the mixture with my lighter. . . ."

I watched as he flicked his lighter and held the flame under the spoon.

I watched the water and heroin mixture bubble and change color, and I watched him suck the mixture up into the syringe. I watched him put the syringe into his arm and push down. I watched the syringe flush with blood as he let go halfway; then he pushed down again and this time the entire bloody mixture emptied into his arm.

I know what you're thinking. How could I sit there and watch him do this? Why did I not get up, run back to my house, tell my parents? Tell someone? If anything, maybe that could have helped him. But I just froze; I didn't know what to do. I didn't want to frighten him or anger him.

His eyes rolled back as he slowly melted onto the steps behind him, belt still around his arm, mouth wide open. *What the fuck just happened? IS HE DEAD?!* I didn't know what to do. I didn't want to be there. I didn't want any of this. He quickly came to, making moaning noises and slurring his words. The corners of his mouth had little white drops of spittle. His eyes were so heavy he could barely keep them open.

"How do you feel?" I awkwardly asked him, trying to remain calm.

"Imagine an orgasm but times a million."

As he was talking, he gave me a faraway smile. It was like he wasn't there; he wasn't sitting on the steps with me. He was off somewhere, floating.

As I sat there with him, as freaked out as I was, I thought that if I could find out where he got his stuff, I could tip off the police. Maybe that would save Matt. But he wouldn't tell me.

I was quickly hit with the realization that I couldn't help him, and so I knew I had to go. This wasn't safe, this wasn't fun, this wasn't me, this wasn't what I wanted my life to become. I had to go.

I managed to get out an excuse. "I have to go, or my parents are going to kill me." And I ran off before he could protest.

I couldn't sleep that night. I ran through the night's events in my head over and over. I couldn't get past how he'd looked after he had shot up. It was like he'd died right there before my eyes. He was supposed to be a rebound after Allen, a distraction. How the fuck did I end up sitting in a dimly lit stairwell with somebody shooting up in front of me? No one had prepared me for how to deal with this type of situation. I was just getting used to having friends and relationships—I wanted to keep them, not end them. And I had certainly never dealt with someone who was on drugs. The truth is that even now, nearly two decades later, remembering that night on the steps with him still haunts me. Every time I think about it, that same fear washes over me. This moment, just like all the other moments of my life that showed me the horrors of addiction, got filed away as something I could never unsee.

AFTER THAT NIGHT, I tried to avoid him as much as I could, giving him excuses not to see him, saying I had castings and shoots after school. I needed time to figure out a clean break from this situation. A couple of days later, he asked me for some money again. "Hanukkah's coming up, and my family doesn't trust me with money. Do you think I could borrow some to buy them gifts? I'll pay you back, promise." He was shaking and scratching his arms. I didn't know why he was doing this at the time, but now I know he was withdrawing. But back then, his erratic behavior was the craziest thing I had ever seen.

"Why are you scratching yourself?" I asked.

"It feels like my bones are itchy." I started to feel bad for him, imagining what it must be like in his head. But then he asked for money again, and I knew he was playing me.

"I don't know, Matt. I need money to buy my Christmas presents." I managed to wiggle out of it.

I decided I couldn't be alone with this anymore; I needed help, and he needed help. The next day, as soon as I got the opportunity, I went to find his sister. His younger sister, Ashley, was in my year in school, and at break, I marched up to her on the playground.

"Hey, Matt asked me for money for Hanukkah gifts. He told me that your parents don't trust him with money. Is that true?"

"No, my parents have already given him money for Hanukkah gifts. . . ." Her voice trailed off, and her big eyes just stared at me, shocked. She had just realized he was using again. "I need to tell my parents."

Later that day, I was pulled out of class by Mrs. Hopkins. I went up to her office, where she quickly cut to the chase and asked me, "Did you steal two hundred dollars?"

"No." *Wait, what?*

"Are you dating Matt Levine?" *What the fuck is going on? What do these two things have to do with each other?*

"Yes," I answered.

"Did you steal money for him? Someone is claiming you did," she continued. *Um, what?! Me? Steal money? Wait, he stole money from me!* I didn't throw him under the bus here, but I did realize that our relationship was way past its expiration date and nothing short of a disaster. I had to get out.

But before that happened, I had to deal with my parents. The school had called them. They didn't believe that I would do something like that (thanks, Mum and Dad), and to prove it, they sent the school my bank account information to show that I had access to enough money from my modeling. I didn't need to steal. I was cleared, but now that my parents knew about Matt, they asked me if I was dating him. I told them I was, but also that I was ending it.

The next day I broke it off with him over the phone.

"I'm sorry, Matt, but it's over. I can't do this," I said, finally.

"But, please . . . I love you . . . ," he said, his voice quivering.

"Bye." I hung up.

I did it. I cut him off.

I got back together with Allen, and shortly after that, I heard Matt overdosed. He survived, but it was frightening to know that he almost died. I heard that he partly blamed me because I had broken up with him while he was in such a fragile state of mind. He thought I should have been more sensitive. As I heard these rumors spread, I thought to myself, *Fuck you. Don't put that responsibility on me.*

I felt bad for Matt, but he needed to take responsibility for his own actions. And that made me realize I did, too. I finally saw my own red flags swaying in front of me. I was in trouble. I was hanging out with the wrong people. I was going down the wrong path. I didn't want to waste my life. I had to pull back, but how?

As is often the case, fate intervened. My grade was a particularly tough group—there were a lot of kids doing hard drugs. As the year wore on, the drug situation got more and more out of control, and the school administration started to get involved. One day in late spring, our entire year was in the assembly hall taking the mock GCSEs (similar to the PSATs in the United States). At the end of the exam, school administrators asked us to remain in our seats and began calling out random names—or what we thought were random names. We all looked around, confused, mouthing to each other, "What the fuck?" Then a pattern emerged—all the names called out belonged to the "druggie" kids. A few students in our school had been doing ice—that is, crystal meth. This shit is serious and stupidly addictive. We had seen an uptick of use at our school, and I can't believe this, but Chelsea and I had been curious and had talked about trying it. Luckily, we hadn't gotten our hands on any yet. Talk about an intervention from the universe.

When they read out the last name, they let us go on our break, where we stood on the playground, asking each other what was going on. In the next class (which was PE), the second roundup started. The first group had obviously snitched and given teachers a list of names that had not been on the administration's radar.

"John Lloyd, Mia Kang, David Chen . . ."

Wait, what? My name had been called. *Uh-oh.*

I was sent to my house office. When I entered the small, poorly lit room, Mr. Chillingworth was behind his desk. I tried to look as innocent as possible.

"Do you know why you are here?" he asked.

"No," I answered simply. But I kept thinking, *fuck, fuck, fuck, fuck, fuck.*

"Are you involved with drugs?" he asked.

"No," I answered quietly.

"Do you sell drugs?" *WHAT?! Fuck no.*

"No."

I sat there dumbfounded as I went through the names of the first round in my head, trying to figure out who named me, who had used me to help themselves out of trouble. *I bet it was fucking Anika.* Anika was a formerly quiet and studious girl who had quickly turned into a rebellious druggie. Now, don't get me wrong, I knew what I had done to wind up in that office, looking at a possible suspension. I was cool with the dealers who sold hash, and I knew kids in school who wanted it. Technically, I guess I sold drugs. Hear me out: I knew where to get it, and I knew people who wanted it, so I sometimes just connected the two dots. I wasn't profiting on it—I saw it as literally helping friends out. If I was going to pick up hash, I'd just pick up some extra for friends who wanted some, too. They must have asked Anika where she got hers from and she said my name. Snitch.

"I don't know what you're talking about. I'm not a drug dealer," I continued. "I don't need to sell drugs. I make money. I model."

"So you have no issue taking a drug test?"

"No problem," I answered.

I played it cool on the outside, but inside, I was freaking the fuck out. Still in my PE uniform, I waited for my parents to come pick me up and take me to the drug testing center. As I waited, I wondered what my dad's reaction was to having been called to pick up his daughter to take her to a drug test.

My dad pulled up to the school in his dark green Jaguar and perfectly tailored Lanvin suit. I could tell he was absolutely, outrageously livid. I imagined him coming in screaming and taking me by my neck and shaking me, much like Homer Simpson strangling his son, Bart. Instead, he walked in silently, right past me. He coolly spoke to my teachers, backing me up. "If Mia says she didn't do it," I could hear my dad say, "I believe her. Let's see what the results are." My dad managed to get them to agree that if the drug test was negative, my suspension would be off. We walked out of school, and he curtly told me to get in the car. I did exactly that. My mother sat silently in the passenger seat. As we set off to the drug testing center, my dad finally broke the silence.

"Listen. Do you smoke marijuana? You're about to do a test, Mia. The consequences of it being positive are that you will be suspended. This will go on your permanent record. It will affect your university applications, which will affect your future. You need to be smart right now. You need to be honest with me, and we need to figure this out together."

Before I tell you how I answered, I want to point out that for the first time in my life I felt like my dad and I were a team. It was rare to feel like I was getting *real* attention from him. He was trying to help me. It felt nice, safe even.

"Sometimes," I answered him. I had suddenly regressed to acting like a little girl. I was sitting on my hands, my feet pigeon-toed, as I looked down in shame.

He tried to contain himself. He had just put his reputation on the line, saying that these accusations were wrong and his daughter was not a liar (oopsie). He clenched the steering wheel and, although his mouth became more pursed, his tone remained calm. But he was still on my team.

"Okay, let me ask this question, Mia. Will this test be positive?"

"Um, maybe?" I answered sheepishly.

"Okay. Okay. When was the last time that you smoked?"

The previous night I had snuck out of my house and smoked a joint with Alex. *Think, Mia, what are your options? Do you lie or trust that he can actually help you through this?*

My dad could tell that I was hesitating. "Mia," he said. "It's important for you to tell me the truth. We need to figure out a way through this."

"Last night," I said quietly.

Mum and Dad looked at each other, and I knew what they were thinking. *What? Mia? Taking drugs? Last night? But she was just home, asleep.* In one day they found out that not only was I not the good girl they thought I was, but I was also a liar. *Our Mia? That can't be.*

"Okay . . . ," he said under his breath, trying to calm himself. He decided to call his brother—a doctor—for advice. I am sure that asking his brother how to get his degenerate daughter out of a drug test was the last thing he wanted to do.

"Listen, this is the situation. Mia smoked marijuana last night and she's about to go do a urine test. How can we get this test to be negative?"

My uncle said, "It's impossible. The most you can do is drink so much water that it's untestable, or maybe you'll create a false negative."

My dad thanked his brother before hanging up and pulling over at a roadside store where he bought three huge 1.5-liter bottles of water. He opened the back door of the car, threw them onto the back seat next to me, and ordered, "Drink all of them by the time we get there." I did what he told me—I downed the bottles as if I'd been lost in the desert for days. Still guzzling water and feeling incredibly full, we pulled up to the drug testing center.

I had to pee more than I've ever had to pee in my whole life.

Once I was out of the loo, I sat down and assessed the waiting room. It was filled with all the other kids who were pulled out of class, all sitting quietly with their parents, heads hung in shame. As I waited, I had to use the bathroom a few more times. The nurses at the station totally knew what the fuck was up. This was not their first rodeo. When it was finally my turn, I went into the cubicle with a nurse who watched me pee (again, yes, I still had more than enough in me to go), so there was no chance of cheating. I handed the nurse the sample—and let me tell you, it was clear. Clear as water.

"Well you're certainly well hydrated," the nurse remarked. Yup.

"I just came from PE. I've been hydrating," I explained.

I went back to the waiting room and sat with my parents until we were called into the doctor's office. He had all of my school records in front of him. They were making the rounds, for sure.

He then looked at my parents and asked, "Can I talk to her alone?"

My parents left the room.

"You have a bright, bright future ahead of you. But you are caught up with the wrong crowd, and you are doing dumb things."

He was right.

Somehow, the test came back negative. Whether my test was really positive and he helped me out, or the urine was untestable, I'll never know. Either way, I was thrown a lifeline that day, and I knew it. I was not suspended. My record remained clean.

I may have gotten off the hook with the drug test, but my home life was fucked. We had gotten out of a hairy situation unscathed, but my parents made sure that I was on lockdown for the next few months. I went to school and came straight back home. My clothes were inspected for that impossible-to-deny cigarette smell. My school bag was searched for any paraphernalia. I had no social life.

Chelsea was on lockdown, too. Her parents had had enough of her shit. Everyone, in fact, was on lockdown. Chelsea and I had our timetables rearranged by the school, so we didn't have any classes together (we were seen as a distraction for each other). Chelsea eventually got sent back to school in the UK. It was so bittersweet. I was crushed to see my best friend go; we assured each other we would write, call, text. It would all be okay. I was devastated to lose my confidante, partner in crime, and best friend, but looking back now, I know it was a good thing. Together we were like a powder keg of volatility, and who knows what sort of dangerous path we would have walked down if we hadn't said goodbye.

As much as it sucked, lockdown did help. My dad really tightened the reins. He knew that I knew better. I wanted to be better for myself. I trusted that my dad knew what was best for me. When he told me that my social life was going to hinder my opportunities for success, I listened and didn't resist. Yes, I fucked up early, but at least I got it out of my system while I was young. After all, my grades and studies were important to me, and I knew I wanted to go to university. Not just any university, but Oxford, like my dad and my uncle. Neither of my brothers applied, so I wanted the chance to continue the family legacy. And I had nearly ruined it. My dad knew what it took to succeed, but he also knew how to balance hard work with some fun. When he said, "You're just play-ing; you're not working," I listened to him, finally. I respected him. He scared the shit out of me, but I also craved that kind of fatherly guidance. I could tell that both my parents were disappointed, and that was the worst feeling, worse than their being angry at me. For this, I wanted to do better. I wanted to try harder. I needed to discipline myself and remain focused on doing well on the GCSEs and later, the A levels.

So all the students buckled down, studied, and took the GCSEs. When the results came back, I was shocked. There are twelve sub-jects covered in the GCSEs, and I didn't do as well as I had hoped. A big blow. I knew I was smart. I knew I was an A student. I knew I had all the potential in the world, but my scores hardly reflected that potential. As a matter of fact, my school record, report card, and GSCEs weren't reflecting that, either. My performance records were going to get me accepted into a university—or not. My future and my goals were all in jeopardy. Why? Because of nothing else but *me*. Because of that punk-ass teen that I had turned into.

These grades were not at all acceptable to me or my father. He was livid. I stood in front of him while he went through my report and yelled at me, and I just took it because I knew I was a disap-pointment. This wasn't the future that I wanted, either. This was a pivotal moment that pushed me to really hunker down and start thinking seriously about what was ahead for me. Modeling wasn't my endgame at all—I just saw it as a side hustle. I actually wanted to work in finance. Economics and finance had always fascinated me, particularly how we create entire financial ecosystems yet have very little control over them. In just one day, the markets could go up or down, depending on what was going on in the world. (I followed all of it, too, by subscribing to *The Economist* when I was fifteen.) Anyway, a financial career—or Oxford—wasn't going to happen if I didn't take control of the situation. I had been distracted; I took my eyes off the ball. I was fortunate to be given an opportunity with modeling and a social life, but I didn't know how to handle it. I let my grades slip. I focused on having fun without thinking of the consequences. I needed to stop messing around. I needed to do better. I needed to slow down. I needed to ace my A levels. I needed to get into a top university. Full stop. Discussion over. It was time to get serious.

5. BEANS AND YOGURT

—

LIKE A MOVIE FADING TO BLACK, my short-lived punk-ass life was indeed over. I went to school and I came home. No seeing friends. No spending time with Allen. I was under lock and key until I earned my parents' trust back and got my grades up. One more mistake and I would be off to boarding school in England (a threat my parents used whenever I pushed the limits). And there was no fucking way I was doing that—I finally had a circle of friends and a boyfriend. I was not giving those up.

For the next few months I kept my head down. Every day was the Mia Kang version of *Groundhog Day*: school, home, study, sleep. I could call Allen and text my friends, but it was 24/7 focus on my grades. No modeling jobs. No drinking. No naughty business, except for cigarettes, which I hid with utmost stealth. I'd leave early in the morning, saying I was going to get breakfast on the way to the ferry, which I guess wasn't really a lie—my breakfast was composed of two Marlboro Lights. I'd carry a can of deodorant (I didn't even wear deodorant, and I still don't) to fumigate myself before I walked into the house after school. I secretly smoked on my balcony when my parents went to sleep (it was a shared balcony). I would slide the door open so slowly, millimeter by millimeter, to be as quiet as possible.

With all this time at home, there were two major downsides. One, I was alone with my mum more, so I tried to keep to my room. My mum had never consistently drunk every day; instead, she had periods of bingeing and periods of sobriety. She'd take up a religion or read a self-help book that seemed to give her the motivation to get sober, but then a personal crisis would arise and she would inevitably fall off the wagon. When I'd hear the click of the beer cap or pop of the wine cork, my whole heart would sink, because I knew she was beginning a drinking binge.

In those times, I could say that I needed to study and stay out of her way. But when my dad was home, they fought. It seemed like one long, constant fight that never let up, and now that I was older, I better understood that this wasn't typical parental behavior. I began to resent both of them for it. That sort of animosity and negativity can bear down on a person, especially an adolescent, and I tried my best not to let it get to me.

I had other issues to worry about. In my last two years of school, I had put modeling on hold, so while I wasn't as obsessed with being the skinniest I could be, that didn't mean my eating disorders just vanished. I was still trying to figure out how I could eat and stay skinny with absolutely zero metabolism. I'd try all kinds of diets: eating fruit only, and the popular Atkins diet, to name a couple. I'd also try tricks like eating with a tiny spoon for the ultimate in portion control, or chewing food a hundred times before swallowing. In fact, at one point I tried eating only condiments and sauces. But nothing stuck, because my body was already so damaged. My weight yo-yoed as I searched for a way to live and eat without worry and guilt.

Because I was on lockdown, alone in my quiet room, I had all the time in the world to indulge my own worst inclinations about food. The silence only made louder the voice in my head telling me that I needed to be skinnier. That voice was *always* talking, preying on my insecurities, telling me I wasn't good enough or thin enough, but it was so much louder when I was alone.

My body dysmorphia continued to play mind games, too. I was in no way happy with how I looked at any point, and I compared myself to pretty much every image in a magazine and every person

I came in contact with—both men and women, but especially women. I'd see a female, scan her body, and mentally record what and how she ate. I'd wonder if she had the same food insecurities. I would watch everyone around me eat, jealous that they had such a normal relationship with food. Strangers in movies, people on the playground, even a random person sitting at that table in Starbucks; it didn't matter who. At times, I even resented Allen for his healthy digestive system—how ridiculous is that? No doubt about it, comparing myself with every other human 24/7 was exhausting.

I also had more time to look at shit online, specifically the ana and mia blogs. I'd buy magazines and flip through them while, again, obsessing over how skinny the models were. Guilty, self-loathing thoughts would creep in and take hold. Starve, binge, purge, starve, binge, purge. I would try to get away with eating one small thing a day, just like when I first lost the weight. Controlling my diet with such obsession and precision made me feel like I had control over my whole life.

But I didn't have that kind of control over my body, and it would start giving out. One night, I fainted when I was in the kitchen, making dinner for my parents. (I wanted to cook for my parents to watch them eat, just like I had with Allen.) I hadn't eaten in so long, and my body had had enough. My parents chalked it up to dehydration, combined with the heat coming from the stove that I was standing over as I cooked. I knew better, though. I was spent. To them, I didn't look like a sick person. I was thin, but not rail thin like the more extreme cases of anorexia, so why would they worry? Mental disorders and addictions aren't as easily recognizable as physical diseases, so by the time something like anorexia really starts to manifest, it's already well into its development. The signs are much harder to recognize.

Something kept telling me that this behavior wasn't healthy, though. *This can't be how normal people live their lives, can it?* I was starving myself just to maintain my weight and stop myself from ballooning. If I did eat, I tortured myself with earth-shaking guilt for doing so. But in my constant comparison of others, I knew that other people didn't go through what I went through. I'd watch other kids eat lunch, and they didn't seem to cry and flog themselves for eating. I started realizing I had a problem. Scratch that, I *knew* I had a problem. I was miserable, starving, bingeing, and flooded with guilt, tired of the overwhelming cycle. I decided to confront my parents about my eating disorder.

I thought that maybe if I sat my parents down, I could open up and let them know what was going on. I had been debating whether or not to have a conversation with them for several days, and I finally felt brave enough to do it. After my dad had come home from work, I asked, "Can I talk to you guys?" It was the first time I had ever said that. As you know by now, we were not a very communicative family.

They looked at each other, concerned, and replied in unison, "Sure."

We sat down at the dining table, as I anticipated a long conversation—who knew what they were expecting to come out of my mouth? Was I pregnant? Was I addicted to drugs? I cut off their wild speculation by quickly blurting out, "I think I have an eating disorder."

My dad breathed a sigh of relief and shifted in his seat. I was wasting his time. He put his hands on the seat to push himself out of the chair as he said dismissively, "Mia, you don't have an eating disorder. You like food too much."

He walked downstairs to the living room, and my mum followed.

The conversation was shut down. *No, you are wrong—you have no idea*, I thought. They dismissed me and my issues. Granted, he had a point. I did, and still do, love food. It's wrong to think that people who love food can't possibly have an eating disorder, though (overeating is a disorder in itself). A deep love for food is the perfect tinder for conditions like anorexia or bulimia. People who love to eat food tend to overindulge, which can lead to guilt or self-hating thoughts, which can in turn lead to purging, or restriction, as a punishment. And the cycle continues.

They didn't take me seriously, perhaps because I didn't look sick. I had a second cousin who had unfortunately passed away from bulimia a year or two prior. Before she died, she physically embodied what it means to have an eating disorder. I believe my dad felt that unless something was visibly wrong, there was no need to worry. But they couldn't possibly have understood the psychological toll of the disease's demands, like my intense fear of gaining even the slightest weight and how that distorted my perception of my body. And I guess part of me understood that they didn't want to deal with yet another issue. The drug incident was bad enough; I'm sure they didn't want to think about the possibility of their daughter having an eating disorder.

We didn't talk about it again. Disappointed that I was reprimanded for even thinking that way, I decided to put aside my hope that my parents would help me. I was on my own.

In fact, the incident weirdly made me feel motivated to keep going. If I didn't look skinny enough for my parents to think I had a problem, then maybe I didn't. If I wasn't alarming anyone, well then, maybe I had more weight to lose. Let me stop here and underscore how wrong I was. I clearly had firmly entrenched myself in eating disorders, and I rationalized the irrational. Like any addict, I would find any excuse to keep it up, just as an alcoholic will find any reason to drink.

Over the next few months, I slowly gained my parents' trust back. They could see that I was studying hard and doing well in school, so they gradually allowed me to see Allen. We'd hang out at his place or go to the movies, but I had to stick to an early curfew and my mum always checked in with him to make sure I was with him. In all seriousness, it was this time with myself, through the remainder of high school, that I learned a good lesson: how to balance work and play. I had gone so far off the charts with my recklessness that I had neglected my studies. With time on the sidelines, I soon came to see that there could be a balance of both. I could temper my social life and modeling so they didn't impede my studies. It was like what Celina Jade had told me years ago on that ferry ride: Anything is possible with self-discipline. And I knew I had insane amounts of that. After all, there was enormous self-discipline required to starve myself for days on end.

And I was still figuring it all out. In year thirteen (my last year in secondary school), I was seventeen, and Allen was eighteen; we had been together for nearly four years. He was applying to colleges in the States, and I was applying to universities in the UK, which only meant one thing: It would be the beginning of the end for us. He was someone I had grown up with, and he was a dream boyfriend and first love who tried to protect me from everything. I had thought we were going to stay together long-distance and then eventually get married, like some high school sweethearts, but that didn't happen. It would have been too hard to maintain a long-distance relationship once we were on different continents. In the meantime, we acted like we had for the last four years. We were always off and on, so it should be no surprise that there was no definitive end to our relationship. There was no fight. There were no long, tear-filled conversations, no blubbering "I can't live without you" by text. We'd always break up thinking we'd get back together, just like we had done in the past, so this time didn't feel any different. We'd still see each other in classes; we had the same friends; we went to the same parties. It was always complicated (you know, the Ross and Rachel "we were on a break" type of shit).

With this last break with Allen, I wanted to have a bit of distance. I always liked having something that was outside of school; I still felt like I didn't fit in. As time went by, my parents had eased up on their restrictions, and they let me pick up modeling here and there after I proved I could handle it. I also started hanging out with a group of girls from a few different schools. I had met them model-ing, and it was nice to have a group outside the confines of my own school and the circle of friends I had with Allen.

One night, while the rest of the schoolkids were still going to the same bars that were sure to accept their fake IDs, I went clubbing with my new friends at Dragon-i, which was the Studio 54 of Hong Kong. Hong Kong's rich and famous—the crème de la crème—went there to see and be seen. Every night, throngs of people would stand in line outside, hoping they'd pass the test: Bouncers would only let in those who looked hot and those who had money to spend. Defi-nitely a far cry from the dive bars that I was used to.

I had on a pleated gray miniskirt, a white backless halter top with a draped neckline, and, of course, heels. Standard early 2000s uniform. A little tipsy, we took a cab to the club, and I handed over my comp card (sort of like a business card for models) at the door. They stamped me with a flame insignia for the model table. In clubs and bars that want to attract a certain clientele, models can eat and drink for free. It's very common for the clubs to have a table or even a VIP section reserved for "pretty people" with free booze to entice them to stay. A stamp gets you taken care of for the night. We drank, people-watched, and danced the night away. *So this is what it must feel like to be an adult.*

We were on our way to hit the crowded dance floor when a male model I knew, Kieran, came up to us. After some small talk, he introduced me to his friend.

"This is my friend Victor," Kieran shouted to me over the pump-ing '00s hip-hop as he pointed to a tall, stunning Pharrell look-alike standing off to the side of the dance floor. No lie, he was the most beautiful man I had ever seen. Wearing a beanie to cover his shaved head, he had buttery-smooth skin. His gray designer T-shirt accentuated his biceps, and he wore a rosary around his neck. At six foot two, he stood a head above people in the crowd. We started talking—you know, the typical topics at first: "Where you from?" and

"What agency are you with?" This quickly led to flirtation. We started dancing, and we inched closer and closer to each other with each song. At some point, he kissed me softly on the corner of my mouth.

Like with Cinderella, the clock struck two A.M. (my curfew was a little later than Cinderella's), and I had to leave the ball. I had to make curfew.

"I've gotta go, bye!" I said quickly after we exchanged numbers, and I raced out to make it home on time. He probably thought I was playing hard to get, but the truth was I was fucking underage. He didn't know that, though; I told him that I was eighteen, even though I was seventeen. He was twenty-four. I know, I KNOW, what was I thinking?? But I was young and stupid, and gaga over his handsome face. I told him I was eighteen because he wouldn't have given me the time of day if he knew I was only seventeen, especially since he could have his pick in a room full of gorgeous models, actresses, and celebrities. For a guy like *him* to like *me*, well, I took that chance even if it meant lying, which, at the time, I thought was a brilliant idea. I didn't think how wrong this was—to base our relationship on a lie. In my mind, this was the only way I was going to stand a chance.

The next few days were everything you would expect—the stomach somersaults and butterflies every time I texted and he texted back. All I could think was that I'd better not fuck this up. *Oh my God, he likes me.* I was still so young and naive—I felt lucky to even have his attention.

In the very beginning, we'd meet up for coffee or to grab lunch or to just sit in the park, talking, kissing, and going for walks. I continued to lie about my age (although he knew I was still in school and lived with my parents) and my experience in the modeling world, even though I had put it on the back burner while I focused on my academics.

I learned a lot about the industry from dating him—the good and the bad. For the first time, I saw how modeling was a mismatch of what was perceived and what was real. Everyone thinks models live the high life: traveling in private jets and yachts, drinking champagne, and getting free clothes. Yes, that exists, but it is rare. With model competition even higher, it was that much harder to reach the top echelon of the industry. (Today, most models squeak by, barely making a living. In 2017, the average annual pay for a model in the United States was under $40,000.[3])

With Victor, I saw a much less glamorous side of the shiny, glitzy industry. As gorgeous as he was, Victor was just another male model among thousands of models. He had to work harder than the next guy to get the job. When he arrived in Hong Kong, he was given an apartment by his agency, but it was bare bones. It was just a room—no windows—not much bigger than a parking space, and the bathroom was so tiny that the shower was over the toilet. And that had a folding door because there wasn't room for a full-sized one. *Teeny.* Victor's grueling schedule and claustrophobic living arrangement were indicative of the real working structure of the industry. It burst my bubble. Because I was just modeling on the side, I hadn't really been privy to full-time modeling and how competitive it all was. Seeing through Victor's perspective made me realize there was absolutely nothing special about being good-looking or aesthetically pleasing. There are a million gorgeous people all trying to stand out. Still, even stripped of its shine, the modeling world gave him something I craved: independence. I craved being an adult, living on my own and being in control of my life. To be honest, if I hadn't met Victor, I probably wouldn't have gone into modeling full-time, or gone as far in the modeling world as I did. Being exposed to his success and his connections was a formative moment in my life.

---

3 Valeriya Safronova, Joanna Nikas, and Natalia V. Osipova, "What It's Truly Like to Be a Fashion Model," *The New York Times*, September 5, 2017, https://www.nytimes.com/2017/09/05/fashion/models-racism-sexual-harassment-body-issues-new-york-fashion-week.html.

And even though there were tough circumstances, I saw how Victor was making a name for himself, getting worldwide contracts that typically placed him in one city for three months at a time, and working with iconic photographers. He told me that he made money, but he sent everything back to his family because they were from a small, poor village in the Philippines where they don't even have running water. He also told me his mother was suffering from crippling arthritis and diabetes. He said he could have been living like a king, enjoying the fruits of his labor, but he lived in that dingy apartment and sent everything home. A hot Robin Hood. A selfless hero to his family. That was extremely sexy. It presented a stark contrast to how I grew up because my mum was very money-oriented.

Ultimately, her behavior made me want to make my own money and be independent; I did not want a future where I was reliant on someone else. With Victor, I tried to prove to myself that (a) I was not my mum, and (b) I didn't give a shit about money, just freedom.

My relationship with Victor became a crazy distraction from my academic future. I knew that after my A levels, I'd be taking a gap year, a popular thing to do for students who were not yet eighteen, the minimum age to go to many universities. A lot of people would get a career-related internship, but I had decided to model full-time. I still needed to get into a university, though, and Oxford was at the top of the list. My dad had gone there, and he was excited at the prospect of one of his kids following in his footsteps.

There was a flurry of applications, essays, and interviews with a handful of universities I was interested in. My interview for Oxford was coming up in December, and I should have been preparing for it—it was *Oxford*, after all—but I didn't. I took my eyes off the prize. I was so fascinated by Victor and the modeling world that I started to lag on school studies and uni applications. I let my relationship with him throw a wrench in the work-play balance I was working so hard to achieve.

When the Oxford interview rolled around, I was not ready. I had been at Victor's apartment and got ready there. I put on a black pencil skirt and a white T-shirt with a Japanese art print on it. The skirt said "I am serious and smart," while the casual, artsy T-shirt said "I have some personality." Altogether, the look said: Formal but casual. Atypical. I wanted to stand out among the sea of Asian geniuses. I looked in the mirror, straightened my skirt, put on a pair of heels, and went on my way. That was the extent of my preparation. Who the fuck did I think I was? I had applied for the philosophy, politics, and economics program at Balliol College, one of the toughest to get into at Oxford. I went into the interview thinking that my smarts and personality would get me by. I thought I could wing it. I should have been excited, nervous, scared. Instead, I was treating it like I was going to brunch with my friends.

As I walked into the waiting room of the administration office, I saw Anika sitting in one of the chairs, waiting to be called into her interview. *Well, isn't that interesting. I wonder if she had the drug bust stricken from her records in exchange for snitching?* I did my best to avoid eye contact. It wasn't long before I was called and led down a long hallway into a bright, sterile office where a female interviewer was waiting for me. I was handed a laminated sheet—it was an academic article on a popular economic policy. I was asked to read it, and then the interviewer asked me several questions about the material. They weren't straightforward questions with simple answers; rather, they were thought-provoking questions designed to reveal how the student thinks and processes information. They wanted their students to think for themselves, beyond being book-smart.

And, well, I cannot remember for the life of me the questions that were asked, but I do remember my performance. Or lack thereof. I fumbled and fell over my words. I answered her, but I wasn't fluid, and I wasn't quick. I needed extra time to gather my thoughts. I wasn't operating at 100 percent; I was more like 70 percent, which isn't good enough for Oxford. They are looking for the best in the world. I was not being best-in-the-world material. The best in the world prepares.

When the torture was over, I got up, reached my hand out over the desk, and shook my interviewer's hand. As I did so, I could feel the seam on the back of my skirt rip. *No fucking way.* I could not be sure of the damage without looking in a mirror, but it felt like it slit right down my ass crack. *OH. MY. FUCK. This is a scene out of a movie.* As I said goodbye, all I could think was, how in the world was I going to turn around and walk out of this room without her seeing my ass?

Oh my God, what do I do? In one movement, I let go of her hand and tried to twist my skirt around enough to move the rip to the side. As much as I tried, my skirt wouldn't budge. I fucked this up on so many levels, and this was just the cherry on top. I went through the five stages of grief in about ten seconds: denial, anger, bargaining, depression, and acceptance. Finally, I settled on the fact that I *knew* that this was never going to happen. My torn skirt and I would not be attending the University of Oxford.

I went outside and chain-smoked five cigarettes, trying to process what had just happened and figure out what my next move was going to be. I knew what I couldn't do, and that was call my parents. My dad had been *so excited* for me. He was probably waiting by the phone, eager to hear how it went. He would want to know all the details, every question asked. Unfortunately, he would be finding out that the family lineage of Oxford graduates ended with him.

I sat alone. I didn't call anyone. I didn't even call Victor. As I puffed on one cigarette after the other, I relived the interview. I went back through every question. I could have answered every single one better. I should've worn a different fucking outfit. I should've fucking prepped. I threw away my one chance.

At seventeen years old, I didn't have the maturity to break down what really happened, so I blamed Victor for distracting me. But now, with 20/20 hindsight, I see the blame falls directly on me. I did not focus, even though I really wanted to go to Oxford. And I found myself asking the question I had asked so many times: *Why?*

As I traveled back home, I spiraled. I spiraled because I knew I did poorly. I so wanted to have a great job and give my future kids a good life, just like my dad had done for me. I got the grades, but I fucked up this second step. I feared that everything else would crumble, too.

I tried to reassure myself that I was applying to other good schools, so if I didn't get into Oxford, there would be one I would get into. Both of my brothers didn't get into their first choices, but they still went to great universities. That was a comfort.

When I finally went home, I was inundated.

"So!! How did it go?!" my dad asked.

"Good," I responded. I downplayed everything, but I did tell him that I didn't think I had answered the questions well enough. My dad was all about perfection, so he would interject, "Oh, you should have mentioned this article in the newspaper the other day. . . ." He gave me all kinds of "You should have done this, should have done that . . ." advice. This was nothing new.

"Okay, well, it's out of our hands, right?" he said finally.

Though I didn't have control over the outcome of that interview, I did have control over my A levels. In the British education system, the curriculum typically ends before the end of the school year, and there are a couple of weeks given to study for final exams—the GSCEs and, later, A levels. Students stress out over this time—the outcomes are do-or-die when it comes to getting into a university. I hadn't performed as well as I would have liked on my GCSEs, but A levels are a higher qualifier and thus more important in the eyes of universities. My poor GCSEs and poor showing at the Oxford interview gave me a good kick in the butt—it made me work really hard for my A levels. I needed to ace them.

As I tried to regroup, Victor's visa ran out, and he had to go home to the Philippines while he waited for a visa renewal. Thank God my big distraction was taken away from me; I needed complete concentration for my exams. And looming after them was full-time modeling. I needed to be ready for that as well. So in order to do that, I started the craziest hard-core eating regimen I've ever done in my life. My mantra was "starve and study."

On a paper calendar, I created a schedule for myself and worked back from six weeks and eight weeks (depending on the exam). Each day I created two boxes to check off: (1) a subject to study that day, and (2) what I was to eat. Here is a typical day:

Morning: A tall glass of a green smoothie that was sipped slowly and swilled around my mouth fifty times before I swallowed. Then I would go on my balcony and smoke a couple of cigarettes to kill the hunger, and go sit at my desk and stick to my strict study schedule from nine A.M. to twelve-thirty P.M. My study methods were a bit unconventional: I'd write and rewrite everything I needed to know on pages and pages and pages. Then I'd do it all over again. The writing was for me the most effective way to rehearse the information in order to retain it. Everyone has their styles of studying, depending on how they optimally learn. This was mine.

Afternoon: a quick cigarette break and some water. Around four o'clock, I would take a break. I would take out a ninety-calorie fat-free, sugar-free plain yogurt from the fridge, and in a glass bowl, I'd measure out a fistful of dried black beans. I'd go to the living room with my provisions, sit on the couch, put something on the TV, and eat. It didn't even matter what was on. This was always the happiest part of my day. I'd first eat the small portion of beans, emptying the bowl bean by bean. It would take me about twenty minutes to finish this "meal," as I chewed every little piece until it dissolved in my mouth. Then I would eat the yogurt with the smallest spoon I could find. I'd dip it in the yogurt and lick it off and dip it in and lick it off to make it last longer. I'd swirl it around my mouth until it basically dissolved.

The beans were filled with fiber, and the yogurt, probiotics. I had started eating fiber and probiotics because I noticed that I'd stopped pooping. Constipation is common with anorexia, because you are not eating or drinking enough to keep your gastric system running smoothly. As a result, it struggles to push through food and liquids. I noticed I would go only every couple of days (you should go every day), and when I did, it was painful. I didn't need a doctor to tell me that that was a bad sign, so I researched information and read up on fiber and probiotics and how they helped keep the system "moving." Beans and yogurt became my entire regimen.

After eating, I would be flooded with guilt, so I would exercise.

I had floor-to-ceiling mirrors in my bedroom from my dancing days, so I would turn on some music, sit in front of the mirror, and do crunches and squats. I'd use my mother's two-kilo weights and do exercises until I built up a sweat and the guilt dissipated. Only then would I stop. Sometimes it was five minutes, and sometimes it was an hour.

Evening: I would spend a couple more hours reviewing what I had learned from the day. Then I would put my books away, pull out a few fashion magazines, put on the TV or open my laptop, and obsess over models. I'd watch videos of models walking down runways and study their bodies. I dissected every girl, every brand, and every designer. I knew I was about to go into this world full-time, so I wanted to know as much as I could. I wanted to know names; I wanted to know what agencies they were with; I wanted to know what campaigns they were in. I analyzed the models' bodies, comparing them with mine, like I did when I first started out. *Okay, I need to get to that wide of a thigh gap. I need my collarbones to stick out like that. Oh, look at that, my waist should really be twenty-three inches.*

I would practice catwalking in my room and videotape myself, mirroring the walks I'd seen on Fashion TV. I'd hit playback and critique them. I would take photos of my thighs to track the progress of the gap I had been striving for. And I wrote down my weight and measurements in my thinspiration book.

This is what I did every night for about eight weeks. I would study for my A levels during the day and study modeling at night. I had the same level of intensity for both. I would wake up and do it all over again the next day. It would take me a long time to fall asleep, though, because I was so hungry that my stomach wouldn't stop growling. I'd wake up in the morning and peel off a sheet of skin from my lips, caused by excess acid that had churned up from my stomach.

There was a last little stretch before the exam, and then a two-week period during which the exams took place. To reward myself at this time, I introduced a chocolate bar—a Kinder Bueno hazelnut chocolate bar, to be exact. I would get my mum to drive me in the golf cart down to the plaza to the 7-Eleven, where I'd buy it. Now, you would think to save myself some time I would buy a box, so I wouldn't need her to drive me every day. However, I knew that if they were in the house, I'd binge. I'd devour the entire box in one sitting. That couldn't happen, so I'd rationalized that it was good to get out, get some fresh air, and take a break from studying, so my mum took me every day.

I'd walk out of 7-Eleven, unwrapping one of the bars, my mouth watering in anticipation. There were two individually wrapped bars in one packet, so I would open one, break off a piece, pop it in my mouth, and let it dissolve. Then, like in some corny TV commercial, I'd close my eyes and drift off into my own world to savor each piece as long as I could. (Cue the wind fan now.) I would finish it before I got home. Then I'd go to my room, so overwhelmed with guilt that I'd start manically doing little exercises, trying to make myself feel better.

This regimen was extremely draining, though, and I had started feeling deflated. One day, as I sat on the carpet in the living room looking up at the ceiling, my mum came in and sat down next to me.

"Are you okay?" she asked.

I just started crying, "I'm so tired, Mum. I'm so tired and I . . . I . . . I can't do this anymore."

She thought I was talking about the exams.

"Don't worry. It's almost over. You're doing so well. You're studying so hard, you're doing the best you can do. I see how many hours a day you're studying. Don't worry; everything is going to be fine. You're almost there." Little did she know that I applied this pep talk to my eating issues. It had been six weeks of solitary confinement and starvation. I was almost there; I'd done such a good job. Everything she said that day I took as an approval to continue my eating regimen. But I don't blame her—I was good at hiding it in plain sight. She'd tell me that it was good to not eat too much, because eating too much would make me tired and not want to study. Or she'd agree that my small portions were the way to go. I took it as a justification to continue. So I sat and picked at my beans, one by one, and ate my yogurt with the world's tiniest spoon, and no one questioned me.

As the exams came around, the only thing I changed in my diet was the addition of a banana before the exam, because my teachers told me that bananas release energy slowly. It did help—I was able to sit and concentrate without being distracted by my hunger.

The time had come. My A levels. I was taking three subjects—math, economics, and fine art. I did it. I pushed through with an insane focus and drive. (*See what happens when you prepare?* I thought.) After one of my last exams, I knew I had done well, so I decided to celebrate by going shopping on my way home. I wanted a pair of jeans that Victoria Beckham had designed for Rock & Republic. (Yes, the Spice Girls were still in my life). I bought a pair in size 21—the smallest size they had in the store. The size models wore. I didn't even try them on at the store. I bought them as motivation: I knew from the number on the scale that there was a good chance they'd fit (I had lost another twenty-five pounds by this point), but I figured I could diet until I fit into them, if not. When I tried them on at home, though, they fit. They weren't easy to button up, but they fit. Being able to get into them, as tight as they were, was the affirmation that I had been wanting.

Oh my God. Maybe I did it. Maybe I'm there. Fuck yes.

After our exams, my class teacher, Miss Mead, took our whole class out for dinner. It would be the first time I'd eaten a proper meal in just about two months. I was five foot nine and a half and down to about 110 pounds. I had so much anxiety going into the dinner. I felt that this was a test and that it might throw me off the regimen that had been working for months at that point.

You know what I did? I binged my heart out. I ordered steak, and I ate the entire slab of meat. I hosed all the potatoes and vegetables that came with it, not to mention the entire basket of bread, and then cake for dessert.

I sat across from my teacher, Miss Mead, and she said at one point, "You've lost so much weight. Tell me your secrets!" *Oh, you don't want to know.*

"I just eat vegetables and fruits and try to stay away from carbs," I blurted out (at the time, the Atkins Diet was a big trend, so it seemed like the right thing to say). As I stuffed my face with more potatoes, I was secretly beaming. That thrill I had gotten earlier when I first lost weight came rushing back—someone recognized my efforts! It was paying off again. Yet the same conflicted feeling came back as well—I didn't want to be found out. I wanted to keep my secret safe.

That night, as I lay in bed, I first tossed and turned, wracked with guilt over all the food I ate. But that eventually drifted away and

I fell into a deep sleep, as it was the first time in a long time that my stomach wasn't growling, keeping me awake.

EXAMS WERE OVER. My gap year of modeling was set to begin. I was excited for what was to come, but my agency had gone out of business, so I needed to get new representation. I wanted a big agency to help me give it a real go. My first stop: Victor's agency. It was a prestigious agency with lots of famous models and celebrities. This being my first big agency experience, I was super nervous. I tried to look as model-like as possible. That meant looking as simple as possible. The industry didn't want to see models projecting too much of one particular style. It had to be understated, and denim, black, or white fabrics acted as a blank canvas, ready for any sort of look. So I went in wearing a pale denim skirt, a plain white tank top with spaghetti straps, and flip-flops. Then, when I arrived at their office building, I changed from the flip-flops into sky-high heels to make myself seem longer, taller, and leaner.

I took a sleek elevator up to the agency's offices, where a set of large, intimidating frosted doors greeted me. After taking a deep breath, I rang the bell. I was buzzed in, and I entered a large room where six bookers sat behind their desks. I could feel eyeballs laser-beam to me, scanning, assessing me from top to bottom.

I walked in slowly and timidly uttered to no one in particular, "Hi."

A tall, handsome, well-dressed man stood up from his seat and said, "Hi, can I help you?"

I stood there with my portfolio in my hand and answered, "I, uh . . . I emailed about . . . about coming in. I'm Mia." *Come on, Mia, keep it together.*

I could still feel all of them scanning me, eyes up, eyes down. Measuring my body in their heads: *Hmmm, she is probably a twenty-three waist and thirty-five hips. Five foot nine and a half . . .*

I had so little confidence that I didn't know what to do. I just looked down at the floor.

"Sure, just fill out this form and we'll take your measurements. I'm Joey, the head booker here." Joey, I would find out, used to be a model. Standing at six foot one, he was muscular and good-looking, with a bit of stubble on his face.

He sat me down on the couch so I could fill out the application form. While at first he was distant and formal, Joey warmed quickly and became quite animated and excited. Sitting down next to me, he peppered me with questions. "Can I see your portfolio? What school did you go to? How come I've never seen you before? You know, you're beautiful. You look just like this girl Gaile. She's a top model in Hong Kong. . . . Wow. You really look like her!" Of course, I knew who Gaile was. She was on so many of the magazine covers I had obsessed over in my makeshift model night school.

I couldn't believe what was coming out of his mouth. I was convinced that they were going to shut me down. *"Oh, sorry, half an inch off. So, that's a no from us. Thank you, anyway."*

But instead, it was: "We'd love to represent you. How did you hear about us? Are you going to see any other agencies?"

I'd done it. In a weird way, that felt like more of an accomplishment than finishing my exams.

"No, no, no," I assured him. "I want to sign with you guys. I'm dating Victor, and he told me to come here."

"Oh, amazing. Super cool. We love this. Where do you live?"

"Right now, I live in Discovery Bay with my parents, but I'd like to find my own apartment. Can you guys help me?" I asked.

"Sure, no problem. We find apartments for many of our models."

That's how it all unrolled. I signed with them that day, and not even a week later, I moved into a model apartment as the agency started to book jobs for me. The icing on the proverbial cake was that Victor was on his way back to Hong Kong. He was going to live with me.

For so many years I couldn't wait to get the fuck out of my dysfunctional house. I had spent my entire childhood counting down the days until I would walk out the front door for good.

And here I was, leaving.

Finally.

Here I go.

6. THIGH-GAP YEAR

THERE IT WAS, IN BLACK AND WHITE. My signature on a piece of paper was my golden ticket out of my house and school, away from my parents, and to being on my own. I was officially a full-time model and, unofficially, a full-fledged adult. I was stepping out into the unknown, and I really had no plan, apart from the fact that in sixteen months I was starting university. I had no idea what was going to happen, other than trying to get work in Hong Kong. If it went well, I'd hopefully travel to other countries.

Would I be any good? Am I even going to book a single job? How am I going to compare to real, full-time professional models? Such thoughts definitely crossed my mind, but I wanted to see where the year would take me, so I just planned to take it one step at a time. That first step was moving into my very first apartment in Hong Kong, which was set up by the agency.

I had packed up my things like the house was on fire—I couldn't wait to get the fuck out. My father, who was away on a business trip, was resigned to the fact that I was going to do what I wanted to do, but my mum seemed to think she could make me stay by yelling at me.

"You can't do this. This is illegal. You're only seventeen! Still a minor!" she screamed at me, following me from room to room as I gathered my belongings.

She was right. I was not yet a legal adult.

"But you don't even want me here! There's no way I'm staying another day in this crazy house," I responded, not caring. I hastily finished packing, throwing anything and everything into my suitcases. My comeback seemed to quiet her. She never even asked me where I was moving to.

I left without saying goodbye and schlepped my bags to my new apartment on Wan Chai Road, in a very congested part of town that bordered Causeway Bay and Wan Chai. Passing a huge food market that sold everything from dried meat to exotic fruits, I checked out the drapery of hanging carcasses and men cleaning the daily catch and throwing guts on the ground. Whiffs of raw meat, fish guts, and the popular durian fruit, which has an odor described by food writer Richard Sterling as "turpentine and onions, garnished with a gym sock," created a fragrance specific to Hong Kong streets that melted with the humidity of about 98 percent. The famous saying goes, "Smells like hell, tastes like heaven."

I walked up to what was now my apartment building, opened the heavy metal gate, and entered. I took the rickety elevator up to the fifth floor. I walked to my apartment door (my own door!) and felt for my key in my bag. Excited and nervous, I took a moment to massage the key (*my* very own key!!) between my fingers before inserting it into the lock.

This was the sweet taste of independence that I had fantasized about for my whole adolescence. I had seen Victor's model apartment, so I was pretty certain it was not going to be like *America's Next Top Model*, where all the girls lived in one huge, modern, and beautifully decorated penthouse. But it didn't matter. I didn't need much. I didn't care, either, as long as I wasn't living at home anymore. I opened the door (to *my* own apartment!) and looked around. My eyes scanned a room that must have been no bigger than a two-hundred-square-foot box. The room had bare-bones amenities. To the left of the entranceway, there was a kitchen counter with a sink, a plug-in hot plate, a microwave, a kettle, and a mini fridge. Mounted on one wall was a tiny TV, and against the other, a double bed. On the far wall, I had a window that looked out onto a generic concrete building across the street. The bathroom had a tiny sink, and the shower hose was over the toilet. The bathroom door was a bi-fold door, because there wasn't even enough space for a full door to swing open. It was a sparse and teeny apartment, but it was *my* sparse and teeny apartment. It was tight even for me, let alone Victor, too. But splitting the rent was more attractive than space.

The building's entire fourth and fifth floors were filled with other models from my agency and other agencies. The close quarters gave the building a dorm-like feel—not that I really knew what that felt like at the time—and I settled in quickly. Although the apartments weren't decked out like ANTM, we did get our own version of Tyra Mail. Like clockwork, every day at 6 P.M., we would each get a text message with our itinerary for the following day—often there were six, seven, even eight casting appointments lined up. We were up early every morning, running around from casting to casting, day after day. I easily adjusted to this new lifestyle. It felt ready-made, and I could just slide right in.

Some castings were looking for "editorial" models who were best suited to magazine features, brand campaigns, or runway. The fashion industry's still-restrictive preferences limit models to a certain look for editorial. They're usually very thin with angular bone structure, which best fits sample sizes (there's no Photoshop on the catwalk), and a striking look. Other models are better suited for commercial work, such as catalog and TV, where it is more about the smile and attracting the customer base. While I had been modeling for several years at this point, I was never classified as either an editorial model or a commercial model, as most girls are. So my agents had me go for everything. I jumped right into the frying pan.

It was an exciting, yet dizzying, time in my life. With so many castings every day, I experienced a constant yo-yo of emotions.

Every time I walked into a room and heads craned in my direction, I would feel that familiar sense that all eyes were scanning my body from head to toe. Sometimes it was obvious that the client liked you . . . or didn't. If they had no interest, they'd take one look at me and close my portfolio or flip through the pages while talking to the person next to them, or hit me with a "you can go now." Sometimes, if they liked me, they'd have me try on clothes. If they didn't fit, well, that was the *worst*. I'd leave that appointment, deflated, only to have to run to the next one, putting my game face back on. The days were filled with constant ups and downs, and that yo-yoing was entirely dependent on other people's approval.

If I didn't book the job, I would beat myself up and wonder why I didn't. *Well, if I looked like [insert random model name here], I would have gotten it,* or *If I were half an inch smaller in my hips, they would have loved me.* HOW FUCKED-UP IS THAT? Since models all see one another at the same castings, everyone finds out who books what jobs. Naturally I (and I am sure most models) would then compare myself with those who did get the gig. It was a constant competition, certainly in my head, but also, bewilderingly, in reality.

Eventually, I learned that I couldn't take it personally (or at least I had to try not to). I had good practice with this: The blunt superficiality of the modeling industry was nearly identical to the bullying I had endured in school. Both caused the same debilitating insecurities to bubble up to the surface—that horribly anxious feeling that I was shit, whether it was from a client who rejected me for a job, or a group of kids who made fun of me.

Over time, it made me develop a thick skin. I walked into castings constantly reminding myself that no one could book every single job. With time, I learned how to detach myself emotionally. It's funny how it always turned out that the ones I thought I got, I didn't, and the ones I thought I bombed, I got.

It helped that I became friendly with some of the other girls. It was hard not to, since we were in such tight quarters and doing the same thing day in and day out. We borrowed each other's flat irons, traded makeup, and swapped clothes. We could be each other's shoulder to cry on if a client or agent complained about our weight. It was great companionship, yet in the back of every girl's mind was the nagging acknowledgment that we were each other's competition. Plus, we were on a crazy-ass schedule, coming and going all the time—a few months in one city, then a few months somewhere halfway around the world. It took me some time to understand just how transient this life was. I was making new friends, but it wouldn't be long until we would have to say goodbye. Maybe our work paths would cross again, but maybe they wouldn't. Nevertheless, we were all going through a very similar experience, since we were all living in a bubble—or rather a fishbowl—where our livelihoods were based on looks and where we were judged every day, for better or worse.

In turn, we all internalized this judgment. It perpetuated the fears, insecurities, and defense mechanisms we had built up to get us through the grueling process. The weirdest thing is that we all felt like what we experienced was normal. Nobody had any perspective. Everybody had similar issues with food, weight, and self-esteem. No matter how many jobs we booked, nobody was really content with themselves, because there was *always* room for improvement. We had to be so conscious of how we looked—it was our job. So when we did hang out—and there was a lot of downtime—all anyone ever really talked about was dieting and working out. (That is not to say we didn't know how to relax. We'd often go out together on off days, shopping, exploring the city, or going to the cinema.)

We traded weight-loss secrets and exercise tips with one another. There was one Australian model, Tara, whose favorite trick was eating prunes. She told me to eat a few prunes every day, which would give you the runs, making your stomach flatter. The male models weren't much better—they had the separate pressure of needing to be muscular, but not so muscular that they no longer fit into the clothes. "Lean" was the name of the game, so doing push-ups and sit-ups or downing protein shakes while we were hanging out was totally normal. They'd talk about little tricks they'd do, like when at a casting with their shirt off, they'd stand directly under a light to enhance their muscle definition. When the boys in our crew went out, their drink of choice was vodka and water. (As if a joke out of the movie *Zoolander*, these guys swore by the combo because the way they saw it, the water rehydrated and counteracted the dehydrating alcohol to avoid the dreaded puffiness.)

Sometimes these guys would take diuretics—pills to help with water retention—before doing underwear shows and other shoots where they needed extreme definition. Back then, they were super easy to buy at any local pharmacy without a prescription.

There was no shame in any of this, because our livelihoods were dependent on it. It was the world we lived in. I got public approval for the first time to do the things I had been doing behind closed doors. Everything that I'd previously done alone and in secret could now come out into the light and be spoken about—shared, even—with this like-minded group. It was as if I stepped into a living and breathing ana and mia blog. It provided me with the encouragement to be even more excessive. I began trying anything and everything to keep my weight down, starting with caffeine pills, because I was told that they boosted metabolism and curbed hunger.

Back then, it was not uncommon for some agents to provide "diet pills" to their models. Yes, you read that right. I was never given any, but I've seen girls take all kinds of pills given to them by their agents. Many were given diet or weight-loss pills to suppress appetite and lose weight for a big campaign or a fashion week. Some were given speed-like pills to keep their bodies burning calories (so much so that sleep was derailed). Some girls were given a hefty prescription of sleeping pills so they could lie in bed and try to sleep, sometimes for days, even weeks (yes, weeks), comatose through the painful starvation, and wake up ten pounds lighter. A case of water would be kept next to their beds to keep them hydrated and fill their stomachs as they tried to lose as much weight as possible.

Next up, laxatives. In addition to shrinking down a little bit before a show, laxatives became a strategic move for me, helping me get rid of everything I ate. The food would just go out the other end. Since I couldn't eat and then throw up at a job, I would take laxatives and just shit it out later. It was more discreet (writing this now, I can't believe I actually rationalized this!?). More important, though, I took laxatives for the same reason I developed bulimia: to get rid of that crippling guilt after I ate. Taking a couple of laxatives, or a handful, meant that I didn't need to worry about getting fat, because I knew the pills would make it all go away. It would all be okay. I would take either Dulcolax, a stronger pharma laxative, or Senokot, an herbal alternative, depending on the day, how much I ate, and when I could poop. Dulcolax is much faster-acting. Senokot digests more slowly, and there is less cramping. If I were at a job and flooded with guilt from whatever I had eaten, I'd ease my guilt by popping the Senokot so I didn't have to immediately run to the bathroom. I knew it would be coming out of me soon. I eventually ditched the "healthier" laxative, though, and my dependence on the Dulcolax escalated because I liked the immediate results. The directions recommend taking one or two tablets a day, max, but soon I was taking ten, twelve, even the entire pack in a day. It got to a point where I couldn't go to the bathroom without them. The cramping from the induced diarrhea would get so bad that at times I'd end up lying on the cold tiles of the bathroom floor to get relief from the sweats that inevitably came with the dehydration and overheating. Knowing I was fucking up my body (and really, who wants to shit like that?), I tried to wean off them in different ways, going back to taking natural laxatives and fiber supplements, but nothing really gave me the results that regular laxatives did. Again, I found myself stuck in a vicious cycle.

However, by modeling industry standards, the results were spectacular. I whittled down to the smallest I'd ever been, which gave me the ability to do runway. I was ninety-eight pounds at five foot nine and a half. I WAS TINY. If you can believe it, I was still slightly too big for Asia's aesthetic. No muscle definition, no curves, no butt, no boobs. The look was to practically disappear when turned sideways, with narrow-as-a-coin-slot hips (about ninety centimeters, or thirty-five inches). Once I got to this goal, I became obsessed with maintaining it. I HAD to keep my hips at thirty-five inches and my waist at twenty-three inches. I would repeat this goal to myself at any point of temptation: *twenty-three inches, twenty-three inches.* I wouldn't—I couldn't—eat anything, because I'd gain weight immediately. I had no metabolism whatsoever. Victor, who was back in Hong Kong after a few months in another market, was living with me at this point, and he got me into protein shakes. They were not quite solid food, but it was a step up from starving myself, and they filled me up while keeping the calorie and fat counts as low as possible. A lot of male models were crazy for them, as well as protein bars, preworkout supplements, and fat burners. I was essentially living off liquids and laxatives—that was how my body was functioning.

Not only did *I* put pressure on myself to be as small as I could be, but my agent bore down on me as well. Until very recently, in fact, going into my agency to see the very people whom I relied on to get me work was the most terrifying thing in the world, and I know countless models who feel the same way. Just by walking through the agency doors, I am always subject to judgment and, most likely, a comment on my appearance. The fear and anxiety brought on by having to go there for even a small task like picking up comp cards or a check were palpable. Once, while I was going over a contract with Joey, top model Ase Wang walked in. The first thing one of the

On set filming a TV commercial when I was seventeen
years old and modeling full-time. I hadn't eaten a
meal in four days in preparation for this shoot. Seoul,
South Korea, 2006.

bookers said to her was, "Wah! You gained weight!" Ase stopped in
her tracks and bit back, "No I didn't! I've lost weight!" I was in awe
of her not crumbling into a million pieces after being told such an
awful thing. The strength, the resilience, the bravery. She didn't fear
these people, and I thought, *One day I'm not going take that kind of
shit either.*

To add to the anxiety, a lot of models were monitored and subjected to weekly measurement check-ins, and there was a financial motivation to stay small. Models were given weekly pocket
money that the agency would advance from the money the models

brought in. The agency would front the expense—in addition to their flights, rent, cell phone bills, and anything associated with their work—but models were to pay it back from their earnings. At the time, the allowance was approximately five hundred Hong Kong dollars per week, or roughly sixty American dollars. That's less than ten American dollars a day for food and transport. (No wonder the models were so skinny. They had to keep their budgets tight, which meant limited money to spend on food, even if they wanted to eat. We also walked everywhere, to burn extra calories, rather than splurging on cabs or public transportation.) If measurements were off, the pocket money was withheld for that week. They withheld the model's own money if her measurements increased. This was all spelled out in the contracts, but I never subjected myself to that system. I hated the very idea of owing anybody money. I used my savings to cover my living expenses, so I didn't have to rely on the agency.

WE WERE GETTING PRESSURE FROM ALL SIDES—our clients, our agents, and of course, ourselves, the worst critics. There was no room to breathe, no room to take a break for even a moment, or to have a bad day. There was a constant fear of being told, "You gained weight," "You look fat," or "You don't look good"—all comments I have heard far too many times. It was as if we weren't allowed to be human. Have your period and feel bloated? Nope, not allowed. Your skin broke out because of stress? Nope, no excuses. We had to be perfect mannequins at all times.

Victor wasn't much help. I would have thought being a model would have given him some perspective that allowed him to be forgiving and encouraging, but that was not the case. In fact, our relationship became toxic, and he got more and more manipulative. He would prey on my insecurities, especially my number-one insecurity: my weight. He often made snide comments about how I should either work on certain areas more in the gym or maybe lose a couple of kilos. He'd make it seem like he was trying to help me, but he was breaking me down so that only he could build me up. I didn't see it as controlling back then; I only saw his criticism as fact.

If there was ANYTHING to help me lose more weight, I was down for it. Really. If you'd told me that drinking the milk of my deceased childhood cat, Nicky, would make me lose five kilos, I'd do it. One night, I had been freaking out about a particular fashion show I was about to do. I had been doing a lot of runway shows, and for some reason I was really torturing myself over this one. One would expect the worry and insecurity to stop after landing the job, but no, the worry only dissipated after I'd *finished* the job. I also lived in constant fear of being "canceled" and sent home (it had happened to me a few times). Maybe the clothes wouldn't fit well the day of the show; maybe I wouldn't photograph well; maybe they'd change their minds about my look.

All these thoughts were circling in my head as I looked in the mirror. I yelled at my body, "I am fat. I am fucking fat. I shouldn't have eaten yesterday. What was I thinking? They are going to just send me home. The other girls are so much skinnier than me."

I didn't think that I was a little overweight, or just built differently than the other girls. I looked in the mirror and wholeheartedly saw a fat girl. That was body dysmorphia, another common disorder that goes hand in hand with anorexia. It made me see fat that was simply not there. It is crazy how the mind is so strong that we can trick ourselves into believing something that is patently untrue.

Victor heard me and said, "If you're really that worried, then take these tomorrow morning, and you'll pee out like five kilos of water." (I didn't stop to think that a good boyfriend would have told me to stop worrying rather than pushing diuretics. I thought he was the best boyfriend ever for helping me be as thin as I could.)

He handed over two little white pills. I put them on my bedside table and went to sleep, hoping they'd be the saviors that Victor promised.

The next morning, I popped the set in my mouth and swallowed them with a gulp of water, and sure enough, almost instantaneously, I needed the bathroom. I'd walk out of the bathroom and have the urge to pee again not even five minutes later. *Victor, no kidding, this shit works.*

I got to work in time for the show's rehearsal, followed by hair and makeup. I must have peed about fifteen times. I probably lost more than five kilos of water. I looked lean. I was all bones and skin. By showtime, however, I was feeling light-headed, wobbly, and weak. Everything felt like a monumental effort. Putting one foot in front of the other took an enormous amount of energy, as my body felt like a concrete slab and my muscles cramped up from the lack of water. I became so dizzy it took all my concentration (what little I had at this point) to not just collapse. Blinking was an effort. I had no water in me, and without water to make everything function, it felt like my body was shutting down. But I did it. It was so extreme that I knew I couldn't go this route all the time, but FUCK, it worked. The second the show was over I took the rehydration salts that Victor had given me to offset the diuretics. Dehydrate to get the job done, and then rehydrate to recoup.

It was pure torture, but so damn effective. After that day, diuretics became part of my bag of tricks when I needed to shrink down as much as possible before a job. My routine for getting ready for a show now looked like this: The day before and day of a runway show, I ate absolutely NO SOLID FOOD, unless you consider a handful of laxatives to flush out my system and two diuretics the morning of the show food. After the show I'd binge, then pop ten laxatives. I'd take a handful of pills every day: appetite suppressors, caffeine, metabolism boosters, fat burners, diuretics, if desperate—anything to get me to shrivel down to the smallest possible Mia I could be. You know when fighters cut weight before a fight? I was living like that continuously.

AS THE WEEKS WENT ON IN HONG KONG, the days bled into each other. It was almost like the motto from *Jersey Shore*: Gym, Tan, Laundry. But for us, it was gym, diet, castings. We always had the nights to look forward to, though. They were our time to let loose. In a lot of cities, all the major nightclubs, restaurants, and bars have promoters who invite models to dinners and promotional events, and Hong Kong was no different. Each venue had a model promoter (model PR), usually also a model, who would get paid to fill up the place with pretty people. When there was a big casting, the PRs would come and introduce themselves, taking numbers so they could later send invites to their clubs' dinners and nights out. We'd all go, since it was comped. I enjoyed going, not so much for the food, but because I liked socializing and taking in such glamorous venues. Just a few years prior, I had dreamed of getting into these glitzy places, where the rich and famous flocked, and here I was, getting to go behind the velvet ropes myself.

Not many of us ate much at these free and fancy dinners. Most would pick at and move food around our plates; a few may have saved themselves for the free food, however, and ate a real meal. Dragon-i on Mondays was a favorite because they promoted what was called Hungry Mondays. It was playfully named for the fact that there were no club promotions on Sundays, which meant no free dinners. The models who hadn't eaten since Saturday were hungry as fuck. Clever, but also sadly accurate.

Early on, if I had a shoot or a casting the next morning, I would be a sensible professional and go home after dinner; if I didn't, I'd stay out. That didn't last too long, though, as it dawned on me: *I get to hang out in the city's hottest and most exclusive venues six nights a week?! Well then, I am going to enjoy this occupational perk as much as I can!* So I started going out pretty much six nights a week. All night.

This quickly became routine, and nights blended into days as I started showing up to jobs virtually straight from the club. So much of modeling is waiting around; there is so much downtime—between rehearsals, waiting for the show, in hair and makeup, waiting for another model to finish their shots—so we took that time to nap it off. We all did it. We could get away with staying out all night because, luckily, youth was on our side; we could go to a job with no sleep and a little hangover and still look good (with the help of a little extra makeup). I was enjoying my life as a full-time model and all the perks that came with that. So far, my partying wasn't interfering with my work, and I continued to get good bookings and make good money, so no one said anything. Yet.

One weekend, Victor and I flew to Manila for a getaway. We had gone out with one of his uber-wealthy friends, Sonny, to a very exclusive club. At some point in the evening, he invited Victor to the bathroom. Victor turned to me and said, "Hey, come with me, I have something fun for you."

Sonny led us to the club's VIP bathroom—so VIP had its own bouncer who stood outside it. As we walked up, it was obvious he knew Sonny, so he let us in.

We piled into a super-swanky, candlelit bathroom, and he took out a little bag of white powder. He made three lines right on the counter next to the sink, as Victor rubbed his hands together in excitement.

"What is this?" I whispered to Victor. I had an idea of what it was, but I wasn't sure.

"Coke," he whispered back, as he bent down to the marbled counter to snort a line.

"I've never done it before."

"Just do a little bit," he replied as Sonny did the next line.

When he was done, he handed me the rolled-up note, gesturing for me to take the remaining bit lined up on the bathroom sink.

I felt scared. Very scared. No one asked me if I wanted to do it, and if I'm honest, I didn't want to, but I felt pressured to hurry up and just do it.

I took the note in between my thumb and index finger, bent down to the counter, and snorted half of the line. It stung my nose, and it had a pleasantly sweet chemical smell to it. I handed the note back to Victor, who was happy to take the rest for himself.

I didn't know what to expect exactly, but I thought I would feel out of it. I kept drinking water, expecting a big rush like with Molly or Ecstasy. Instead, it was subtle. It just made me feel awake and ready to go. I felt like myself, but with a little buzz. I was more confident, assertive, and talkative. *Hmmm, this feels good.*

That was it. It was love at first sniff, and the start of a toxic romance. Little did I know that what took place in a random exclusive bathroom in the Philippines was going to impact my life for years to come.

THE NEXT NIGHT WE WENT OUT AGAIN, this time to a bar with a group of Victor's friends. I had a great idea to make the night even more fun.

"Yo, can we go get more coke?" I quietly asked him.

As with any romance, I set out to get to know my new lover. I wanted to know what it was about, how it worked, what the limits were. I got familiar with the numbness that would spread from my mouth to my forehead. I loved how I became more outgoing, less inhibited. I liked that I could drink more when I was high. I could have a drink and get a buzz, do a line and kind of sober up, and get a different kind of buzz. Drink, line, drink, line, drink, line, drink, line, until I was wired. Next thing I knew, it would be seven A.M. and I'd be wide awake with no appetite, looking for an after-party. It was easy to do because it seemed like the entire industry was doing it, and every nightclub was flooded with it.

Coke was certainly easy to get. There was an abundance of rich men who love to party with models and who would just hand it out to get us to hang out with them. (Sad, I know.) Or I could just ask any promoter, "Can you get coke?" and he'd figure it out. Someone would give us lines or little 1-gram baggies every time we went out. I never paid a dollar for anything.

It became a nonstop party. I started living off an insane cocktail of cocaine, laxatives, diuretics, fat-burning pills, and liquids. You know what the bizarre thing was? As I write this, it all sounds so extreme, but in that crazy, fucked-up world, it was normal, boring even.

What wasn't normal, though, were the thoughts I started having. The laxative addiction had gotten so bad that I couldn't poop without them and I couldn't eat without taking them immediately after. I started to feel trapped in a never-ending loop, and there seemed to be no exit door out of this physical dependency as well as the constant self-loathing and doubt, guilt, and paralyzing insecurities. It. Was. Exhausting. And I thought, *If I am going to feel this way every day, three times a day, for the rest of my life . . . I'd rather tap out right now.* Unfortunately, this feeling wasn't a one-off, as I'd contemplated ending my own life a few times. I never told anyone nor ever acted on my thoughts, but it doesn't lessen the pain of having such thoughts in the first place. I would quietly fight these feelings for a long time before I really dealt with them properly.

Until then, I hid my pain and tried to continue on, pretending everything was okay. After a few months working in Hong Kong, my agency wanted me to try another market: Singapore. This country was a great stepping-stone for any aspiring model looking to bulk up her portfolio of quality editorial work that's in English—an important detail when building an international career. I had gotten my A level results back (and got straight A's, phew!) and, at this point, had been accepted into several universities, of which I chose to attend the University of Bristol in the UK. That was nearly a year away, but it was still good to know that I had a game plan in place after my gap year. Victor managed to relocate to Singapore as well. Our Hong Kong agency had a sister agency in Singapore, so I signed the contract, booked my ticket, said goodbye to my Hong Kong friends, and left.

LET ME STEP BACK A BIT. I didn't take this move lightly. I was actually nervous when I left Hong Kong. I was still only seventeen, leaving "home" for the first time. I was leaving everything that was familiar to me. In Hong Kong, even though I was living a life independent from my parents, they were still relatively nearby. In Singapore I'd be starting over in a way, learning the ins and outs of a different culture, as well as having to navigate a new city.

I was also taking a huge step up in the hierarchy of modeling. I knew I could work in Hong Kong, but could I make it work overseas? I felt like I was swimming with the bigger fish now. I thought, *What if Victor gets work, and I don't? What if I get in debt with my agency because I made no money?* I was a ball of nerves as I arrived in Singapore.

The agency arranged for me to live in a "model apartment," which was one apartment with six other people: two girls from China in one bedroom, me and two models from Kazakhstan in another, and one of my bookers (agents) and her girlfriend in the third. Having a booker living with us was very common in the modeling industry. They were like chaperones, and they monitored everything we did, everything we ate, where we went, and when we came back. No boys were allowed, and they monitored what time we came home from a night out. With a huge percentage of the model population being minors (myself included, at the time), it was probably smart. Victor had a similar setup. He was put in an apartment of all men and their booker. It was strange to be away from him all of a sudden, after living with him 24/7, but we made do.

When I arrived, I met my roommates, who had already been working in the city for a while.

"Hi, I'm Regina," one introduced herself in a friendly voice before pointing to the other girl. "Zis is Irina."

"Hi, I'm Mia. Where are you guys from?"

"Kazakhstan," they replied in unison. I had never met anyone from that country before.

They were welcoming and friendly to me, and they showed me the ropes of my new neighborhood. And the truth was that whether or not we had common interests or similarities or even spoke the same damn language, we bonded over our mutual insecurities and search for constant approval. Not only was I here with all my issues, but I was living with all of these other girls' issues, too. Regina had been told that she was "too big," so she was constantly working out and trying to eat as little as possible. Another roommate, Mandy, was also obsessive. On Sundays we'd watch movies, and while the rest of us would be sitting on the couch, she'd stand, because she thought it burned more calories. I'd wake up in the morning and she would already be out walking. Her whole life revolved around burning calories.

Even crazier was the fact that she wanted to be a chef someday, so she would spend all day cooking an absolutely insane amount of food. I mean, a colossal amount. She'd make all types of different dishes—roasted chicken, pasta and meatballs, stews—just so she could set it out for all of us to eat. She'd sit there and watch us, and ask us how it tasted. Obviously, we picked here and there to spare her feelings, but the sad part is that none of us wanted to even touch it. She was eating vicariously through us, much like what I used to do with Allen, only we weren't really eating either.

I'd wake up and go to sleep knowing that everyone in the house was doing whatever they could to be as skinny as possible. If someone was feeling bad because an agent yelled at them or they couldn't fit into clothing on set, we all knew what it felt like. We tried to help one another not be eaten alive by our insecurities.

Like in Hong Kong, all of this exposure to other models' deep self-doubt made me feel like I didn't have a problem. Almost everyone in the industry suffered from the pressure to look a certain way and conform to a specific standard of beauty. (In hindsight, in my almost two decades of working in the industry, even the girls who have thought they had a healthy relationship with food and exercise have still been deeply affected by the pressures of the industry in some way, shape, or form, either consciously or unconsciously.) The extremes we went to to fit the mold were universal to modeling. It made me feel like there were people far sicker than me, around whom I saw the serious extremes of anorexia. I saw girls who were so skinny that every rib and vertebra stuck out. I have also seen girls covered in soft, downy hair—a condition called lanugo, the body's way of protecting itself against heat loss because there is no fat to warm itself.

Singapore reminded me of Disneyland, with its perfectly groomed plants and flowers and immaculate, litter-free sidewalks. It was much more buttoned up than Hong Kong, too. Chewing gum was banned, and you could get fined if you forgot to flush a public toilet. It shouldn't have come as a surprise that the punishment for drug possession, if the amount was high enough, included the death penalty. It was a pretty austere place because of its strict laws. Even if you bumped into somebody on the street, they would be overly apologetic.

All that to say, in moving there, I didn't think I'd be able to get up to too much trouble. But let me tell you, trouble was every-where, if you looked for it. The same system was set up there—go to castings, meet the promoters, get invited to parties. Boom. Behind closed doors, unlimited drinks poured, and cocaine—and any other drug, really—was readily available. The common factor in every city was that rich people wanted to hang out with beautiful people, and they would pay for all the drinks and drugs (and anything else) to do so. This was the place where things took a turn for me.

Still only seventeen, I went from one party to another until it all started to blur together. We'd be invited to penthouse soirees that lasted for days, with dozens of models constantly flowing in and out of the suite. I would party for two or three days before crashing and going home to sleep. One time I showed up to work a fashion show still high off a cocktail of Ecstasy, alcohol, weed, and cocaine. I don't remember much from the day, although I do remember gurning as I walked the runway. What's gurning? It's an involuntary clenching of the teeth and jaw, a common side effect while on MDMA and Ecstasy. Attractive, right? The client didn't think so. Needless to say, they complained about me to my agency. I don't blame them. I was getting cocky with how far I could go.

At another show, I was so out of it, feeling shitty from a hangover/comedown, that I snapped at my dressers and other staff around me. Comedowns happen after those mood-altering drugs leave the bloodstream, and the body, once high with happy chemicals whirling around in the brain, suddenly nosedives into a profound sense of anxiety and sadness, in addition to feeling physically sick. It can fuck with your entire existence, especially if it's a bad one. So that day, I was erratic and rude. No wonder that client also complained about me. My reputation had been stellar up until that point, but my lifestyle was starting to interfere with my work. At the time, I didn't really give a shit. Isn't that horrible? I was just so young and self-involved, and I had no idea about the importance of professionalism and reputation yet, but that is no excuse for bad behavior. One day, while looking for pictures from a recent fashion show online, I came across a blog written by someone who had worked on that show. He wrote that I was a nightmare to work with (going as far as calling me a bitch) and that he would never work with me again. *Ouch.* This comment was there for anyone to read and would exist online forever. That was not me. I didn't want to be known for that. I didn't want a bad reputation. He was right, though; I was being a moody bitch, and I should have known better.

As I struggled with the ins and outs of modeling, Victor struggled, too. He didn't seem to be getting the gigs he needed to make enough money for his family back home. I had gone with him on that trip to the Philippines and saw how his family was living in squalor. Their home was actually a wooden hut with no real roof, running water, or beds—just mats on the floor. There were cockroaches running around everywhere. His mom was in poor health, and had a little sister and brother he wanted to support through school, and there was no father in sight. I appreciated where he came from and how humbly his family was living, so when he started asking me for money to send home, of course I said yes. I wanted to help. It felt good to help. I gave him one or two thousand Hong Kong dollars (about $150). But then the emails started. I would get notes from his mom about how the washing machine was broken and how, with her arthritis, she had to painfully wash clothes by hand. She never asked me for a handout, but she might as well have. Next thing I knew, I was going to Western Union to wire her money for a new washer.

I liked the fact that he seemed so close to his family. It was something I didn't have and wanted to be a part of. Up until this point, I hadn't had much contact with my parents since I had moved out of the house. I had left home on bad terms with my mum, so I wasn't really surprised. Then one day, while I was still in Singapore, my dad called. My dad never called. Not wanting to be yanked back to the reality of my family, I didn't answer. And then he tried again. And again and again. I knew something was wrong. When I finally answered, he simply said to me, "Your mum has been hurt in a car accident."

I paused.

"Will she be okay?"

"Yes."

"Was she drunk when it happened?"

"Yes."

That's when I hung up. I had heard all I needed to. I felt a lot of emotions in that moment, none of them sympathy. After the call,

I sat and thought about my reaction: *Was I a sociopath for responding like this? Was I too cold? No.* I decided that I was tired of the alcoholism, the fights, the abuse, and I needed to protect myself by creating a distance from her, both physically and emotionally. I eventually found out what had happened to her: My dad had been driving the golf cart when it flipped over turning a corner, and my mum was injured. She was stitched up across her upper and lower lips. Weeks later when the wound still wasn't healing, they went back and discovered chunks of her tooth were still embedded in her lip. Her looks were never quite the same (thank God she was okay otherwise), so this accident took a toll on her in many different ways.

Even when I found this out, I was not ready to mend fences. Having my parents back in my universe caused a regression in me that I didn't need or want. I was moving to my next destination, Tokyo, and I was excited for a new adventure.

That is, until I found out that Victor was cheating on me.

One night, Victor and I had stayed in a Holiday Inn. As we couldn't sleep over in each other's apartments, we did this a lot. I was using his phone, and a message popped up: I LOVE YOU. The sender's name was Linda.

When I say I lost my shit, let me tell you, I. Lost. My. Shit.

Victor had been living a double life. He had another girlfriend in another country. When he would fly out to her, he'd tell me he was going away for a job or going back home to see his family. When he was not with me, he was with her, and vice versa. He was playing both of us.

"Get the fuck out of my hotel room!" I screamed (I had paid, of course) as he tried to wiggle out of being caught.

"You're a lying, cheating son of a bitch!" I cried as I slammed the door on him.

I changed my flights to get out of Singapore ASAP. My move to Tokyo couldn't come soon enough.

Thank God I was moving to another country, one with a completely different scene, and one without Victor. It was one of the biggest fashion capitals in the world, and I was excited to get there and get to work. When I arrived at my new accommodations, a cute little boutique hotel, I realized that, unlike in Singapore, I didn't have to share a space with other models. I had my own hotel room. My booker would meet me in the morning, take me to my castings, and drop me off at the end of the day. With the language barrier, my booker acted as my translator, but it was very much like the movie *Lost in Translation*. The cultural gap was much more significant, and I couldn't just go around sliding into society like I had in the other cities. I wasn't meeting other models or model PRs, so I wasn't going to parties or club events. I wasn't living the life I had expected to live in Tokyo. Although the city was crammed with millions of people, I was incredibly lonely.

In this isolation, I let my eating disorder go into overdrive—it was easy to do without anyone watching. I'd have a milkshake or protein shake, and that would be my food for the day. Liquids only. Who was there to tell me differently? No one. I'd often drink alone in the evenings just to pass the time (usually Bailey's because it was slightly filling). As long as it was liquid, I was okay. I would go to TGI Friday's and order a milkshake and sit at the bar, desperate to make friends with any English-speaking people who walked in.

I would call Joey at my agency and cry, telling him how lonely I was. With all this time on my own, I started to pine for Victor. I was as naive as he was manipulative, and I felt like I couldn't survive without his validation. This was especially true in Tokyo, where I was modeling in a new city with my insecurities at an all-time high. Feeling vulnerable, I reconnected with him. (I know, I know, you must be thinking, *WHAT?*) We started talking on the phone all the time, but even with that lifeline, Tokyo got so bad that I decided to terminate my contract early and go back to Hong Kong. There, I was back to my old ways on my old stomping grounds: going out as many nights as I could, staying out as late as I could, doing as much blow as I could, and then going to work the next day.

In Hong Kong, I met with Paolo Tomei, the head of his eponymous modeling agency based in Milan. At the time it was one of the biggest agencies in the world, representing many of the industry's top supermodels. Many of the models I used to stare at in magazines and on fashion TV shows were represented by him. He was known for having a good eye for finding the next supermodel and was in town meeting with Hong Kong models to scout new talent for Europe. My agency picked me to meet with him. I sat there as he looked through my book, my nerves so heightened they felt almost visible.

"I see something in you. I think you can go very, very far in this business," he said. I remained quiet as he flipped through the pages, although I am sure my heart was pounding so loudly he could hear it. I eyed a pile of comp cards on the coffee table—proof that he was meeting with *all* the top girls in Hong Kong. *Wow, I can't believe I'm here.*

"I want you in Milan for the next season . . ."

I couldn't believe it.

That was one of the greatest moments of my life—my invitation to Milan, the home of Gucci and Prada, the mecca of the modeling industry, where only the best can succeed. I couldn't wait. But my agency in Hong Kong had a different reaction; they didn't think I was ready. They encouraged me to stay and get more experience. They said I'd be swimming with the sharks. They were convinced I was not ready for that kind of competition. In my head, I was all for it. I thought, *If I'm destined for success, what's the difference if it's in a few years or now? Bring it ON. I'm ready.*

At the same time, Victor met me in Hong Kong. He had ended his other relationship, and he was extremely remorseful. We rekindled our romance.

"Let's go to Milan together. Let's start again," he said.

"Okay, let's try." Was this a smart decision? No. Again I ignored the red flags waving right in my face and decided to give him another chance.

In Milan, I quickly realized that my agency was not kidding. "Cutthroat" is too weak a term to describe what I experienced. It was also the first place where I was really exposed to worldwide fashion campaigns—the ones you see when you flip through a fashion magazine or walk through a mall. Milan was the fashion capital of Europe and my modeling debut outside of Asia. Top models, top brands, top pay—the stakes were much, much higher. There was more money on the line, which took my eating issues to new levels.

I stayed in a hotel that primarily accommodated models, with two girls assigned to each room. They came from all over the world to try to make it in Milan. There were girls from Australia, Brazil, eastern Europe, *everywhere*. And every one of them was just trying to be skinnier than the next, because the competition was outrageous. My first roommate, from Russia, walked around naked and, every once in a while, ate one little square of white chocolate. Nothing else. Another girl ate only frozen peas. She'd microwave them and eat them, one by one. There was also a fifteen-year-old from Poland who was so skinny that she no longer menstruated. By comparison, the fact that I hadn't yet pushed my body to its limits made me feel like I had permission to push it even more. So I did. I increased my intake of my pills and laxatives, and halved the protein bars. I'd eat only half of a protein bar in a day, dividing it up in even smaller portions to take bites throughout the day.

We would receive itineraries under our doors for the next day by six o'clock the evening prior. The next morning, we would race off to castings, like clockwork, sometimes ten to twelve in a day. At my first casting, I signed in and I received a number. I was 252. There were 251 other girls I was competing with ahead of me and God knows how many after me—what the fuck? How was I going to book anything? I needed to starve more (I mean I was already starving—what more could I do?). The competition was just fierce. Let's put it this way: Being pretty with a winning personality was nothing unless the size was right. The pool got more and more insane, and there were more and more looks to compete with: a mix of stunning eastern Europeans, girls from Brazil, porcelain-skinned Asian girls, dark-skinned girls, girls with freckled skin, blondes, redheads, girls with Afros—every possible look you can imagine. Everyone had one thing in common, though: They were fucking skinny.

With the incredible competition, I was getting pressure from all sides. One day I had popped by my agency to pick up comp cards, and an agent called me over.

"Mia! Mama Mia, can you come here, please?" he said with a thick Italian accent. I walked over to his desk, where I could see he had pulled up an image of me in a bikini on his computer screen. He zoomed in on my thighs and said, "You see here? This is your problem area. It's too big." He then pulled up an image of another model in a bikini and zoomed in on her thighs. He pointed to the screen and continued, "You see her? She looks good. You need to go to the gym and do leg exercises to make your thighs smaller. Don't you agree, Francesca?" He nudged the agent sitting next to him. She glanced over at my photo and concurred. "Mmmm, *si*. You don't look good." No mincing words. Fuck, I need to starve more. I didn't party at all in Milan; I was focused on booking jobs. I wanted this, a lot.

I was doing well there, landing a few good jobs and in the running for huge campaigns like Diesel and Valentino. It felt good; there was a buzz in Milan I hadn't felt before. Something was happening—*I* was happening. My agency kept encouraging me, saying that I was right about to pop. "One more season. One more season, and you're there." Paolo Tomei wanted me to come back for the next season, as I had almost booked a couple of career-changing jobs. "I see so much potential in you. You could really make it all the way," he said. I, of course, believed him. I was a small fish in a big pond, but this was the first time I felt like I could make it. I wanted to make it.

IN JUNE, I CALLED MY DAD. I wanted to tell him how well things were going and that I wanted to stay for one more season. I was about to make a name for myself *internationally*. I could be one of those models I'd stared at on Fashion TV or whose magazine spread I'd taped to my bedroom wall. I felt *that* close.

How could I leave now?

He crushed that fantasy real quick, letting me know how he felt about it in no uncertain terms.

"If you don't go to university this year, I'm not paying for it. If you miss the cutoff, you pay for it yourself." University is *very* expensive in the UK if you're not a UK resident. He added, "Do you want to be twenty-five in a room of eighteen-year-olds? The learning curve is not the same. . . . Just do it."

I promised I would, come September. My dad rarely stepped in and gave me advice, but when he did, I generally complied.

Meanwhile, I would remain in Milan to finish out the few months I had left. I had landed a callback for an Esprit campaign. I *really* wanted it—Esprit was a popular brand in Hong Kong when I was growing up. I wanted to do the campaign for sentimental reasons—for little Mia.

I wanted to book this as a personal achievement.

To prepare, I did not eat solid food for two days, took a laxative the night before, and on the morning of the appointment took a diuretic. I got there, tried on some sample clothes (which included oversized puffer winter jackets, nothing that would reveal my tiny figure anyway), and took snapshots, all the while feeling like a fucking raisin, just shriveled up. I got through it, though, nerves and all. It was a blazing hot day, especially for so early in the summer. I sluggishly walked out and went to find a tram stop to head back to the hotel, feeling weak, light-headed, and drowsy. I had gotten on the tram when, whoosh, my legs gave out and I went down. Lights out. I had fainted.

I don't remember much of it, but I do remember coming to with kind strangers helping me off the ground and putting me in a chair. A pregnant woman stood up and gave me her seat. That upset me, but I felt so lifeless and weak I couldn't refuse. Sitting there, I thought, *How the hell am I going to get back home? How the fuck did that happen? I don't feel okay. I need to get myself together.* I got off the tram and went to the nearest café, bought two bottles of water, and downed them.

You'd think that I would have taken this incident as a sign that I was pushing myself too much. My eating habits were catching up to me, and I was damaging my body. But I ignored all of the warning signs that my body was giving me. I was so deeply entangled with my eating disorders that of course continued to starve myself. I was booking great jobs and making money. I had even made a few friends, and I was waiting for Victor to arrive. One day, I had been walking back from the last casting of the day with a girl whom I had met there, Jess. We were heading toward her apartment, which was on a very long street, and I planned to use a tram to get home from there. As we walked, out of the corner of my eye I could see a guy perched on the side of a building with a bicycle. He had a mullet, a mustache, and a colorful purple and white tracksuit jacket with matching shorts, straight out of the eighties.

As we walked by him, Jess chatted away, totally oblivious, but I kept an eye on him. I didn't trust him. That's when he moved his shorts to one side, exposing his dick and his balls. Afraid, I uttered, "What the fuck?"

"Wait, what?" my friend asked.

"That man just flashed his dick."

It was gross, and I was frightened. He then got on his bike and cycled ahead of us.

As we arrived at Jess's building, we said our goodbyes and I kept walking. The guy reappeared, ditched his bike, and began following me on foot. At that point, I started to panic. I looked up and suddenly realized that there was not another person on the street. Just me and this weirdo.

I panicked and called Victor. He was still overseas, but I wanted advice on what to do. "I'm being followed. This guy is following me and showing me his dick. What do I do?"

"Try to stay calm. Don't go into any buildings, 'cause he's going to follow you. Try to find somebody, anybody, so you are not alone."

So I picked up my pace, practically running in my little summer dress and ballet flats, bag over my shoulder, my phone in one hand, my portfolio in the other. I looked over my shoulder. He was closing in.

And he was jerking off.

By this point I was hysterically crying. Finally, I saw a woman in the middle of the street, at the tram stop. A beautiful sight. Sobbing hysterically, I ran to her as he closed in.

I managed to reach the woman and flung myself on her, circled around, and crouched down behind her. As she started yelling at him in Italian, I peeked out behind her shoulder and saw him masturbating. I don't know what she said, but, as we could hear the tram approaching, he finally scurried back to his bike and rode off. We didn't call the cops. I just wanted to go home, lock the door, get in bed, and stay there.

The next day, I called my agency and told them what had happened. I was still in shock. Traumatized, I didn't want to leave the hotel. I didn't want to go anywhere. I didn't feel safe. I didn't want to go on public transport. I didn't want to do anything. Unfortunately this was just one of many harassments I endured there. I wasn't the only one. Many girls had similar stories of sexual harassment and assault, not only in Milan, but in various cities. Whether it was in the subway, on a tram, or on the street, many women had been catcalled and harassed.

It was after this incident that Victor arrived, and I was so happy that he was there. I was looking for a savior and protector, and I was convinced that was him; I was so vulnerable and weak, I buried how he had treated me. I just wanted to feel safe again.

Once we had finished our working season, we decided to go on a trip to Rome for a week. I had just gotten paid, so I had brought a few thousand dollars with me. It was a big relief to get away and have a romantic holiday. I even let loose a bit, eating and acting more like a human and less like a model. I wanted to focus on my mental and emotional health after that horrible incident. I enjoyed the fresh pizza and delicious ice cream in Italy. I definitely gained a little weight (which Victor wouldn't let me forget). We were able to relax and do cool touristy activities like visiting the city's historic sites. We really reconnected. He was sweet and romantic, and by coming back in my life at the right time, I saw him as my knight in shining armor. Or so I thought.

One evening, in our hotel room, I went to take some money out of the stash that I had brought with me, but it wasn't there.

I had put it in my laptop and had bundled the two with some clothes. But now, I couldn't find the money. I frantically went through everything, turning the entire place upside down.

"Victor, where the fuck is my money?"

"I don't know. Let me help you look."

Nothing. I just couldn't understand where it went. I went downstairs to ask the concierge if anyone had been in our room.

They said they couldn't check the CCTV unless I filed a police report.

Back in the room, I felt like I was losing my mind.

Then it hit me. There was one more place we hadn't checked yet: Victor's suitcase.

I looked at him and blurted out, "Can I check your suitcase?"

"What the fuck are you saying?"

"At this point I'm not ruling anything out. I have checked this entire room. The only thing I haven't checked is your suitcase," I huffed.

"Are you asking if I took your money? That's so fucked-up that you would even accuse me of that. You have lost your mind."

"Well, I want to go through your stuff, then."

"Fine."

I opened the luggage. I rifled through its contents, and right when I thought I'd gone through everything, I found it hidden at the bottom, under his T-shirts.

I wasted no time. I took the money and said, "I'm getting the fuck out of here."

I packed up my shit and left, without giving him time to explain.

That's it. I'm done with him, I thought. I got on a plane, and I went back to Hong Kong. It took all that for me to realize I was in a relationship with someone who was manipulative and narcissistic. He was the one who cheated. He was the one who was putting me down, telling me I needed to lose weight. Now he was the one stealing from me. He was the bad guy, but I felt like a sucker.

Back in Hong Kong, I settled into yet another model apartment and buried myself with work, but I was still heartbroken over Victor. My ego was also hurt; he had made a fool out of me. Matt, Victor, and other men I was attracted to seemed to fit a pattern. Did my choice in men have anything to do with my own insecurities? Did I not respect myself enough to run away from those damn red flags when I saw them? These thoughts would continue to rack my brain for years.

About a month later, the doorbell rang. I answered the door, and there was Victor. I couldn't fucking believe it. He must've gotten my address from the agency.

"I want to work things out with you. I came all the way from the Philippines to win you back."

I didn't want to see him; I didn't want to be with him. But I felt bad that he had come all this way. He looked terrible—genuinely miserable. After all, it was a big, romantic gesture that you see in Hollywood rom-coms—dropping his life and traveling so far to win back his girl. He poured his heart out, saying he had been miserable without me. He seemed depressed. He said he couldn't eat or sleep and was almost suicidal. I told him I was just trying to work as much as I could and I didn't need this drama right now. But I couldn't throw him out on the street. Once again, I took on his problems as my own.

He explained everything away—that he was not in a good place after the breakup, but he promised to get his shit together. To be honest, I was scared to kick him out. I was terrified to do anything that would anger him (sound familiar?), so this eighteen-year-old sucker let him stay. The first thing he did when he entered my apartment was to drop his bag and empty his pockets of little baggies of pills, mostly Ecstasy, onto my desk. *Damn, he must be all kinds of fucked-up right now*, I thought. I knew from past experiences with Matt and my mum that I needed to be careful around him. I knew enough not to do anything to poke the bear.

We agreed that he could stay with me until he felt better and got his shit together enough to get back to work and set himself up. Then we could talk about the possibility of an "us" again. The problem was, after a week or so, he wasn't getting better. He wasn't even trying to get better. Every night he would sit at the tiny desk with his laptop, depressed, and do drugs. He would stay up all night and sleep all day. Since I felt uncomfortable around him, I would try to avoid him as much as possible, going out and staying out as long as I could, meeting friends for a movie, drinks, anything, so by the time I got home, I could tell him that I was tired and wanted to go straight to bed.

I would get up in the morning and leave. Even if I didn't have anywhere to go, I would go. The only times we had any interaction were nights where he'd take whatever drugs he was taking, watch porn, and come into my bed.

While I was sleeping, he would hold my arms and pin my legs down and force himself on me while he was high. All I could do was cry through it. I felt powerless to stop it. I felt trapped. I didn't know what to do.

I stayed in this horrifying, abusive situation for about two weeks. Two weeks too long. As you read this you may think, *Why didn't she just leave?!* As most abused women will attest, though, I was paralyzed by fear, and he preyed on my low self-esteem. When you are in an abusive relationship, it's very easy to lose yourself. I didn't see a way out of it.

I finally broke down to my sister Anouk. I needed to tell someone what was happening. I was desperate to figure a way out of this. I was too scared to kick him out, but too scared to leave, because I knew he'd find me.

"I can't go home. I can't deal with this, but I don't know what to do," I cried to her.

"You *have* to get away from this guy. He fucking lied to you. He's stolen money from you. He's fucking raping you. You have to get away from this man. Now."

"I don't know how."

"Book a plane ticket to London. You have to go anyway to start university, so go early, go work there. Change your phone number. Change your email address. You just have to go. Don't contact him. You have to cut him off."

She was right. That very afternoon, I waited until he left for a basketball game with his friends, and then I packed up all my shit and went to a friend's house. A few days later, I was off to London. It was the best damn thing I ever did. I don't regret much in my life, but I regret my relationship with Victor. I was abused in so many ways, and I don't know why I just took it. He broke me down, while I was constantly living for people's approval. He was all bad, and he preyed on how young and vulnerable I was. I was never so wrong. It would take me a long time to figure out why I let myself to be manipulated, abused, and shamed by someone like Victor, and to see a connection between my long-standing insecurities and my romantic choices. Unfortunately, that wasn't my last abusive relationship, but I did learn how to walk away with this one. And I was proud of that. It came down to respecting myself. I was letting these abusive situations shape me, and I deserved better. Who knows where I'd be if I hadn't left. I certainly had more growing up to do, but leaving was probably the most adult—and positive—thing I had done in my life.

7. UNI AND ME

GOODBYE, VALENTINO. *Sayonara*, Prada. *Adios*, Marni. It would have been nice. But when my father tells me to do something, I do it. So I went to university. At the time, I felt like I was giving up a lot—a golden, once-in-a-lifetime opportunity to go far in my modeling career—but looking back on it now, I see it was probably one of the best decisions I ever made, next to finally ending it with Victor. It was good to be thousands of miles away from him; there's nothing like some distance to give you breathing space to heal the hurt. I had a new phone number, new email, a new apartment. It was a fresh start, and it seemed as though there was nothing but brighter days ahead.

I was off to the University of Bristol—not Oxford, but still a "red brick" university (one of the top in the UK) about two and a half hours outside of London. Bristol is a thriving, beautiful city. Though it's a university town, it has a culturally creative personality all its own. Along with its amazing arts and music scene, it's known for being the birthplace of drum and bass and the hometown of the infamously elusive artist Banksy.

I was going for a double degree in philosophy and economics, which takes three years in the UK compared with four in the States. I planned to drive to London when I had modeling jobs, but modeling would take a back seat to school, as my dad and I agreed. I wouldn't be pursuing the career-vaulting trajectory of runway work and campaigns that would necessitate my traveling for months at a time. I felt like I was doing something *normal*, which, ironically, felt really out of whack, since my life had been anything but normal. As an overweight kid, I never had a normal school life, and later, I almost ruined my education by fucking up, so this was a chance for a do-over. I was eighteen years old, doing what normal eighteen-year-olds do. It was another opportunity to start over, but with the promise of more permanency this time.

It also made me stay put for three years. Live in one place. My gap year had left me in a constant state of flux: I had moved from city to city, country to country, each of which had its own language, culture, and rhythms. Each move necessitated hitting the restart button, only to have to do it again a few months later. It took courage and gumption to pull off that lifestyle. I welcomed the challenge and embraced it wholeheartedly. But after more than a year of living out of a suitcase, the constant pick-up-and-go was exhausting, and I yearned for stability; I wanted to grow some roots and make some friends.

Arriving at Bristol, I moved into a dorm (we called them "halls"), something akin to the apartments I had lived in with models, but the vibe was obviously different. The students were all about books, not looks, and instead of rushing to go-sees and castings, I was rushing from class to class. I was using my brain again. It. Felt. Incredible. I was being challenged in ways I hadn't been for a while, and I loved it. It also gave me a routine, which I hoped would help in shutting off my self-abusing devices.

I also had a great guide through the transition. My brother Malcolm, who had graduated from Bristol several years earlier, gave me advice on what clubs to go to and where to hear the best music.

"One piece of advice: Don't tell anyone you're a model, not at first, okay?"

"What? Why? That's something I'm so proud of."

"There's a preconceived idea that all models are full of themselves. If you let people know, you're going to seem like you're full of yourself. Not a great way to make friends."

Never in a million years would this have occurred to me. Being heavy and bullied as a child, and then later, with all my eating issues, I was just so fucking insecure. I never thought that I was beautiful, so I didn't understand what he was advising me to do, or rather, not to do. Plus, I always felt that modeling was something I *did*. In my eyes, it did not make up who I fundamentally was as a person.

"I'd like to make friends, but why wouldn't I tell them about who I am and what I do? I think it's really cool what I've achieved," I told my brother. My dad, as well as all my siblings, had found their lifelong friends at school, so I anticipated that it would be the same for me. Before my gap year, I hadn't been used to making very strong connections, outside of Chelsea and Allen. But my year of modeling was essentially a crash course in starting up conversations, socializing, and making fast friends. In the end, though, because of the transience of my lifestyle at the time, those friendships didn't last long. I wanted to find that group of friends who'd be there for me through thick and thin.

"Just trust me and don't tell them at first," he said, and ended the conversation.

I DID TELL THEM. Well, I didn't do it on purpose. It was the first night of induction week (I know, I know, I couldn't even make it past my first day), and we had opened our dorm doors for a meet and greet. Everyone was hopping from room to room, mingling and drinking, getting to know each other. I was with a group of people in someone's room, and we were sharing photos—family photos, baby photos—whatever we had on our phones. I was sitting on a bed next to a girl as I scanned the photos on my BlackBerry (remember those?). I scrolled past a bunch of modeling shots. She popped her head over my shoulder and asked, "Is that *you*!?"

I remembered what my brother had said, but, mulling it over right there and then, I decided not to lie.

"Yes, that's me," I answered a bit self-consciously.

"Wait, you model?"

"Yes . . ."

"Let me see!" she said, grabbing my phone. "Do you do it in your free time?" she added as she scrolled through the photos.

"I've done it professionally, but now I'm doing it here and there as I get my degree," I said as she started passing the phone around. *Oh well, the cat's out of the bag!*

Everybody started peppering me with questions. "What kind of stuff do you model for?" "Have you been on any magazine covers?" "Would I have seen you anywhere?"

It's not that bad, I thought. They're not judging me.

I answered their questions as nonchalantly as I could, hoping I didn't sound full of myself. Because I certainly wasn't.

As the night wore on, I started noticing similarities in the way the other girls dressed, did their hair, and wore their makeup. Everyone neglected to tell me that, in going to Bristol, I would be entering a tribe of the UK elite. I was observing what the UK calls "rahs"—the young and posh British set—in their natural habitat. Think of Prince William as their king, and Kate as their queen. When I was there in 2007, more than half of the students were from the top quarter of the UK's most affluent families. Bristol was their breeding ground.

The rah uniform was head-to-toe: Jack Wills sweatpants tucked into Ugg boots, and a preppy polo shirt. The girls favored spray tans and bleach-blond hair, either overly teased and slung over to one side, or in a "this cost me three hundred dollars but it looks like I just rolled out of bed" tousled look. With names like Clarissa, Purdy, and Posie for the girls, and Jonty, Rupert, and Wilfred for the boys, all of them had gone to prestigious schools like Winchester, Eton, and Harrow.

They all seemed to know one another, too, having gone to the same elite schools and with families that socialized in the same circles. I started to feel out of place—really out of place. *Wow, I don't think this is for me. I am not like them.* Then I thought, *Well, fuck, I'm going to have to adapt. I'm going to have to fake it till I make it if I'm going to get through university.*

The next night, we had a formal welcome mixer organized by the university that took place in each hall's main building. I steeled myself as I walked there from my dorm alone. My thoughts seesawed between hope and dread. Before I went in, I had a cigarette and gave myself a serious pep talk. Okay, a few cigarettes.

As I walked in and headed to the bar, the first person I saw was Lucy, from the previous night. She had a sweet spot at the end of the bar, surrounded by a posse of girls—*wow, she already has a posse.* I decided to just go in and do my best to make friends.

We all started talking—the girls were all really friendly and seemed interested in getting to know me.

Lucy asked, between sips of beer, "So did you go to public school or private school?" I found it odd that the first question they asked me was where I went to school.

"What are public and private schools? I grew up in Hong Kong. We only have local schools and international schools."

Lucy reframed the question: "Like, a government school or an expensive school?"

Ooooh, so she is asking me if I'm rich or poor . . . I get it now.

The terms "public" and "private" in relation to school are the reverse of how they are referred to in America. In Britain, public schools are tuition-based, and private schools are government funded. I could tell that where they went to school was important to them; it was how they defined themselves. Then here I came, without even a working knowledge of what the hell the difference between public school and private school was. *Okay, I am not going to fit in.*

"I went to an international school," I answered, hoping that answer would put her at ease, and it did.

I spent another hour at the bar, bouncing from group to group, being asked the same question over and over. Private or public school? Meaning, are you rich or poor? Will you fit in or not? Are you one of us or not? *Wow, this is a big deal to them,* I thought. This was not a big deal to me. After half a dozen attempted interactions with different groups, I kind of lost hope in finding a connection. I was also feeling gross after all that beer. I decided to sneak out and go back to my room. I left thinking, *Okay, maybe I won't make friends on the first day. I will eventually make friends at some point, though, right? I don't know if I can fake it until I make it here. This is going to be the next three years of my life. Fuck, I hope I make friends. But if I don't, it will be fine—I'll just be invisible—I've done that before.*

This is what I was considering as I reached the stoop outside my building and lit up a cigarette. There were several students already smoking there as well. I walked up and we started talking, introducing ourselves. I noticed the Chinese gentleman first because of his accent.

"Hey, where are you from?" I asked.

"Hong Kong," he said.

"Get the fuck out!" was my reply.

"I'm Henry," he said. And Chinara was from Nigeria, Paulo from Italy. All foreign. It was a great counter to the party I had just left. After having lost all hope that I would find people like me, here I was discovering that the school actually had an amazing international demographic. *Here is my tribe.*

After that night, we became fast friends, thick as thieves—especially Chinara and me, probably because our rooms were opposite each other. No one was cliquey in this group, because we were used to being the minority or being outcasts. Chinara went back to London all the time, like me, so the university wasn't the social epicenter for us, as it perhaps was for other students.

When it came to the academic piece of school, I loved it. I loved my classes. I loved using my brain. It had only been a year since I had been in school, but I'd missed it. I feel like there are two sides to me—the dorky introvert, and the social, rule-breaking extrovert—and the two certainly struggled for my attention at university. I felt that school satisfied both: That excited, chubby nerd inside me screamed "Yay!" and my fun, social butterfly side was also excited for what was to come. I felt like everything was lining up.

When I was growing up, my dad used to say, "University is where you go to learn what you love from those who live what they love." That is sort of how I decided to focus on philosophy. I had never studied it before, never even picked up a book on it before, and I wasn't even entirely sure what that field of academia was. This was the perfect opportunity to find out and enjoy it. As I delved into the subject, it really taught me to *think*. Growing up in Asia, the work ethic is very regimented and orderly—one remains within the lines. Generally speaking, academia in Asia is all about excelling and acquiring the knowledge to get a "respectable" job, like being a doctor or a lawyer. So to study philosophy—to be encouraged to let my thoughts wander, to ask big, complex questions and have deep, philosophical discussions—was incredible. This nonlinear thinking was a welcome counterpoint to studying and memorizing hard facts and equations. It's funny, because anyone who gets a degree in philosophy will inevitably get asked, "What the hell are you going to do with a philosophy degree?" I didn't have an answer at the time, but studying Hume, Kant, and Descartes helped with independent thought and opened up a world to me that was so much bigger than the microscopic one happening on campus.

Lectures were filled with more than a hundred young adults, sitting, taking notes, and listening. Seminars took place in smaller groups of ten, where we'd discuss what we had learned in the lectures. Working toward a double degree in philosophy and economics, I had thoughtful, weighty discussions with other students and professors, and people were *listening* to me—not looking at me. What a change from modeling. I pondered important issues, like the measure of matter, rather than worrying about the measure of my waistline. I loved the open-ended questions, the debates, the existential dilemmas that seemed to confound even the professors; it all went to the core of what it means to be human.

I felt like I was starting to forge a future, on my own terms.

And then I let my recklessness throw me off course yet again.

ONE NIGHT, I was with a bunch of girls from my dorm pregaming in one of our rooms. We were all sitting in a circle on the floor and somebody pulled out some cocaine.

YES!!! Hi, old friend! my rebellious half thought.

I was excited for a couple of reasons. One, I loved cocaine (but you know that); and two, it was something I excelled at. A lot of the girls were just trying it or hadn't done it before, but I was a coke aficionado. I was the expert. I got a credit card out, broke the powder up and cut the lines, rolled up the note, and gave everyone their turn.

Like an excited puppy, I posed the all-important question to Emily, the girl who brought the coke to the party: "Where'd you get it?" I was in a new city, so I needed to be hooked up with a dealer. She gave me a number. *Let the games begin.* As we continued, I noticed who was doing it and who was not. Chinara was doing it. I realized that she had a very similar appetite for it, and it became a big factor in our friendship.

It wasn't long before I found more people who did coke, and I built a little crew around Chinara and me. It all progressed very quickly. I believed that all the shit I'd pulled in high school—the fact that I'd managed to survive, graduate, and get into a good university—was proof that I'd be all right this time around as well. *I know what I am doing. I know when to stop.* But very quickly, I got carried away. I became the party girl, and I was the one who bought in bulk and handed out grams like candy to friends. Before I knew it, I was doing so much cocaine that I was blowing through a lot of the money I had made from modeling, and I was going out most nights each week, hitting every one of the city's clubs.

You must be thinking, *Girl, why are you doing that? We just read how excited you were to be on the hallowed grounds of academia, using your noodle, and getting a good education. Why are you falling back into drugs?* I went to Bristol to better myself and get a good education, yes, but I was also just blending in with the crowd. Society tells us that college is an allocated time to be wild, rebellious, experimental, and just a little out of control. The Brits like to party, and Bristol was a party town, so this was what it was supposed to be. Studies took a back seat as I concentrated more on my social life. I let myself get distracted by the excitement of being in a new place and starting a new chapter in my life. I figured I could do what I did in my last years in school when I pulled it together in the end and aced my A levels.

I was giving the minimum input, thinking I would still get the maximum output. I was relying on my natural abilities. When final exams loomed at the end of the first term, I did study. Well, I crammed. I went back to my ol' standby "starve and study" routine to do so. My weight had gone up and down that year, mostly because mealtime was more of a social activity, and it was very British to end up in a chip shop at the end of a night out and eat an enormous amount of french fries covered in cheese.

When I went back into that starve-and-study mode, it went pretty much unnoticed, possibly because everyone was too busy dealing with their own shit. Although the academic environment was incredibly different from that of the modeling world, I saw the *same* fucking issues with food and eating. Body issues are every-where, no matter who you are or what you do; the entire female gender is burdened by society's standards of beauty being placed on women. Many female students worried about gaining weight, comparing themselves with other girls or models and celebrities; they worried if they were pretty or thin enough, sizing themselves up against impossible ideals. Some would take extreme action if they felt "less than." Louisa, a girl who lived in the room next to mine, would eat just a bowl of frozen peas, as I had seen girls do in Milan.

But I always knew I'd be modeling through the summer holidays. So I locked myself in my room for a month and created a strict timetable for studying and eating, like I had done for my A levels. I focused and shed weight by once again depriving my body of food, all the while hyping myself up by telling myself that it was going to feel great when it was all over.

All my cramming in the eleventh hour would not be enough: I received my end-of-year results, and guess what? *I failed.* I got 19 percent—you read that right—in my quantitative methods mathematics class. And I *love* math. I'd never gotten such a low score in anything in my life (not even PE). I tried my best to excuse my way out of it. I sat with my tutor—a British term for a mentor or advisor—blaming my performance on culture shock. I tried as hard as I could to gain sympathy as the foreign student who was having a hard time adjusting. They didn't bite. Nope, nada—I failed, and that was it. I could continue on to my second year, but only as a student of philosophy, the subject I had done well in. Weirdly enough, my brother also failed the first year of university and switched from physics to history of art. Since I wasn't the first, my dad, thankfully, wasn't so shocked when he found out about my massive fail. Clearly, it's not uncommon for students, many of whom are on their own for the first time, to party too much their first year at university. And my brother turned out great, so I think my dad was okay about it—at least that was how it seemed to me at the time.

Even without his anger, it was a hard pill to swallow. I needed to fucking study. I had let myself get distracted by my friends, by the fun, by not having enough discipline. The beauty of exams is that they're straightforward: If you put in the work, you will do well. But I partied my way into a failing grade and nearly derailed my education.

AT THE START OF MY SECOND YEAR, I was just a philosophy student. I lost the sense of structure and practicality that had come with economics and math classes, which was a nice balance to the airy, loose, and intense study of philosophy. It messed with my head. I was left to ponder big, abstract, and existential realities, and it left me feeling untethered. When a teacher asked us to answer the heady question of whether we're all just brains in vats, I couldn't wrap my head around the intangibility of it all. I missed problems with concrete, yes or no, right or wrong answers. I had moved into a house with two girls, and I took to smoking weed all day, which helped me drift and ponder over such elusive topics.

I was more studious and got better grades, but it wasn't easy. I still wanted to have fun, as I was still discovering who I was as a person. What music do I like? Who did I want to hang with? Where was the best party? I wanted to continue enjoying my college experience.

And so I did. If it was a weeknight, we'd do coke until deep into the night. If it was a weekend, we'd go out to a drum and bass, dubstep, or hip-hop party and smoke some weed, maybe do some coke, and some MDMA.

Let's talk about MDMA for a minute. (MDMA is known as "Mandy" in the UK, "Molly" in the US.)

The drug may make you feel great for a few hours, but the comedowns are torturous. One night I had gotten so fucked-up that I woke up the next evening in a cold sweat and with a mouth so dry that I had a hard time dislodging my tongue from the roof of it. My head, pounding with pain, felt as heavy as a cinderblock. My mood—on a scale from one to ten—was a negative five. I never felt this bad from coke or booze. *Is this it? Is my body going to just give up?* My body implored, *No more, Mia, please. Let's not do that again.* I managed to move my aching body enough to un-cocoon myself from my bed covers, reach for my laptop, and Google, "Can you die from a comedown?" I couldn't find anything specific about dying, but I did find out that MDMA releases such an enormous amount of serotonin, and the brain becomes so significantly depleted of this feel-good neurotransmitter, that it takes a few days to replenish its reserves. As a result, those few days of recovery make the user feel as low as the drug made them feel high. (They don't call it a come*down* for nothing.) It was messing with the chemicals in my brain (coke did, too, but so far in my experiences, the effects were tenfold with MDMA). I was fucking with my head, literally.

One day after a bad trip, I decided MDMA wasn't worth the comedown and I would stick to what I knew: coke. So when everyone would be getting super high on MDMA, I'd be doing shitloads of coke.

One Sunday morning, my alarm clock went off at ten and I hit "snooze" four times before I remembered why I had set it the previous night. My dad was due to arrive any minute—he had flown in for a visit, which was a *big deal*. He never came to visit me, but here he was, flying from Hong Kong to London and then driving all the way to Bristol.

He would be showing up in twenty minutes, and I wasn't up or ready. I had gone out the night before (surprise) and had done too many drugs (surprise), so I was hungover and running on only a couple of hours of half-assed, tweaked-out sleep. But I knew my dad was excited to take me out for lunch.

In those few precious minutes, I scrambled through my room and hid all the paraphernalia, wiped all the coke residue off my desk, threw out the ashy pile of cigarette and joint butts, and coyly placed books and pens on my desk. I even opened up one book to give the impression that I had been studying all night. Before long, my dad was rapping at the front door, and I quickly looked in the mirror and realized I hadn't even showered or attempted to put myself together in the slightest.

After we got to the restaurant and ordered, I barely ate. I also barely was able to give him answers beyond grunts and nods to his questions; I just sat there, head in hands, miserable and grumpy. *Nice to see you too, Daddy. Thanks for coming all this way. Sorry I am essentially lifeless.* I have no doubt he knew what was going on, but he didn't say anything. Do I wish he had? At the time, I was relieved, but now I wonder if it was yet another missed opportunity for me to change course from the road I was going down.

By the time my third year rolled around and school became more challenging, I knew I needed to tone down the partying to graduate, and that's what I did. The curriculum was less about going to lectures and more about independent study and writing dissertations and papers, so it took more effort on my part to keep up. I managed to focus. I had moved into a semi-detached townhouse with five girls. All of my housemates were bright and studious, like me, and also, like me, enjoyed partying. I had managed to find a good balance of the work hard–party hard mantra, and I was getting by.

And then my first panic attack hit.

It was 2010, the end of my final year of uni, and exams were approaching. Everyone was in full study mode. I had been sitting at my desk for hours and hours every day, contemplating questions like *Is my experience of consciousness the same as other people's experiences? Who decides what morality is?* I was getting so caught up in my thoughts—thoughts that had no answers. It felt like I was opening one door and then the next door and then the next, with no end in sight. It started to give me a dull pang of apprehension, because life and all of its messy complications were so unknown and there were no answers. One day in a seminar, we were discussing a concept from Descartes, who posited that perhaps a sort of evil demon of "utmost power and cunning has employed all his energies in order to deceive [us]." In other words, our senses can play tricks on us, and our perception of reality and consciousness could all be bullshit. I remember getting fed up. I raised my hand and asked, "We've been sitting here for an hour. Why the hell are we discussing all this? We're never going to know, so why does it matter?"

"Welcome to philosophy, Mia. Glad you can finally join us," the professor said.

That eerie feeling of the world being infinite gave me a sense that no one had control over anything. It was an uncomfortable feeling.

After class, I went to go grab an espresso with my friend Hani before we got back to studying. Suddenly, I felt sick. My heart was fluttering and my palms were sweating. Hani chalked it up to a strong batch of coffee, so I went back to my house and tried to ignore it and study. That's when it happened.

My heart was beating what felt like a million times a minute, and I started to sweat.

Thoughts raced as I tried to catch my breath, but I couldn't seem to control my body. I felt tingly all over, almost numb. Feeling helpless and overwhelmed, I couldn't figure out What. Was. Happening.

Holy shit, am I having a heart attack? A stroke? I feel like I'm dying.

I lay in my bed and tried to close my eyes. But the more I thought about it, the worse it got. Not knowing what to do, I called my sister. She listened patiently as I breathlessly told her how I was feeling.

"I was just studying, trying to wrap my brain around some of the things we were discussing in class, unanswerable things, and all of a sudden I had a feeling of doom that all 'this'—the world, our relationships, our life—is out of our control. Here I am, three years into questioning these things and studying theories that I can never truly know the answers to. And it finally hit me—we are all going to die, and everything means nothing!"

"This sounds like a panic attack," she told me after I described what I was experiencing. She reasoned that what I was studying was causing me an extreme amount of anxiety, and my body had gone into shock.

Anxiety is hard to explain to someone who has never dealt with it. It's like trying to describe a color or how love feels. You can't really understand it unless you've felt it. To this day, I still struggle with anxiety. Some days are better than others, but I know it is something I will be dealing with for the rest of my life. I also truly believe now, upon reflection, that it was bound to happen to me, and I do think a partial catalyst of its onset was my drug use. All of that shit going into my body and fucking with my brain chemistry definitely made me more susceptible. It took me a long time to get to that realization, though. I had a lot more learning to do, and I didn't yet draw any correlation between the two.

In the meantime, I had managed to pass my exams and graduate from Bristol. My mum and dad flew from Hong Kong to the UK to be there for the ceremony. During uni, my relationship with my mum continued to be on and off. At times she'd be sweet and check up on me, or I'd call her to see how she was doing. I'd go home during the holidays and see them. Leading up to graduation, however, she was going through a rough time and was drinking again, so things were not good between us.

My dad had made reservations at the nicest restaurant in Bristol to celebrate, and as we sat down in a cozy banquette, I saw that we were among a sea of families marking the big day as well.

During dinner, my mum proceeded to drink a lot—a LOT. *This is not going to end well,* I thought. She started to get belligerent, and there was nothing we could do to stop the impending tsunami.

"Mia, you're a drug addict, and a troubled child," she sneered out of nowhere.

She raised her voice as she delivered more insults. My dad was powerless in stopping her. I could feel eyes turn toward our table. My friends were at the restaurant with their families; one of my professors was with his family at a table nearby.

"You're a fucking drug addict!" she shouted, holding her glass of wine.

Mortified, I stood up and walked away from the table and out of the restaurant. I got in my car, and I just drove. I didn't even know where I was going. I drove and drove as I sobbed.

I drove until I got tired. I was out in the country somewhere, so I got a room for the night at a Premier Inn, where I spent the entire night and into the next day crying. Then I checked out and drove back to Bristol. I ignored texts and calls from my dad, from friends who either had seen the entire outburst or heard about it later. I didn't want to talk to either of my parents. I didn't want to see them. I couldn't talk to my friends, either. I was so humiliated. I decided on my drive back that I didn't want to have anything to do with my mum anymore. I *couldn't* have anything to do with her anymore.

I ignored the drunken, crazy emails she sent me. They were simple, to the point, and very often filled with typos to the point of incomprehension. She once sent me a note that simply read: "You are a thousand-year-old snake."

That's it, I thought. *Nope, Mum, I am not tolerating this anymore. I won't let you take your pain out on me anymore.*

8. REPRESSED MEMORIES

—

THE PAIN OF GRADUATION DAY did not help with my anxiety. It should not come as a surprise that it, in fact, made it worse. I felt more and more untethered, unable to keep a hold of any sort of control that I did have. I felt an urgency to take back some of that control and create a bit of structure in my life. I needed to live in more of a factual, black-and-white, binary world where there would be little room for my mind to spin out like the Tasmanian Devil. So, in the fall of 2010, I decided to go for an intensive one-year master's degree in finance and financial law at the University of London. I would still model when I had the time, but I wanted to further my education in a subject that I loved as well as do something that would help me land a good job in finance.

The school had a big international population, so the campus was filled with students from all around the world. Unlike uni, when everyone goes because they are "supposed" to go, getting a post-graduate degree requires a heightened level of passion, dedication, and focus. There was an air of competitiveness, and I thrived on it. I knew I needed to be committed to succeed here.

In my first class, our professor gave us an icebreaker where we went around the room saying our name, where we were from, and then—cringe—a guilty pleasure.

One girl who was sitting two rows behind me—a beautiful, petite, immaculately put-together Asian woman with sleek, thick, long hair swept over to one shoulder—spoke up: "Hi, my name is Dominique. I'm from Malaysia, and my guilty pleasure . . . my guilty pleasure is trashy TV."

I instantly turned around and said, "There is nothing to be ashamed of in liking trashy TV! What show?"

"I love *Jersey Shore*," she said, laughing.

"SAME!" Believe it or not, that was that. We were instant best friends.

Soon after, I invited Dominique to pre-drinks at my apartment before we went out to a club. She brought her friend Yasmine, who was Indonesian-British. Witty, intelligent, educated, cool, and Eurasian, we all clicked instantly. We had similar backgrounds in international schools in Asia, so being together felt like a slice of home. The night got even better when I found out that Dominique and Yasmine did coke, too. I took out my stash and encouraged everyone to help themselves if they wanted any. I don't even remember where we went, but it didn't matter: We had the best time. The kind of crazy night you can only have when it's the start of something. And it was. This was the beginning of a beautiful friendship with a core group of women, but it was also the beginning of yet another fucking crazy year with coke.

No matter how much I told myself I needed to focus, that this year would be different, I was soon back to my old ways. I hadn't yet said it out loud yet, and I don't think I even realized it for myself at the time, but it's quite clear looking back at it now: I was an addict.

When I wasn't with Yasmine and Dominique, I was traveling to visit my boyfriend at the time, Dev, whom I had connected with over the summer at a music festival. Dev worked in the music industry and was living in Holland because he had overstayed his UK visa. I would meet him there, or wherever he was touring. Soon I was going to castings in the morning, classes during the afternoon, and parties at night, and traveling on the weekends, hardly realizing I was quickly spreading myself too thin.

The coke fit in with my manic lifestyle, and all the partying started to blend together—same shit, different reckless days and nights.

I would never go anywhere without multiple grams of coke; whether we were at a club or a house party, we would pound line after line after line and drink so much that we'd more often than not find ourselves feeling totally wired. Once, Dominique, Yasmine, and I got ourselves to the nearest bathroom, where Dominique took the toilet, Yasmine took the sink, and I took the tub as we all vomited in our designated areas. Just. So. Gnarly. Sometimes I'd catch a glimpse of myself in the bathroom mirror after doing coke and think, *Who is that?* and a brief whiff of shame would wash over me. I knew deep down what I was doing was unhealthy and reckless, but I'd shake off the feeling, fix my hair, and walk out of the bathroom so I could continue the party. Questions about why I was doing this and how could I slow down would have to wait. There's no point in taking a good look at yourself if you're not yet willing to do the work to change.

If I took a cab ride home after partying, the view was always the same: I'd look out the window and watch people on the street as they went about their day, going to work, taking their kids to school, or starting their morning run. People living normal lives. I felt like such a waste of life. My dread of watching the sunrise stayed with me. When I got home, I would still be so wired that I couldn't sleep; my heart would pound, and my eyelids wouldn't even fully close because they'd keep fluttering. As I tossed and turned, my mind would race: *Did I do too much? I'm fucked-up. Am I losing it? Please just wear off already. Was this worth it? Why did I do this to myself? I just want to sleep. PLLLLEEEEAAAASSSEEE. This is torture.*

I would eventually feel better, and then somehow make the choice to do it all over again—a cycle I was doomed to repeat. The cycle of an addict. It very easily goes from having fun to having a problem. I was sliding down a steep, steep hill, and fast. But because we all did it, I never thought I had a problem. As I write this now, I see how close this rationalization was to my food issues when I was modeling—everyone was so extreme about their weight, but I didn't think there was anything wrong with it.

I was trying to find some balance in my life, but I was doing so in a very destructive way. And I continued my harmful eating habits. Around this time, my weight went up and down—I'd have a shoot and starve, then I'd binge when it was over. Food is a very important part of the Asian culture and lifestyle, and so it seemed like whenever I was with my Asian friends we were eating. They were so tiny and petite, I'd inevitably compare myself with them. I observed how they ate, jealous that they could eat as they did and stay so skinny. To keep up, I'd starve myself, so I could then binge when I was with them.

WE WERE SURROUNDED BY DRUGS—everyone in London seemed to be doing them. According to studies done back in 2002, roughly 80 percent of all banknotes in UK circulation were contaminated with drugs—and 99 percent in the London area. There should have been a study on keys, too: I used my house keys to snort coke so much that one time when I came home at fucking nine A.M., they didn't fit in my door. Powder had solidified in the crevices of the key. I had to call a locksmith who knew exactly what the problem was—he had seen it before. Our crew had expanded, and everyone we hung out with was doing coke. So even though I was acquiring a bigger appetite for it than my friends, I still rationalized it away—*Who, me? I don't have a problem. Everyone is doing it.*

Then there was Dev. He did a lot of coke, too. Being on the road four days out of the week just begged for that kind of lifestyle. He performed and toured so much that I'd often find myself in random hotel rooms, waiting for him backstage in his dressing room, or watching the show from the side of the stage. Whether it was Croatia, Romania, or Germany, I was surrounded by people I didn't know, speaking a language I didn't understand. So I'd do coke by myself.

Sunrise or sunset at a music festival that Dev was performing at. That period of my life was such a drug-fueled and anxiety-ridden blur that I don't remember any more details. But even looking at this photo makes me feel uneasy. Somewhere in Europe, 2011.

One night, somewhere in Europe (I can't remember exactly where, as all the towns blurred into one another), after the show we went to an after-party at a club. I went to the bathroom with him, and we huddled in a stall as we did lines.

"Let's do another one," I suggested, excited.

"Okay." He cut two more lines on the toilet seat.

"Let's do another one," I said, insatiable.

"No, Mia, you've had enough."

Ouch.

"You're basically calling me a crackhead."

"You've had enough. You don't need a third line right now."

He took the bag—my supply—and left.

At the time I was furious he did this. I didn't see that I was out-snorting my friends, and now my boyfriend. It was as if I was on a merry-go-round going faster and faster, but the truth is that I didn't want to get off.

I WAS ON A CONTINUOUS HUNT FOR COKE. If I couldn't get in touch with my dealer, or manage to get it elsewhere, I would go home feeling like the entire night was a waste. Fuck my friends and parties—I was on a hunt for cocaine. I was not going out to have fun. I was going out to get coked up and then get more. In the moment I loved it more than I loved my boyfriend, perhaps even more than I loved my friends. It was the love of my life.

But I would deny, deny, deny it to anyone who called me out on it. That is, until I heard a rumor about me, spread by a guy I hardly knew. He had been going around telling people that I was such a cokehead that I had had a nosebleed on set at a photoshoot. One person told another person, etcetera, and the rumor eventually got back to me. I picked up the phone and I called him.

He barely had a chance to say hello before I ripped into him.

"A, you don't know me, and B, that *never* happened. I have never been at a photoshoot where I had a nosebleed. Why the fuck would you say that?" I asked angrily.

"Well, that's what I heard," he answered quietly.

Okay, so he didn't start the rumor—it had been going around. *Is that how I'm seen? Am I getting a reputation?* I had never had a nosebleed at a job. (That is not to say I never had a bloody nose. I had nosebleeds a lot, but I never got one at a job.) I had so many other things to be known for: modeling, my intelligence, my personality. I did not want to be known as that girl who was a cokehead.

As my addiction developed, my anxiety worsened. Actually, being on coke is similar to having a panic attack in some ways: The heart pounds; palms sweat; the breath comes hard and fast. I'd lie there, mind racing, as I would try to put together pieces of what had happened the previous night. The anxiety would ramp up every time I thought about my inevitable "coke chats." When people are high on cocaine, they don't shut the fuck up. They keep talking. So I would inevitably ask myself, *Oh my God, what did I say to [fill in any person from the previous night]? Oh, I blacked out—what did I do?* This rabbit hole of questions would add to my agonizing anxiety and my sleepless nights.

But I would wake up and want that numb feeling coke gave me again. It made me feel like a better version of myself. I liked the Mia I became when I was high more than the Mia who was sober or not on cocaine. I have always thought that coke is a drug for insecure people—and in hindsight, I see so clearly that I was very insecure. I was doing it to access that "better" version of myself. I took the drugs to like myself; I know now I didn't like who I was without them. Coke made me feel so confident that I forgot about my insecurities.

Before I'd go out and meet anybody, even if it was just to meet my girlfriends, I did coke to bring out the Mia that I preferred to be. On the flip side, when I was coming down, I looked at it as turning back into the Mia I didn't want to be. And really, I was doing so much that when I did come down, I wasn't coming back to that baseline of "normal Mia." There was Mia on coke and there was Mia coming down—the normal, regular Mia was seen less and less. I started losing myself and losing my grip on reality. I got to a point where I wasn't even enjoying it anymore. The first two lines were always fun, but anything after meant a nervous urgency to maintain the high. Eventually I knew how the end of a night would play out: I would have fun for a bit, but the fun would wear off and I would end up with anxiety attacks and sleepless nights. The drug was seriously losing its allure.

In the meantime, I reached the end of my master's program (remember, I was in school?!), and it was time for my final exams. Now, this wasn't my first rodeo; I knew what I needed to do. I locked myself in my apartment and ramped up my foolproof, tried-and-true routine of "starve and study," knowing that I'd be back to modeling after exams, just like in previous years. I stocked up on packets of instant Cup-a-Soup. I would just have one of those a day right at 4:00 P.M.—the same schedule I had done when I was fucking seventeen. The plan was to study, lose a bunch of weight, and ditch the social life, drinking, and drugs. Nothing else but preparation. These studying periods were my own crazy version of bootcamp, a strict, tough-love regimen to get focused and get through what I needed to get through. And it worked—I actually aced my exams.

SOAS
University of London

Master's degree graduation from SOAS, University of London, 2011.

After graduation, I hung out with Dev, who had come back to the UK, and we were finally able to be a real couple who lived in the same postal code. I didn't need to work yet, as I had money in the bank, so I had some time to figure out what my next step would be.

It got to the point where I'd do a line and the anxiety would kick in almost immediately. I'd do a line and my heart would flutter. The uptick in anxiety was affecting my rest. I could never get a good night's rest. When I did, I had extremely vivid dreams. For a couple of weeks, I kept having the same nightmare over and over. I first attributed it to anxiety, but I couldn't shake the uneasy feeling that accompanied it when I woke up.

My dream went like this: I was home in my parents' house in Hong Kong. I was about five, playing in the living room. There was a man there, too, but I couldn't see his face. We'd play, and then he would bring me to my bedroom and make me pick out an outfit. I would pick something, but he would pick out another brightly patterned skirt instead and ask, "Are you sure you don't want to wear this?" I put on whatever he picked (it was always a skirt), with the instructions to leave nothing underneath. Then he'd take me to the bathroom, lock the door, and make me lie down on the floor. I lay on a bathroom mat and closed my eyes. As I lay there, he sat down next to me, pulled up my skirt, and put his fingers in me. He never got too close; he sat upright over me, like a doctor performing surgery.

When he was done, he touched the inside of my ankle and told me, "If anybody asks, I touched you there."

To make sure I would answer correctly, he'd ask again, "Where did I touch you?"

I pointed at my ankle and said, "There."

Every time, it was the same scene. Same bathroom mat. Same skirt. Same touch on the ankle. *Don't tell anyone.*

I'd wake up with a bolt, crying and sweating. Early one morning, I sat upright. Then it hit me: *I don't think this is a dream. I think this really happened to me.* At first, I couldn't figure out if I had just had the dream so many times that it seemed real, but it was so fucking vivid that I couldn't shake the feelings that came with it. After the umpteenth time, I needed my suspicions to be confirmed.

I built up the courage to call my sister Anouk.

"Anouk, I need to talk to someone . . ." And I told her everything I remembered. I added, "And I have this weird nagging feeling that this really happened to me." I described the skirt to her: mid-calf length with a crazy eighties print with orange, yellow, and red shapes.

Anouk was quiet for a minute. Then she finally said, "It did."

WHAT?

Anouk broke down. "I am so, so sorry, Mia. I remember that skirt. I never saw anything, but I had a feeling something like this happened." I understood her confusion, her trepidation that maybe she suspected wrong. She was just a child herself at the time.

"He" was someone close to the family.

My head was spinning. I was confused, upset, and disgusted all at once. *How did I manage to bury such a horrible event for so long? I wonder if he remembers? Does anyone else know?* My questions would have to wait, though, as my anxiety took over and I folded in on myself and cried all day. Correction: days. I didn't realize it then, but I had what's called morbid anxiety, a psychiatric disorder in which a person has intense anxiety that exhibits as fear that she or he is going to die. The anxiety consumed me for weeks, and I wouldn't leave the house. My friends would check on me and bring me food, but I wouldn't go out, somehow convinced that if I left the house, I was going to die. I don't know why I thought that, but I did. Just the thought of walking down the street overwhelmed me with panic.

I was in utter despair. This is how my body reacted to trauma coming to the surface. I needed to stop it. I needed the pain to go away. The pain of knowing seemed worse than burying it all these years, but then again, maybe not. Something told me that maybe this was the reason for the drugs, for the eating issues, for the anxiety.

I made another desperate call to my sister, who told me, "You're just reliving it right now. It's something you've kept buried that's now at the forefront of your mind. I think you need to deal with this—it'll help you."

Deal with it, don't bury it.

FIRST STEP: I told my parents over Skype. Things were better with my mum at this point. I needed to let them know. They were horrified for me, and even more horrified that they didn't know about it. I could tell it was hard for them to take in. But they believed me, and that was big. And it felt good letting them know. Their support gave me the confidence to confront the abuser.

Second, I needed to face him. I needed him to know that I remembered. And I wanted to hold him accountable. For anyone reading this who has been through something similar, I know how scary it can be to do this. I didn't think of myself as brave right then, but I forced myself to be. I knew it was necessary, because no matter the outcome, doing so starts the healing process. I had compartmentalized it and kept it a secret, locking it away in the deepest corners of my memory. Addressing it made it real. As a victim, I questioned myself: *Am I making the scene up? Did it really happen like that? Am I mistaken? What if I will upset him?*

When the abuse occurred, I just didn't get it. I was a child—I didn't even know what was happening. I didn't even know what genitals were. But now, I was an adult, and I wanted to address this. I wanted the confirmation that it happened instead of this vague and painful tornado of emotions and doubt that lingered in my mind. I knew the storm wouldn't go away until I dealt with it—I shouldn't, wouldn't, *couldn't* bury it. I wanted to rid myself of all shame and get what I needed in order to heal, which was acknowledgment.

I couldn't do it in person or on the phone, so I wrote him an email. I needed to get what I wanted to say out and not get caught up with emotion, or worse, chicken out. I told him that I remembered what happened, and I needed acknowledgment from him that he did what he did.

I knew that once I addressed that the abuse *happened*, only then could I work on healing. I've learned that it takes *years* to come to terms with the emotional aftershocks of abuse. There's no rule book for trauma—no guidebook on how to deal with it, because we are all different.

He responded immediately.

He was respectful. He said he remembered. He had his excuses for why he did what he did, but he was very apologetic and offered whatever support he could.

There it was. Acknowledgment.

I neither wanted nor needed anything from him. What I wanted was to be free of the way the abuse had wreaked havoc on my subconscious for all these years, irretrievably altering the person I became.

I have since realized that while you can acknowledge a wound and give it what it needs—some disinfectant, a Band-Aid—you still need *time* to heal. It doesn't go away quickly. In fact, the time it takes to heal can be brutal. Even after talking to my support system and confronting the abuser, I was still morbidly crippled and didn't want to leave the house. I had started seeing a therapist, but it didn't seem to help much. My sleep was more fitful than ever. No matter what I thought about or what I tried to do, or what movie I tried to watch or what book I tried to read, my morbid anxiety came rushing back, and everything went back to, *you're going to die.*

For the first time in my life I was truly reckoning with the extent to which I had felt unsafe, exposed, and unprotected all my life. And even though the abuse had come to light and become a conscious part of my understanding of my life and my decisions, that knowledge was not enough to combat the sheer terror it unleashed in me.

I stopped going out or doing drugs of any kind, and I completely isolated myself. The only human contact I had was with my boyfriend and my three girlfriends who came over to check on me. I felt utterly hopeless, and it put a strain on my relationship with Dev. I was wrestling with the beast that is depression, and it was winning.

I called my parents again. As they picked up, I just started crying.

"I'm losing my mind. I think I need to see a psychiatrist. . . . I think I need to be on some kind of medication to fix whatever is happening. . . . I just think . . ." I hesitated. "I just think that I'm going to die all the time. I am living in constant fear. I can't even function," I said through my tears. It was a relief just to admit this. "It feels like I'm spiraling down this dark black hole and I don't know how to get myself out."

My dad told me to come home. They were at our family house in Thailand.

"Take a break. Come to Thailand. Your mother and I are here. I'll buy you a plane ticket."

"Okay."

It wasn't a hard decision to make, because I was so desperate to feel better.

I went to Thailand. Their villa, which rested atop a mountain, was beautiful and had stunning views of Koh Samui. It was paradise. A respite.

I was miserable. The picturesque setting should have alleviated some of the anxiety, but as I did laps in the swimming pool, all I could think was, *I'm going to die. I'm going to die. I'm going to die!* The fear manifested itself in both physical and metaphysical ways: I would literally think that a tree might fall on me or my heart would stop beating, while at the same time fretting over how we all are going to die.

I got out of the pool, wrapped a towel around me, went back into the house, and found my dad. I broke down. "I don't know how to fix my head. I don't know how to stop thinking this way."

My dad didn't really have much to offer me in the way of guidance. He's so fact-oriented and black-and-white, he didn't understand the struggle I was going through and the jumble of emotions it created within me. He told me to just stop thinking those thoughts. But I truly believed I had lost my marbles, convinced I was going to have to spend the rest of my life heavily sedated or in a mental institution.

My mum, on the other hand, understood a bit more, as she struggled with emotional turmoil herself and was always looking for a solution to her unhappiness. I've watched her use alcohol, of course, then religion and spirituality, studying Catholicism, Buddhism and its various sects, meditation—anything that would offer her refuge or an escape from herself. She had been reading a lot of New Age self-help books at the time—books like *The Power of Now, The Four Agreements,* and *The Secret.* I was in need of anything that could help me find peace: I was so desperate to just switch off the anxiety. She suggested a book she had just read (for the life of me I can't remember the title or what it was about). I picked it up and I read it in one day, but I wasn't really into New Age theories like energy, meditation, and crystals—I don't even believe in astrology. I wrote it off as woo-woo nonsense.

A couple of days later, I was talking to Andrew, a longtime family friend who also managed the villa complex—he would frequently come by our house with his adorable little poodle, Nelson.

When we were in Thailand, I'd often "borrow" Nelson and let him sleep in my bed with me. I asked him if I could have Nelson over for a sleepover.

"Sure," he said. "What's going on?"

He had been through some personal struggles and had been in AA for many years, so I suspected he'd be a supportive confidant.

I told him about my morbid thoughts and anxiety. I had never thought I needed medication, but I did know something needed fixing. The therapist I had been seeing before going back to Thailand was kind and gentle, but I felt like she was too removed from my experiences. I still had no idea where to begin with my healing.

Andrew went on to tell me how Koh Samui is known as an island of healing. People from all over the world go there (and to other Thai islands) seeking spiritual discovery because of the island's indigenous crystals, which are known to have healing energy.

"There's a lady on the island that people visit for guidance. I think you should go see her. She may be able to help."

"Honestly, Andrew, I'll do anything at this point. If you can set me up with her, that would be great."

A day later, he came back and handed me a sticky note with a name and number written on it. "I found her. Here's her number. I told her that you'll be reaching out."

Later, when I was with my mum, I mentioned the woman's name—Doreen—and she quickly perked up and asked, "Wait, as in *this* Doreen?" She picked up the book she was reading, and I spotted the author's name on the cover. It was the *same woman*. That coincidence alone was enough for me to trust the process. I don't normally believe in coincidences, but sometimes the universe aligns things for you in a way that you cannot ignore. *All right, even if I don't fucking get this whole crystal energy healing, nonscientific shit, I'll give it a go. I have nothing else to lose.*

I called Doreen and cut to the chase. "I need a session with you as soon as possible. I'm losing my will to live." She answered in a kind voice, which immediately give me comfort. She told me to come over to her house the next day.

My dad drove me to an extremely remote beach that neither of us had been to. We pulled up to a small one-bedroom cottage nestled off the road leading to the beach, surrounded by huge, leafy palm trees. Inside, the furnishings were sparse but functional, outfitted with only a bed, a chair, and a few pots and pans. You really just need one pot and one pan, after all. She had one plate and a knife and fork. I loved the simplicity of it all.

Doreen was wearing a long, flowing, tie-dye dress; her hair was in a pixie cut with a shock of white and little spots of gray. I learned that she used to be a soccer mom living in upstate New York. Married to a wealthy financier, she'd had everything in the world that she could ever want. She gave it all up to find herself, wrote a few books, became a self-help guru, and currently lives in a romantic, beach-front shack in paradise.

We sat on her porch along the ocean as the waves speckled brilliantly in the sunlight. A slight breeze blew the fronds of the palm trees that surrounded us. We sat opposite each other, and she hit record on a tape recorder. We talked for three hours, but it felt like ten minutes. Toward the end of the session, she said, "I know what happened to you when you were a child."

I hadn't told her yet. I shook inside, stunned that she could read me like that.

"That little girl inside you is very hurt. All she's doing is looking for somebody to support her and have her back and take care of her. That's why she's so anxious now. You need to understand that the universe has got you. Do you feel the chair against your back? You see how that chair is supporting you? Do you doubt the chair? Do you think that you're going to fall down?"

"No, I trust it," I said, tears streaming down my face.

"That's what I'm talking about. That support—don't question it. It's always there."

At the time, I didn't quite understand what she was saying—this type of healing therapy was so out of left field for me—but it did click with me on a more primal level. Eventually, I came to understand that my anxiety came down to trust and control. I didn't trust anyone or anything, probably because I'd been let down by those who were close to me. And I had problems with things being out of my control. So, in my fragile state, I didn't trust *anything* that I didn't have control over, which brought on the seemingly irrational fears that I would be struck by a tree, or a car would hit me, or I'd keel over from a heart attack.

"You feel that the chair is holding you up?"

"Yes, I do."

And I did. When we were done, I walked down the porch steps that led to the beach. Each step down, I felt lighter and lighter—as if a huge boulder had been lifted off of my shoulders. The sand felt so good on my feet. I let my toes sink into the powdery beach. My head felt a little buzzy, but a good buzzy, as I looked out to the sea, shimmering in the afternoon sun. *What is this? What is this feeling?*

In that moment, I was anxiety-free.

9. CATWALKS TO CAP GAINS

FOR THE FIRST TIME IN A LONG TIME, I felt okay. I was alive and well. I felt like I could finally breathe again. In just a few short hours, Doreen helped me see clearly what I couldn't see for myself for so many years. I resorted to common defense mechanisms many abuse survivors use to protect ourselves. She shed light on how the sexual abuse affected me in so many ways. It was why I was so over-weight as a child, and why I had developed so many insecurities and control issues.

I had buried the abuse in a desperate attempt to go on with my life. Now that the abuse was out in the open, I could deal with it. Doreen had taped the session and gave me a recording to listen to if I needed it. I did a few times, but what really helped in moments of doubt was to remember the simple yet profound concept that the chair was holding me up; that thought grounded me if I started to feel out of control. I didn't do much more therapy after that, as I felt that I could do the work on myself, by myself. I went back to London after a few more weeks with my parents, not sure what my next step was, but I felt more equipped to handle the future.

But there would, of course, be a temporary backstep: Before I had left for Thailand, Dev and I were having issues, so I figured that the time apart would do us good. Dev saw the worst of me before

I went; I had been a complete emotional wreck around him. With time to think, he realized he couldn't be there for me anymore. He was done, so he broke it off with me within days of my return. The timing of the breakup was terrible, as I was still fragile and raw, and it hit me hard—like two-weeks-in-bed and boxes-of-tissues hard. It was certainly not what I needed after the emotional roller coaster I had just been on (and still was on). But in the end, it gave me that push to start taking stock of my life. When my friends Dominique and Yasmine came over to my apartment for one of their "let's make sure Mia is okay" shifts, I had made a decision that I was ready to share with them.

"I am going to get a job."

What? YES. A JOB. A BONA FIDE OFFICE JOB. I popped open my laptop and started pouring over job sites, and they stayed to help me on my CV over some Sauvignon Blanc.

Time for a major life change.

I always felt more like an empowered, boss-ass bitch when I was focusing on intellectual Mia as opposed to model Mia. While I had insecurities galore about my body, I had no insecurities about my intellect. I decided to do what felt best for me: put aside modeling and start a career in finance.

I immediately hit the ground running with my job search and got some bites. I interviewed for an entry-level trader position in a young, small commodities trading house—tiny compared with bigger companies like Morgan Stanley and Goldman Sachs—in the heart of London. I got the job, which was amazing, because outside of my degree, I didn't really have any experience in the field. I wholeheartedly jumped right in. *Let's do this! Let's use my brain. Let's go from catwalks to cap gains.*

In my position, I was dealing with smaller-client services and assisting with their investments, which meant staying in touch and advising them to buy and sell certain commodities. Part of my job was also "business development," which translated into cold calling strangers and hopefully turning them into new clients. I worked on a commission basis and quickly got the hang of it all. I felt like I was functioning again: anxiety in decline, new job, new work-life balance. Because of that, I could relax and breathe for a moment. I had started going out again, but only on the weekends. And even then, I also used the weekends to catch up on sleep, do errands, and keep up on all the financial news, so I wasn't even going out that much. I had toned it down a lot. If I wanted to go out, I'd go out, but now, I had the structure of a nine-to-five job and that was a good thing for me.

I did have a little trouble fitting in. The office was definitely a boys' club. On the entire team, three of us were female. One woman was a receptionist, and the other was a newbie, like me. Before I started, my brother Malcolm, who had also gone into com-modities trading, gave me this piece of advice: "This is a male-dominated environment. Be one of the boys. You've got to be able to play along."

My dad also warned me that the industry I was walking into was very chauvinistic and high pressure. But he assured me, "If any-body can handle it, Mia, you can." I wasn't worried—having two big brothers, I could definitely handle some testosterone-filled banter. I figured I would be able to take care of myself. And after all I had just been through and the morbid anxiety I had just experienced, I was happy to throw myself into a new job that offered some structure and stability.

But my dad wasn't kidding. I had entered into the fiery den of "lad" or "bro" culture, typical in the long-standing misogynistic finance industry. It's an attitude that still exists all over the world, in every language, even in this post-#MeToo era (although this was pre-#MeToo). In Hong Kong, one of the finance capitals of the world, we called these chauvinists "banker wankers."

These boys (and yes, I said "boys," because they were so imma-ture) were now my colleagues, boss included. They didn't necessarily come with the best education, but they had the gift of gab and charm, which helped them make oodles of money for all the expensive dinners, tailored suits, strip clubs, and cocaine they indulged in. It seemed like they played more than they worked. Sometimes they'd even do coke during the day, using their collar stays as DIY utensils for snorting bumps. (I tried to use my familiarity with coke to get "in" with the boys, but they never included me.) They would sit and talk about the money they had tucked into strippers' panties the previous night and about their female conquests over beers at lunch, constantly deriding and objectifying the female gender as a whole, but it was nothing that I had not seen or heard before. It actually wasn't too shocking for me, but it made for a shitty work environment. As much as I tried to keep up with the banter and participate, no matter how much money I brought in (even if it was more than them), I was always an outsider because I was a woman. I was still just another "girl in the office." I started believing that I was probably filling some sort of gender quota.

Although it was an inane environment, it was good to gain experience and to have a routine. I had to be somewhere at a certain time. I had to dress appropriately. I had to use my brain and keep it sharp. I liked being productive—it made me feel more *normal*—and I was good at it, too. As time passed, the boys became comfortable with having me around, so they didn't hold back with the jokes, which started to become more and more inappropriate. It began with snide comments about me made under their breath—slights about being female, laced with sexual innuendo. The banter then turned up a level, and they added crude practical jokes to their repertoire. For instance: One afternoon I came back from the bathroom, finished up an email I had been writing to a new client, and pressed send. Immediately, I heard a wave of muted giggles and snickers from behind me. I spun around in my chair, circled the room, and found two boys at their desks trying to stifle their laughter.

"What the fuck is so funny?" I asked.

"Read your signature on the email you just sent," one of them replied, in between chortles.

I went to my outbox and opened the file. Those motherfuckers changed my signature to "Suzie Wong." *Fuck, fuck, fuck, that email was to a new client that I'd just secured. Fuuuuuuck.* Suzie Wong is a famous fictional character—a Chinese prostitute, to be specific—from the 1957 Richard Mason novel *The World of Suzie Wong*. The book was such a classic hit that it went on to become a movie, a play, and even a ballet. Pop culture soon adopted the name "Suzie Wong," and people began using it as slang for a hooker.

Their behavior was intolerable. And not just because of some sexist, childish joke that was completely inappropriate for work. They didn't know it, but this hit a trigger for me. When I was younger, my mum accused my dad of having an affair with a woman my mum nicknamed Suzie Wong. Their "joke" hit home for me in a way they could never understand.

My patience was running out. I think having a sense of humor is one of the greatest tools you can be equipped with in life—but what I experienced was sexually and racially inappropriate and completely offensive. I wasn't sure how much more I could take. Surely dealing with this shit wasn't synonymous with pursuing a career in finance.

The final straw soon came: I asked my boss if I could go to the bathroom (yes, I had to ask my boss to go to the bathroom—we all did—crazy. What was this, primary school?).

"No, you're supposed to be getting back to [client A who worked with douchebag company who shall remain nameless]. Deal with it now!"

But I had to go really, really badly. I had to decide which was more important: getting back to client A or peeing my pants.

"I'm going to pee in my chair. I have to go." Not caring about the consequences, I left and went to the bathroom.

When I came back to my desk, my chair was gone.

"What the fuck, guys, where is my chair?"

No one fessed up. There was complete silence in the whole office, except for the sound of typing.

"Mia, you have to get that reply out NOW! Do it," my boss ordered me from across the room.

I had no other choice—I got down on my knees so I was level with my computer and started to write the email.

I had an eager audience. As soon as my knees hit the floor, I heard someone say, "Oops, there she is on her knees again," followed by laughter.

"Fuck you." I stood up and looked at my boss, who was also laughing, and asked, "Are you fucking kidding me? How can you allow this?"

"Come on, they're having a laugh," he quipped. Everything was always, "Oh relax, it's just a joke." I get it. A large part of British humor is about being able to make fun of yourself and participate in trading barbs and banter. But this went beyond that. They were trying to make me feel like I was uptight, as if it was prudish to expect basic human decency at my job.

"Are you serious?" I said. "This is so crazy. I want to report this to HR."

"Go ahead, call HR," he said. I could feel my face blush with anger.

"Fine." But as I was about to pick up the phone, he picked up his phone and said, "Hello, HR speaking." There was nothing I could do.

"Fuck this. This is SO not fucking worth it. I'm out." And I meant it. No way in hell was I going to work in this man-cave of an office for three more minutes. I walked out with two middle fingers blazing high in the air for all to see.

The receptionist called me later, talking into her receiver in a hushed tone. "You left everything at your desk, like your phone charger, everything. . . ."

"Just chuck it," I told her. Leaving those things behind was worth it. There was no way in hell I could walk back into that office after such a dramatic exit.

Luckily, I quickly landed another job as a derivatives consultant at a financial consulting firm. It was a much bigger company, and while I am not sure its size had anything to do with it, the corporate culture was fortunately the opposite experience of my previous job. My employers were supportive and caring. Maybe it was because there was more of a corporate structure that instituted more rules and training programs, but maybe it was just because they simply weren't assholes. Either way, I felt much more at home there.

I did months of training and exams, which I loved. I enjoyed learning, and I felt like I was becoming a real professional. I felt like an adult. I lived in one place, had a job that I actually enjoyed, had great friends, had a routine and stability. And get this: I was eating! I had gained weight, since I was not modeling anymore. The nine-to-five schedule of my job came with the prerequisite lunchtime that I had never had before. Everything was organized around lunch: meetings before lunch, after lunch. "Hey, what are we doing for lunch?" And I was happy to eat. It was still very disordered eating, but it was enough to gain weight, especially since my metabolism was still out of whack. I would still only have a black coffee in the morning, but I would eat a salad and fat-free yogurt for lunch. For dinner, I'd make something for myself or meet one of my girls after work for some food. I no longer felt the burden to be a certain size—no agents eyed me with judgment or chased me with a measuring tape. It was a relief, although it was scary to cross that divide. I had gone from the girl *in* the magazines to the girl reading them. As a woman, I still felt the pressure to keep up with the ideal image that the media portrayed and the standard of beauty that is placed on all women. And just because I was eating and gaining weight didn't mean I wasn't still suffering from anorexia. Eating disorders can't just be turned off. I still questioned every bite, and afterward, guilt and self-loathing would inevitably show up at my doorstep.

My continuing eating issues aside, the new routine felt great, and I enjoyed my job and hanging out with my friends. But I soon found myself feeling unsettled. Unmoored. London can be blanketed in gray for weeks, without even a peek of blue sky. It would be so cold and dark in the mornings that I'd dread getting out of bed. Then it would be cold and dark again by the time I left work in the evening. At this point, I was twenty-five and had been living in the UK for seven years, and as much as I tried to make it my home, I always felt like a stranger. Every morning I would get up and commute and look at everyone on the tube, and it still felt like I was in a random foreign city. As I finished months of training and was about to take on my first consulting project, I mulled over a trip back home to visit my parents. I missed the heat and the sun. And when I had last seen my parents, I'd noticed that they had aged, and it scared me. I felt a pang of responsibility to be there for them. As complicated as my relationship with them was, they were still my parents, and they had been there for me when I was at my lowest with my anxiety. Their presence and the acknowledgment that I was going through something had made me feel taken care of and seen. I felt a strong tug toward my family, and I missed that sense of feeling connected. I wanted to go home. I hadn't had that thought in years.

I had started asking myself, *What's tying me here? I have friends here, but I don't have family here. I could do finance anywhere.*

I didn't set a time limit; I didn't have any set plans. I thought I'd quit my job, go for a few months, and return to London eventually.

So in 2013, I bought a round-trip ticket and moved to Hong Kong for three months to see what would materialize. I figured I'd model a bit to make some money to keep my head above water. And if all went well, and it felt right, I'd start looking for a job in finance. I lived in my parents' house at first while I figured out what I was doing. My brother Malcolm was living in Hong Kong, too. By this point he had built an empire of restaurants, nightclubs, and bars—I was crazy proud of him. Together we enjoyed his success, eating and drinking in his establishments, spending time together. I had always felt at ease with Malcolm—he offered that protective feeling that only a good older brother can provide.

I knew immediately I had made the right decision in going back. There was something about the heat and humidity and all the glorious food. I would just walk around the streets and take in all the smells. I was home.

AFTER ABOUT A WEEK OR SO BACK HOME, I went in to see Joey at my old agency. He met me in the waiting area, giving me a huge bear hug. As we sat in the office, I explained that I wanted to see where modeling would take me—was I still relevant? Would people remember me?

"You absolutely can work again. The market still remembers you. We are going to have so much fun!" The tone in his voice shifted as he added, "But I need you to do something for me. You need to lose weight. You've been living in Europe for a long time, and you know sizes are different there. Bigger. Now that you're back here, you'll need to be smaller. I won't be able to book you a lot of jobs until you do."

This was not news to me. I knew I had gained weight, and I knew Joey would see a big difference in me after not having laid eyes on me for a long time.

I managed to get jobs here and there, but Joey was right—I was too big for the market. In Asian culture, weight is usually the first thing people comment on, especially if you haven't seen them in a while. It doesn't matter how well you know the person—they could be a friend, your mother, or a colleague—if they think you've gained weight, You. Will. Hear. About. It. I'd heard a group of clients talking about me, saying that I was fat. "She's gained weight. Mia's looking fat, she's gained weight. . . ." *Welcome back, Mia, to the craziness that is modeling in Asia.* But it was easy money, and so I kept trying.

I had been enjoying my brother's company and gallivanting around every restaurant and nightclub in Hong Kong, so I wasn't quite ready to restart that starvation mode again. I had set it up in my head that I'd get there in time. I was enjoying myself, and I wasn't up for that kind of pressure again. Because my brother was so connected, everything was at our disposal. And before long, party-girl wreckhead Mia resurfaced. In Hong Kong, though, it was a little different, because I had my brother next to me. I felt safe with him, and I knew that if anything happened, he would look after me.

One night, I was with Malcolm in his apartment. He had a bunch of people over for cocktails, and someone had some coke. I did a line. I did a second one. I did a third one. My brother grew wary as he watched me snort each line. He pulled me aside and said, "Yo, chill." But I did a fourth, and then a fifth. The coke in Hong Kong is largely cut with speed, so the effect was immediate, and an adrenaline rush pierced through me. Everything sped up like it was on fast-forward, with the *Super Mario* theme song playing as the soundtrack to my manic mind. My mind raced as I paced. And paced. I needed to get out of there. I felt an urgency to get out of my skin, even, I was so jittery. The effect was just starting to take hold, though. My girlfriend Tara suggested that we go dancing. *Good, yes, dancing, right now, is what I need.* As the coke and other chemicals flooded my body, it became rocket fuel, and I was ready for takeoff. I had never felt this before.

Tara and I were walking in the doors of a club when I collapsed. Well, I think that's where I collapsed. I don't remember. What I *do* remember is opening my eyes for a second and realizing I was vomiting in a bathroom stall. Then it went back to black.

Darkness.

When I opened my eyes—or pried them open, rather—I found myself splayed out on a sofa in Tara's apartment, clothes from the previous night completely disheveled. I had slept for the whole day, and I couldn't remember much. Dread, fear, and anxiety came swarming in. The room smelled rancid from old vomit, and I was frothing at the mouth. My stuff was strewn across the room. *Oh God, what did I do? Where did I go? What did I say?* All the questions kicked in, followed by a torrent of anxiety, and my thoughts started to spiral.

Okay, let me just rewind. I remember doing fucking shitloads of lines, but beyond that . . . Hey, where are my shoes? How did I get here? Panic set in. I remembered then that Tara had a family dinner to go to, but she let me stay to recover. *Wow, how is it Sunday night already?* I started panicking so much that I had to call someone. So I called my brother, simultaneously hyperventilating and crying. Calling my brother in desperation was a bit humiliating for me.

"Dude, I'm freaking out. I can't breathe. I can't calm down. I don't know what I did. I can't stop feeling like I'm losing my mind. . . ."

He tried to reason with me. "It's the cocaine. You did too much and it's fucking with your brain. Can you do something for me? What I want you to do is put on an episode of *The Simpsons* and try to calm down."

The Simpsons was our thing. We'd always watch *The Simpsons* together as kids (and adults). It was a happy place we both shared. I watched a few episodes until my heart rate slowed and my mind quieted enough for me to take a nap. Five hours later, I woke up and asked my friend Tara to fill in the pieces of what had happened the night before: Shortly after we got into the club, I blacked out, and she managed to get me into a cab and dragged me back to her place.

Was this my bottom? Knowing that I had collapsed and didn't remember a thing scared me. Damn, I didn't even know what happened to my shoes. I loved those shoes. While I didn't go to the hospital that night, I probably should have, because that was the closest I had ever come to overdosing. The anxiety that had waned since my session with Doreen several months ago came roaring back. It was at this moment that I assessed my situation. *My body feels like absolute shit, my mind is in a million pieces . . . for what? This isn't fun anymore. That sweet young girl who was so studious and wanted to go to the best schools and just kill it in life . . . where is she? Look at me now, I'm a fucking vegetable on someone else's couch with dried vomit in my hair and crusted blood in my nose. This isn't who I want to be.* I didn't feel like I had a grip on my mind anymore, and I was scared for myself and my future. I was filled with the immediacy that doing another line could kill me.

I wanted to say goodbye to drugs, nightlife, and everything that went with them. I vowed to never do cocaine again. I decided to refocus that negative energy to something more positive and give modeling a serious go—there was enough interest from clients, and that meant good money. But I needed to lose weight, so I started to up my game with exercise and eating less. I had been living at home where there was only healthy food in the fridge, portions were controlled, weight was checked, and exercise was done every morning. So I started going on hikes with my mum and dad, and then, when I moved into my apartment, it progressed to getting my own gym membership. I tried a few classes—first spinning, then TRX, and more added from there until weight was falling off me. Any free hour I could get, I would go to the gym, to the point where I was doing three or four classes a day, and when there weren't any classes, I would work out on the machines. I avoided socializing to avoid eating, and I walked everywhere to try to burn the most calories; I would take the stairs instead of the elevator. At home, I did crunches and exercises on a mat at any opportunity I could—while the kettle was boiling, while watching TV, or even while responding to emails. Mind you, this was not about fitness or health—this was all part of a master plan to be at my skinniest. I used to joke that every drop of sweat was my fat crying. But it's no joke that I became as obsessive about working out as I was about my food intake.

WITH THE WEIGHT COMING OFF, I was booking more and more jobs. With that kind of momentum, I decided to stay in Hong

On set at a shoot. I was particularly proud of my thigh gap in this photo, despite feeling inadequate and fat while on set. Hong Kong, 2014.

Kong and just ride it out and see where it took me. I was glad I did, as my career was reaching new heights, with bigger and bigger campaigns coming my way. I was nabbing magazine covers and was sought after by international brands. Eventually, I was no longer in the fashion shows; I was being paid to attend them and to be seen at them. I had crossed over from model to "top model" (in Hong Kong, they are also called "celebrity models"). It was around this time that I decided to put myself through Cantonese school at night, because I wanted to take my career to the next level—I wanted to be able to talk to the media and do interviews, maybe even movies. I was working out all the time, but fueled by nothing—I was back to my liquid diet. Old habits die hard, I guess. I'd have a yogurt drink, a fat-free chocolate milk, or a protein shake when I was really hungry and light-headed. This is around the time that cold-pressed juice cleanses became a thing, so I quickly folded that into my routine, often doing three-, five-, and even ten-day cleanses.

IN LATE 2014, a giant cosmetics company was doing a huge world-wide casting for an Asian campaign, and guess what? I got the job! I couldn't believe it. I flew to New York City to shoot it. That job changed my whole mindset, because it gave me a completely new perspective. I'd definitely thought about becoming a top model in Hong Kong as an end goal, but never a global model. Besides, I was twenty-six, and I thought my career was close to being over. A model's life span is pretty much from thirteen to twenty-five. I was already old—over-the-hill in the industry's eyes—so I was shocked that I was picked.

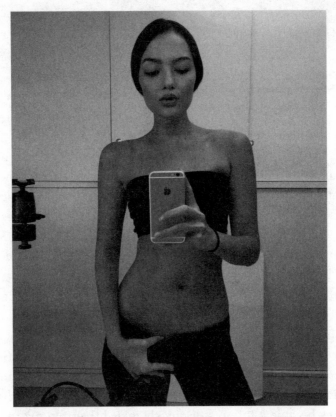

On set at a shoot. Liquids and laxatives were the name of the game. Hong Kong, 2014.

An Instagram post from 2014 in Hong Kong. Caption: "In the gym at 6am, completed a 3 hour workout— spinning, HIIT circuit training and Pilates. Now off to today's fashion show." This was probably the peak of my obsession with exercise to stay skinny. Any hour I could spare was spent in the gym.

I was suddenly at the peak of my career, at heights I had never imagined. I was also *back down to my lowest weight.* I was often shooting twice a day and then going to an event or two at night, squeezing in two or three workouts before, after, and in between my busy schedule. I'd wake up at five A.M. to go to the gym, squeeze in a spin class between jobs, and be back there as late as eleven P.M. for one last workout. My relationship with exercise became obsessive, just like my relationship with food. Working out made me feel the sense of control and accomplishment I felt when I starved myself; however, I was *also* starving myself, practically surviving off air. I juggled both at the same time, and my life became a roller coaster of manic scheduling every day. I searched for the next available time to work out while staving off constant food cravings and temptation. I felt so in control, though. My career was where I'd always dreamed it would be. I was now working side by side with top models whom I used to idolize in Hong Kong, making more money than I ever had, and building partnerships and sponsorships with household brands. The more I succeeded, the more I pushed myself with exercise and diet. I was at a place I thought I would never be, so I did what I had to do to stay there. I knew there were a zillion other girls right behind me, waiting to take my place.

Next up: one of the biggest international sports brands in the world. They had also been looking for an Asian girl for their new global campaign. Joey sent me to the casting. Unfortunately, I had been dealing with some sort of stomach bug that left me throwing up for several hours before the casting. But I went anyway (how could I not?). To test me, they asked that I demonstrate a few exercises on video for them. Just moments before the take, I had been in the bathroom throwing up. I was so weak, but I didn't want to let on that I was sick. I got through it, but I was convinced I couldn't possibly be their girl.

But Joey called me with the good news a few days later. "YOU GOT IT!"

"WHAT?!" I must have stank like vomit, and I definitely was too weak to do half the exercises, but maybe they knew what was up and liked my commitment, my dedication, and my attitude. (This was further confirmation of my theory that every casting you think you bomb, you get, and vice versa.)

Booking this job was a very emotional experience. I'd never done a global shoot on that level before, and to be picked out of hundreds, if not thousands, of beautiful Asian women was beyond

On set at a shoot. I remember feeling thrilled
that the dress was baggy on me—a real feat
for anorexic Mia. Hong Kong, 2014.

my comprehension. Before I knew it, they flew me to Mexico for
the shoot. I had never gone on a shoot like that before—on location,
with a large dedicated team. We spent a week together, and there
was a lot of downtime. We all got pretty close.

When the job was over, I had a sixteen-hour flight back to Hong
Kong. Typically, I would have gone to sleep, but this time I couldn't.
I just cried. I always reflect after a shoot, reminding myself that it
might have been the last shoot I'd ever do; there's never any certainty
that you will get booked again. It's an occupational hazard in this
business. This time, it was hard to go back, because I wanted more.
I had booked two huge American campaigns without an American
agent or representation, so what did that say about my chances of
continuing on that upward trajectory?

A hotel selfie. I'd just arrived for a global
sportswear shoot and was trying to squeeze in a
last-minute workout at six A.M. before my call time,
because I believed I was inadequate and too large
for the shoot. Mexico City, 2015.

It was a taste of something bigger, but also reassurance that
I could do the bigger, more coveted work, which gave me a new
perspective. It gave me a feeling that I could go even further, dream
bigger; I gave myself permission to have loftier goals. It had helped
me to see that I wanted a big career. It was an opportunity few people have, and there was such a short window of time to make it
work. I felt like it would be a waste not to see it through. My education wasn't going anywhere, and I could go back to finance after
modeling. I wanted more for myself, and I wanted to try. Fuck it,
what would be the worst thing that could happen? That I'd bomb
out there and have to come home? Even if I only stayed in New York

City for a few months, it meant an opportunity to experience the Big Apple while I was single and in my twenties. Who in their right mind would say no to that?

Finding the right agency was key, as it would get me the visa I'd need to move there. That summer, I flew to New York and met with a few agencies, one of which was located in a loft building in Soho, a huge open space with exposed brick walls and towering windows that overlooked a bustling shopping street. I walked in, and just like clockwork, all the bookers turned around and sized me up. I had encountered this a dozen times at this point, so I was used to it. I was shown to the conference room, where I was meeting with a booker named Gabe. We exchanged the usual pleasantries and began chatting while he flicked through my portfolio, when in barged another booker, a woman with a commanding voice. Her name was Deborah.

"I don't know who you are, and I know you're meeting with Gabe, but I needed to come and meet you. I think you've got something special, and I want to be your agent." Her hijacking the meeting was such a ballsy move that she sold me right then and there. She was a hustler, and I respected the hustle.

I sat with her as she told me what the industry was like in the States. Then, out of the blue, she said, "I think you can do *Sports Illustrated*."

"Me? Do *Sports Illustrated*?!" I knew the magazine—after all, I had plastered the Tyra Banks cover on my wall—but I thought it was only for girls like, well . . . Tyra Banks! And I didn't realize *how much* of an iconic American symbol it was. The *Sports Illustrated* annual swimsuit issue is part of the fabric of modern American culture. That it could be a remote possibility for someone like me gave me goose bumps.

She told me, "Yes, you could do *Sports Illustrated*. You've got a fucking personality. You're a smart kid. You know, they're meeting people now." She explained to me that *SI* conducts a worldwide model search every year, picking six finalists to be photographed for the swimsuit issue and subsequently voted on by the public. The winner of that search would be featured in another issue the following February as an official rookie.

"I'm not even signed with you guys. I don't even have a visa. I don't know. . . ."

For assurance, she brought in the agency's director to ask her what she thought. "She's not ready," she said, but Deborah still insisted I go.

"Just go; take the meeting. They only meet girls once a year. Let's do it now."

Her hustle and confidence in me made me like her even more. So I agreed to do it. The second the appointment was confirmed, I stopped eating. At this point it was instinct for me, but that doesn't take away the fact that I was really nervous. I asked Deborah if I would be asked to be in a bikini, but she assured me the appointment was just to meet me and talk.

On the day of the interview, I arrived ten minutes early, so I sat outside to have a cigarette to calm my nerves and give myself a pep talk before walking in. I went up to their offices and met with MJ, the editor of the *Sports Illustrated* Swimsuit Issue, in her large office in Midtown Manhattan. On the wall by her desk was a collage of photos of *SI* models over the years—Chrissy Teigen, Heidi Klum, Elle Macpherson. WOW. At that point I had been in the industry for thirteen years. That's thirteen years of obsessing over models and watching the industry change. So to be sitting in that office, where these supermodels had previously sat—the moment was pinch-worthy, to say the least.

She asked me the conventional questions about my life and where I was from, but soon the conversation just flowed. At one point, she pointed at the board and said, "I've done this for a long time. I've met very few women like you." I couldn't believe how well the meeting was going.

She wanted me to do a few test shots on camera to see how I was on film and to see what kind of personality I brought to the table. So I introduced myself and bantered back and forth with the photographer while they asked me questions. Then I left, and that was that.

Okay, I thought, *that was a really good experience. It was great to even just have the interview. How many girls get that far?* I was happy with that. I thought I had no chance in hell at getting the job.

I flew back to Hong Kong, and a few days later I received a short email from Deborah: "MJ loves you and she's putting you in the model search. You'll be shooting for *Sports Illustrated*."

WHAT, WHAT, WHAT!?!?!

I couldn't believe it. I just couldn't believe it. With that, I signed a contract with her agency. They would handle my visa as soon as possible. The *SI* shoot still needed to be scheduled, but I needed to move to the States right away. I needed to start packing.

July 4 was my mother's birthday, so I figured I would bring her some flowers, take her to lunch, and also pick up a couple of last-minute things that I wanted to take from the house. Mum and I had been in an alright place, but I always knew to proceed with caution. When I showed up and went downstairs to my old room, I discovered that my stuff had been cleared out. Everything was gone. Nothing in the closet. Nothing in the drawers. Nothing in the desk. No clothes, no stuffed animals, no yearbooks. No trophies from my childhood dance competitions.

I went back upstairs to the living room, where my mum was sitting, and angrily asked her, "Where is all my stuff?!"

"I cleaned up your room."

"What do you mean?"

"Instead of bashing your mother, you should thank me for cleaning your clutter and your mess."

"Are you insane? You have just thrown out my entire childhood!"

She kept repeating that I should be thanking her for cleaning up my stuff, because all it was doing was collecting dust.

We were standing in the living room, yelling at each other, when I walked right up to her, her face an inch away from mine. I wanted to hit her. I never had done so before, but this time the urge was palpable.

Nose to nose, I yelled, "I barely had anything, and what I did have, you threw away? Are you fucking kidding me?!"

She remained steadfast; she didn't even comprehend what she'd done or why I was hurt. I couldn't take it anymore. I could feel my anger rage inside me, and I knew something was going to happen. It was as if I stepped outside of my body and watched my own hand go up to her face. Like the Hulk, I couldn't control what I was doing. I didn't want to hurt her, but my body was acting involuntarily.

Rage came over me, and I pushed her forehead with my hand. It wasn't a slap or a punch; it was a shove. She fell back three steps from the force. I immediately took two steps back, tears streaming down my face. I looked at her and I saw how shocked she was. My blood was boiling, but I couldn't believe what I'd just done.

I needed to get the fuck out of there. I walked out of the house to the pier, and got on the ferry as if I was on autopilot. My mind wouldn't stop racing—it was trying to make sense of all the emotions I was feeling. I couldn't believe that I had just pushed my mum like that. She wasn't hurt, but she was in shock. She is the only person in the world who can push me to such anger. I was so mad at her, but I also didn't like what it brought out in me. I was so disappointed in her, but more important, I was disappointed in myself. How was I, after all this time, still so shocked and triggered by her behavior? I felt like no matter how old I was, or how far away I lived, my mum always had the power to make me regress to an angry, emotional child.

When I got back to my apartment, I called my sister Anouk. She had been dealing with her own shit with my mum at the time. She had a lot of empathy for what I was going through, yet I remained distraught for much of the day. Later, I was in my bedroom, sitting on my bed with my computer nestled on my lap, when I saw an email pop up from Mum. I opened it. I don't remember the entire email, except for the line: "I only have two daughters now, not three. You're dead to me." Everything after that got cloudy. A wave of heat washed over my body. My heart raced, and my breathing quickened. I was in shock. Tears built up and let loose, streaming down my face as I curled into the fetal position and started uncontrollably sobbing like a child.

Like I did when I hid in my room listening to my parents scream at each other.

Like I did when I was locked in the study after I had been punished by my mother.

Like I did when I drove to a hotel after the altercation with my mum the day of my graduation.

How could my mother not want to be my mother anymore? After all she had done to ME, she got to walk away? I couldn't understand it. If your own mum doesn't love you, who will?

I called back my sister Anouk and read her the email. Anouk tried to help me see rationally. She suggested, "Don't reply right now. Give yourself time to cool off."

I didn't think about it; I didn't gather my thoughts; I didn't cool down. I simply responded, "You were dead to me a long time ago."

It was as if it came out of the depths of my subconscious. She had lost the respect a mother deserves a long time ago. She thought she was disowning her daughter, but I didn't want to let her have the privilege of walking away. I tried to heal the relationship so many times, but she kept disappointing me. For a long time, I had maintained a relationship with her just because she was my mother. As if I was forever indebted to her because she gave me life. And the frustrating part in all of this was that she could be a good mum. A really good mum. The capacity and ability were there, but most of the time, it just wasn't her priority. Add to this the longstanding social code in Asian culture that everything is tolerated and swept under the rug. Family is family. No matter what. But tolerating hurt and mistreatment for the sake of family is how generational trauma is passed on. If there's one thing I learned from my upbringing and relationship with my family, it's that I want to do everything in my power not to pass on the trauma that was passed on to me. So I made a decision to put myself first and break away. I wanted to prioritize my own growth and development as a person, and, more important, my healing. This meant letting go. She was done with me, but I was also done with her.

It wasn't easy, but I needed to move on. I needed to rid my life of her, at least for now. I was successful and independent, yet here I was crying about my mum—something I had been doing my whole life. But in order to become the woman I wanted to be, it was time for me to start taking care of myself, because no one else was going to. For the first time, I truly understood that. When Doreen talked about what was holding up that chair, I realized it was me. I was supporting myself. And I needed to move forward, not regress or spend time trying to cover old wounds or dwell on how my mother treated me. I wanted to take that energy and invest it in *me, my* life, *my* happiness.

I had good things happening that I wanted to concentrate on. Besides, the United States was beckoning me.

10. NYC TO MEET YOU

—

I TRIED TO LEAVE WHAT HAPPENED with my mum back in Hong Kong—I didn't want it to distract me. Now that I was in New York, I was suddenly swimming with the big fish, and I needed to stay focused and not let the fierce competition get to me. I tried not to place any huge, unrealistic expectations on myself, but rather to embrace a "let's just see what happens" attitude. All I could do was show up to castings, walk into those rooms with a smile on my face, and hope for the best. Outside of that, it was out of my hands.

I took it day by day and tried to enjoy the city, since I didn't have a clue how long I was going to stay. Would I be there just a few months, heading back to Hong Kong after the *SI* shoot? Or would New York be my new home?

I was crashing at a friend's big Tribeca apartment. She and I knew each other in Hong Kong, and she so kindly said I could stay with her while I figured out my plan. I had spent a lot of my savings on packing up all my shit, getting a visa, and moving to America, and I knew that I was going to have to pay a year or two of rent up front if I did manage to get my own apartment. So I needed this to work or I wouldn't be able to stay. Luckily, my agency had me hit the ground running, meeting as many clients as possible at as many castings as possible. When I had first arrived in NYC, I had a meeting with Deborah where she laid out the new landscape, cutting to the chase: "Listen, New York is cutthroat. It's the best of the best. You will not work if you're overweight in the slightest. As long as that's handled, you're going to work. It doesn't matter how pretty you are or if you've been on the cover of *Vogue*. If you're not the smallest you can be, you're done. Done, done, done." And at that point, I was apparently too big for the American market. I was probably a small size 4, up from a 2. Size 4 was considered too big to make it in this market, so I needed to shrink down.

To illustrate her point, Deborah found an image of me on Instagram where I was close to my skinniest and, pointing to the image on her phone, said, "Here. Get to this weight. This is how you should look when you do your *SI* shoot. And you know what? If you look like that I could get you in to meet Victoria's Secret, too."

When I arrived in New York, this was the photo that was used as a reference of the size I should be. China, 2014.

Honestly, by that point I had learned to zone out while people criticized my body. I'd learned to fight back the tears and let it out when I got home. I knew that if you don't want anyone critiquing your physical appearance, then you shouldn't be a model. (It's like how if you can't stand the sight of blood, you shouldn't become a doctor.) Occupational hazard. I could handle it, but whether I *should* have had to be able to handle it is a different question. Deborah, bless her, was aggressive, but that is what made her such a good agent. She explained that she had to be so tough on me because New York was so competitive. The stakes were so much higher than anywhere else, so she pushed me that much more to book the jobs she wanted me to do. And she wanted me to go for Victoria's Secret—the ubiquitous pink-labeled brand that was, at the time, every model's dream booking. What girl in her right mind wouldn't want to don a set of feathery-soft angel wings and strut down the runway in teeny-weeny lingerie while being serenaded by a rock star? The brand's yearly show and campaigns moved girls into the stratosphere that few models enter. I loved that Deborah was shooting for the stars. Although I hadn't known her for long, she had earned my trust. She'd been right about *SI*, after all, so she was probably right about this too. I thought I could reach that goal—it was just about shrinking down to the right size. (At this point, clothing size was how I judged my weight. I had given up weighing myself, because I just became too obsessed with the numbers on the scale.)

WHILE DEBORAH WAS ENCOURAGING ABOUT MY CAREER, she also unwittingly caused new insecurities to develop (like I needed any more). I was very vulnerable, so I listened to her, the birdie on my shoulder, eating up all her hard-won advice. She reminded me that I was lucky to be starting a career in the US at age twenty-six, because most agencies are looking to sign fresh young faces or already established models. This line of thinking fueled a new phase of my eating disorder, which now included working out every single moment I could. I amped up my exercise sessions, hitting the gym even more frequently and for longer—two to three hours at a time. You'd be surprised what your body can do on sheer willpower.

She was still not happy with my weight, though, and I was always thrown numbers to beat. "You are still five pounds off. You need to do some more work." Yet, as tough as she was, she also had a maternal energy that allowed her to be a great source of comfort to me. Since I was new in America, I opened up to her about how hard it was for me to be alone. I was struggling financially, and I was so far from home, with no family close by and a freshly severed relationship with my mother. Deborah helped make the transition a little easier.

As for the five pounds to lose, in the context of the competitive modeling world I found myself in, she was right to push. The *SI* shoot was coming up, and I needed to look my best. *SI* was a *huge* coup for me and could be a turning point in my career. Deborah and I pored over the details of the shoot, pregaming and prepping. We looked over previous issues and checked out other models who had graced the magazine's pages. She would point to one and say, "That's what you need to look like. This is the body you have to have." She also told me that there was a certain type of *Sports Illustrated* girl—which was high energy, friendly, stylish, and sexy all rolled into one. She created this image for me, and I felt I had to live up to it. She also warned of girls not being invited back to the magazine because they didn't smile enough or because their bodies weren't in the "right" shape. I couldn't *not* do this; it was so pivotal to my career. I had no choice but to look like these rare specimens of perfection. Her scare tactics lit a fire under my ass. As the shoot got closer and closer, I had to up my game as I had never done before. This was the biggest shoot of my entire life, and if I didn't nail it, it might be the end of my career.

Despite my having next to no income, Deborah recommended that I invest in my body to get it "perfect." So I signed up for the monthly membership app ClassPass and purchased a few sessions with her husband, who was a personal trainer. I was also buying anything cheap and weight-loss related from Groupon—cool sculpting, lymphatic drainage, fat-burning lasers. You name it, I tried it.

I tried to limit my intake of sustenance to mostly micro-portions and liquids. That meant allowing myself to have a couple of almonds or a few squares of chocolate here and there, but the guilt would immediately creep in and I would go work out. I was losing weight and landing great jobs, but there was no finish line. There was always another goal to reach. Another pound or two to lose.

At first, I didn't have a real target date for the shoot to work with—all we knew was that it would be at some point in September or October 2015, for the February 2016 issue. The magazine makes a point of not telling anyone when and where the shoot is until a week before, because they don't want the information to leak out; it was that hush-hush. So I just stayed in the workout and starvation zone, thinking that I would need to be ready at a moment's notice. I finally got the call: We would be shooting in the Dominican Republic. I got my dates, my flights, and the shoot schedule, including the schedules for the five other girls shooting that week. As soon as I got their call sheets, I took to Instagram to check them out. I couldn't help myself. At this point, I didn't need to find out their measurements; I knew what those numbers would be. What I did look up was how many Instagram followers they had. With the rise of social media, models had a new way of comparing ourselves to one another and quantifying "success," which added an entirely new dimension to feeding insecurities. A few of the girls had nearly one million followers! I had only ten thousand or so—hmmm, no pressure.

The night before I flew out, as I lay in bed, the only thought I had was that I was so fucking hungry. *When is the last time I ate? I had a few almonds around one P.M. Shit, I am starving. I'm almost done, though. Then I can eat.* I wasn't excited about the shoot. I wasn't excited about the locale (beach! sun!). My mind just went to the shoot and being finished, so I could binge.

Fucked-up, right? It's fucked-up that I had a *Sports Illustrated* swimsuit photo shoot and I was just excited for it to be over. I didn't enjoy the first-class plane ride. I didn't revel in the personal drivers who took me everywhere. I didn't take full advantage of the fancy hotel with all its perks.

I just sat in my hotel room, waiting, starving, and counting down the minutes until I did my shoot. Earlier that night, I took a selfie—Deborah had asked me for a picture to see what kind of shape I was in (even though what could be done at that point?). She responded, "You look amazing. You did it. Amazing, you're going to

A selfie when I touched down in the DR. This was the photo I sent to my agent, when I was told I finally had reached a good weight. I hadn't eaten solid food for nine days. Dominican Republic, 2015.

kill the photoshoot, you're great. This is the exact shape I need you in for Victoria's Secret." (I know it seems like agents do some pretty shitty things, making girls lose weight, but, for the most part, they are just the messengers for what the market demands.)

The next morning, I got up at four-thirty A.M., and we started on hair and makeup while it was still dark outside. We shot for a few hours and were done by lunch. Everyone was so cool, which made the set relaxed and fun. I played my part, being the best Mia I could be on the outside, yet all I could think of were the minutes that were passing at a snail's pace. I couldn't wait to be done so I could eat something, anything. *I should be enjoying this! SI! I can't believe I'm here! But I'm so hungry.* I couldn't enjoy the moment at all.

When we were done, someone shouted out, "That's a wrap! Mia, you just finished your first *Sports Illustrated* swimsuit photo shoot!" But instead of feeling elated, I felt deflated. I. Had. No. Energy. Left. Not one ounce. I had used it all up being peppy, cracking jokes, smiling and laughing, just like my agent had told me to. Each interaction required such effort.

As was typical after a big shoot, the crew wanted to enjoy a leisurely lunch.

"Hey, Mia, come with us—celebrate!"

Generally speaking, if your client asks you to go for a meal, you go for a meal. It's professionalism 101. But I just couldn't make myself. I was that tired. "You know what, I can't. I'm going to go to my room, I'm sorry. I'll catch up with you guys for dinner, though."

I went back to my room.

And I cried.

And I opened my minibar.

There were a few mini Toblerone chocolate bars, a few bags of Planters mixed nuts, Pringles, M&Ms, and Snickers bars—within fifteen minutes, all of it was gone. The cans of sodas and juices—guzzled. The handful of chocolate bars? Inhaled. The bags of nuts and Pringles? Devoured.

I took three sips of the beer, which made me feel tipsy because I was so deprived. But I continued to binge on whatever was left as I cried, wrappers and empty cans now littered around me. When there was nothing left to wolf down in my room, I ordered room service. Fried chicken. It sounds psychotic, but I had put my body and mind through so much constraint, constantly monitoring myself, keeping myself on track, that I had no control left. It had been a twenty-four-hour-a-day fight for ten straight days against temptation and hunger, a battle against my body's natural instinct to eat. It was the most exhausting and consuming thing I have ever done. After all that, I sat, cried, released it all, and just ate. It felt amazing. I didn't even feel guilty about eating. I didn't feel guilty about anything, because I was literally flooded with dopamine. I

A selfie after I had finished my first *SI* swimsuit shoot. Relief, tears, and the entire contents of the minibar. Dominican Republic, 2015.

was so happy to turn off the part of my brain that had been hard at work for so long.

As I sat there, feeling like a beached whale, I noticed that it was getting physically harder to do this, to test my body like this, as I got older. It felt harder emotionally, too. It was a lot easier to starve when I was younger, but in my late twenties, the strain was showing. When I was done hoovering all the food, I showered all the sand, fake tan, body shimmer, and makeup off me. Clean, I sat on the bed in my robe, crying and drinking another Corona. I'd done it; I did my first *Sports Illustrated* swimsuit photo shoot. I should have been ecstatic. But I was bawling my eyes out alone in a hotel room. *What was all of this really for?*

I had a ticket to Miami the next day, so I went there, holed myself up in a hotel room, and continued the crying party. I ate and I cried. I went to the beach and tried to relax—I needed to decompress and to reassess. I literally just ate, cried, and hung out by myself. I couldn't figure out what the fuck I was going to do.

I thought to myself, *That's it, I'm not doing this anymore. I have to find some kind of balance now, because I need to be this skinny, but I can't be starving myself like that anymore, so I don't know what I'm going to do.* At this point, I hadn't questioned the goal of being as thin as possible; I just questioned myself—my willpower. Was it wavering? I had never considered that my metabolism might be slowing down with age. Women's bodies are always changing, and weight can fluctuate in ways that are out of our control. I questioned my discipline—was it waning? Did I not want this as much as I used to? In the end, I concluded that I had the passion and ambition, and that I still wanted it very much.

Those three days in Miami ruined all the fasting I had done up to that point. My body was retaining everything, because it was so desperate for sustenance. But I went back to New York and continued the hustle. The next thing I knew, I had interest from Guess—a huge, iconic brand whose previous campaigns included famous models from Adriana Lima to Anna Nicole Smith. Their interest alone was a big accomplishment for me as a fresh face in the States.

I would have to remain on high alert and be as skinny as possible for as long as possible. There was no break. I'd check in with the agency so Deborah could assess my progress, but it never seemed like enough. It was like dangling a carrot stick that was forever out of reach. "You're almost there. Three pounds more." Now, of course, I realize that there's no such thing as "there."

It felt like I was waiting for some magical moment to occur, turning me into this content, accomplished supermodel in New York. It never happened, though. I was fucking miserable, my body was a mess, my mental health was a fucking mess, and I was literally living off of cigarettes and liquids. Honestly, if it wasn't for the fact that I had a roommate, I'm pretty sure I would have broken down a lot sooner. The idea of "making it" and everything that entailed completely consumed me. Victoria's Secret was within reach. *I can fucking do it, I can fucking make it. I can be this girl who puts Hong Kong on the map in the modeling world. I can do this.* I'd wake up in the morning and the first thing I thought about was how to make it through the day without eating. What workouts was I was going to do? My last thought at night was, *Okay, let's think about tomorrow. I'm probably going to be a pound lighter. . . .* Everything—every thought, every decision, every move—was centered around my weight. Obsession can take you very far, and that's how I did it. Even though I didn't feel talented, I figured I could probably obsess better than my competition could. To me, all this was part of the hustle.

The hustle worked. The *SI* Swimsuit Issue went on stands in February 2016, and things quickly changed for me. I got a lot of exposure with the press junket. It was an immediate entrée into American modeling. My first photoshoot in America was *SI*, which was unheard of. Models could work their whole career and never get there. I felt very lucky.

Things picked up, and I decided to stay in New York and get an apartment. I found one, signed a lease, and moved into a building with a gym (of course). I started to use that gym all the time. If I couldn't sleep, I would go to the gym and just try to burn calories. I was up to smoking a pack a day because of the hunger. I don't handle winters well either, so seasonal depression got me good that first winter. Maybe it's because I am not used to the cold and darkness; perhaps it was because I was alone in my own apartment; perhaps it was because I still didn't have much money. (There was a bit of a time lag with booking jobs and getting paid for them.) That winter was all about fighting hunger, fighting depression, and fighting off any and all temptation.

In March, I received that fateful phone call from Deborah about Guess requesting my return for their next campaign. I did it, barely getting through another all-liquid diet to get ready for it. My body was telling me it was done fighting. My body was done starving; it was fed up with the laxatives; it was tired of my abuse. Was this a lifetime of food and drug issues catching up to me? Was my body pulling the emergency cord? I had gone through a lot in my life, but after that shoot, I felt more overwhelmed, overtired, and overwrought than I ever had before.

When you're suffering from eating disorders, there is a huge element of control. You stop eating to gain control. You purge to get control. Getting control can be all-consuming. As you have read by now, it got to the point where I would eat and I would be immediately flooded with so much guilt and self-loathing that I would spiral to the deepest, darkest depths of my insecurities. This constant emotional push-pull was exhausting, and the thought of doing this day in and day out, multiple times a day? *Forget it, I would think. I'm not strong enough; nor do I want to live a life this exhausting. Maybe it is just easier to end it.*

I would sit with my suicidal thoughts, convincing myself that that was the only option to get out of this vicious cycle that I seemed to be stuck in. Relief, let alone any real recovery from this, didn't seem possible.

So with every speck of strength I had, I took myself to Thailand, for a ten-day trip where I would soon discover a different kind of fighting that would save my life.

11. MUAY THAI

I DROVE BY IT EVERY DAY.

Each time, I would slow the car down—ignoring the beeping and honking from passing cars and motorbikes—so I could get a good glimpse of the fighters, fascinated by the beautiful dance between them, swinging and kicking, grunting and puffing, drenched with sweat as they fought.

I had been staying in Koh Samui, Thailand, the farthest place from New York City I could go for my emergency detour. To get into town, I had to drive down a short but steep hill, a three-minute drive from my house, into the village of Choeng Mon. Just past two 7-Elevens, three local pharmacies, and the snake farm was the Yodyut Muay Thai gym.

After days of drive-by stalking, I finally pulled into a spot right in front of the gym, shut off the motor, and watched from afar in the comfort of my car. It was particularly hot that day, with the typical tropical humidity that could peel paint off walls. The open-air, no-frills gym, barely protected from the elements by a corrugated metal roof, housed two canvased rings and a large workout area covered by red-and-black checked foam mats and punching bags that hung from rafters. Functional, and far from flashy, for sure.

I must have sat and watched for a good twenty minutes while a group of boys sparred in the rings. (It was more like I stared, which, now upon reflection, must have seemed very creepy, and not unlike how I watched other models when I was a newbie model.) They moved with so much power, so much fluidity, so much intensity, so much focus. Yet, as they exchanged blows, it was just two people standing in front of each other, reacting to each other. I wondered, *How do they know what to do? And when to do it? What's going through their minds?* They were so strong. There was such power, so much beauty in being strong.

Wow, I want to be that beautiful and powerful when I do that, I thought.

When I do that. I wanted to be that powerful, that strong, and it was in *that* moment that I knew what I wanted to do.

It was a huge revelation for me. Muay Thai is the national sport of Thailand. It's known as the "art of eight limbs" because of its eight points of contact—hands, elbows, knees, and legs. I had always found martial arts fascinating, although I wasn't sure why. It may have been because it was *everywhere* growing up in Hong Kong, the home of Bruce Lee and Jackie Chan. When I was really young, my brother Alistair and I would wake up before my parents to play Nintendo's *Street Fighter*. However, as my parents slept, my brother would be the master fighter Ryu, and I'd always be Chun Li, the Chinese female fighter. Beautiful and strong, she could lightning-kick her way through any situation. Overweight and long-considered to have not one athletic bone in my body, I never thought I could be like that myself, but boy, did I *want* to be that confident while doing a spinning bird kick (only maybe I'd drop the annoying, high-pitched girly sound effects). I was also obsessed with mimicking the punches and kicks Sporty Spice used to do in all the Spice Girls videos.

And here I was, twenty years later, sitting in a Muay Thai gym parking lot, itching to give it a go. It was intimidating, though. I had done some kickboxing before in Hong Kong, but this was different. This felt like I was in the belly of the beast. It was Thailand's sport, in its home country, in its language, governed by its rules.

This wasn't some chichi boxercise class where 90 percent of the attendees are just doing it for the Instagram post. Plus, the gym was about 98 percent male. It was not exactly the most welcoming environment for a woman.

I thought about walking into the gym's office, but it was *alllllll* the way in the back of the building, and I would have had to walk through the entire gym—past all the fighters, trainers, and customers—to get to reception. *Um, no.* Instead, I drove home and called from the safety of my house.

Ring . . . ring . . . ring . . . voicemail. Phew.

I managed to eke out a message. The gym's owner, Son, called me back that afternoon. I was terrified of talking to him at first, but he was so nice and accommodating. I found myself making an appointment. I didn't show up for that first session (yup, I was chicken), but I got my ass there the second time around.

That first day, I met Son, who, in person, did not match the chirpy and welcoming voice on the phone. Here, standing before me, was a shirtless, rock-hard warrior in black and gold Muay Thai shorts with a large tribal tattoo that wrapped around his right shoulder. In person, his voice was loud and commanding.

Oh fuck, what did I get myself into?

I also met Gemma, the receptionist and Son's soft-spoken then-girlfriend/now-wife who ran the office—little did I know, she was an absolute Muay Thai beast, too.

I was introduced to Mr. Firstt, who was to be my trainer. Smaller than me—maybe five feet five inches—and only nineteen, he was already a retired champion. He had more than 150 fights under his belt and had been number two in his weight class in all of Thailand, having fought at the famed Lumpinee Boxing Stadium, the most prestigious Muay Thai stadium in the world. That is badass AF. When I was nineteen, I was smoking cigarettes, drinking too much, and occasionally missing my university lectures because I was too distracted by boys.

My first time training Muay Thai at Yodyut. Koh Samui, Thailand, 2016.

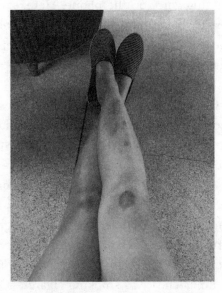

The bruises after my first few lessons of Muay Thai. Koh Samui, Thailand, 2016.

Mr. Firstt and I during one of our twice-daily training sessions. Koh Samui, Thailand, 2016.

Well, those days were over, and now I was looking at a fierce fighter who was most likely unconvinced that this skinny-ass girl standing before him was all that serious about Muay Thai. To be honest, I had my own doubts. To start, he informed me in Thai-style English that I was to learn the basics: jump rope, punches, kicks, elbows, and knees. Then it was to the pads. The temperature had to be easily more than one hundred degrees with 98 percent humidity, typical of Thailand in March and, well, all year round. The place had no air-conditioning, but Mr. Firstt kept me on my toes for more than an hour. Hands down, it was the hardest physical activity I had *ever* done. We didn't take many breaks, outside of a quick sip of water between rounds. I was drenched in sweat and kept wiping my eyes with my gloves so I could see. It was as if I was standing in a shower and there was a continuous stream of water trickling down my face. I probably lost three or four pounds in sweat alone. It was so hot. So fucking hot. I thought I was going to overheat, keel over, and die.

But, fuck me, it felt *great*.

I never felt so alive and so close to death all at the same time.

I was immediately hooked.

I gave myself bruises all down my legs and arms, and muscles I didn't even know I had were sore.

But I didn't care.

I went back the next day, and the day after that.

On the third or fourth day, Son—who had probably figured out by now that I wasn't just some chick who wanted to try this crazy sport on a whim—told me, "You know, the other fighters train twice a day—once in the morning and once in the afternoon. You should, too."

Whoa, do this twice a day? I thought I was pretty tough already. *But most fighters do this twice a day?! Okay, I want to try.*

I STARTED TO TRAIN DOUBLE-TIME. I extended my vacation for another week. Pretty quickly, the training became less about working out and more about technique and improving my skills. I became obsessed, and Mr. Firstt indulged me in that—we would practice for hours on end. At first, we mostly worked on my left kick. Apparently, it was hideous.

Mr. Firstt had let me down gently, "It's not beautiful. You right kick? Beautiful. You left kick? No good. You left kick ugly." (FYI, my left kick is still hideous, but I swear I'll get there one day.)

And that's all we did, back and forth for hours, just trying to get it right. I filmed our sessions so I could analyze my technique and improve it. I'd make him demonstrate on the bag so I could study every single detail.

"Show me," I'd plead. He would oblige and also pull up You-Tube videos of famous super fighters like Buakaw Banchamek to show me how it's done.

"You do like this, okay?" he'd say, first pointing at the screen, then pointing at me.

And we'd go at it again—for days—to try to get a certain technique just right. At the last rounds on pads, when there were about thirty seconds left, Mr. Firstt would make me go ham (give it all I had). For the last couple of shots, I'd give it ALL my power.

He'd build it up and scream, "Mia, power! *POWER!*" (Fun fact: I now have the word POWER tattooed on the inside of my lower lip.)

Inevitably, he would pull the little prank I *always* fell for, just like Lucy pranked Charlie Brown with the football: He would make me give everything I had for the last shot, then move his pad so I would miss and tumble to the floor.

It was a lighthearted joke that ended a crazy, exhausting workout. He'd make it up to me by walking on my back and legs while I was down for the count to get out all the aches and pains. Then he'd fold me up like a pretzel, and carefully unpretzel me. I'd lay on the floor in a jelly-like state before I had the energy to get up. So dead. But so alive.

This became our routine, prank and all. Every day, twice a day, it was me and Mr. Firstt. The more time I spent with him, the more I wanted all the knowledge he had. He was my sensei, and I was his faithful student.

I was also getting more comfortable being in a room full of top-notch fighters. It wasn't hard—everyone was so nice to me—and before long I knew all the trainers by name. I'd walk in and say hi to everyone: to Nong B, a well-known ex-champion who was very polite and kind of shy around me; Mr. R, who spoke English well and was always ready with a smile (and a big fan of the ladies); and Wirat and Eyat, an unlikely pair of brothers, as Wirat was lanky and super friendly while Eyat was the biggest of all the trainers and a bit of a bully.

Then there was handsome Mr. Chit. I call him the Thai John Wayne, who, in his mid-forties, was the oldest of all the trainers and had fought more than 350 fights (we are not sure of the exact number, as he'd lost count). He spoke *zero* English but laughed at everything and anything (seriously, I once saw him chuckling at his own belly button). We became very close. He was wise without words; I could tell he'd seen some shit in his life.

TWO WEEKS LATER, I extended my vacation again.

"I am going to be here another week," I emailed to Deborah, my agent.

"Another week," I emailed her a week later.

It got to a point when she just stopped asking.

"Girl, take all the time you need," she told me. Thank freaking God. I think she could tell that whatever was happening on the other side of the world was doing me some good, finally.

DAYS BECAME WEEKS, and weeks turned into months. After two or three months, some of the fighters were angling for me to push myself more.

"You should join the group training," one of the fighters suggested.

"Wow, you guys think I'm good enough to join and keep up?"

"Yeah. Of course. You'll be fine."

The joke was on me: I had thought my training with Mr. Firstt was brutal, but group training was ten times worse. It was almost triple the workout hours. It's one thing to go and try something new; it's another thing to try something new while you are the lowest on the food chain. I was the beginner, and everyone else was *so much better* than me.

Mornings consisted of a run, stretching, a round of shadow boxing, four rounds on the pads, four rounds on the bags, four rounds sparring, some technique work, finishing with some squats, push-ups, and sit-ups. Afternoons consisted of a run, stretching, two rounds of shadow boxing, four rounds on the pads, four rounds on the bags, four rounds sparring, thirty minutes clinching, then conditioning, which typically included one hundred knees on the bag, and finally, two hundred sit-ups.

As hard as it was, the guys were so encouraging—they never made me feel intimidated. (What I was telling myself—my negative self-talk—was a different story.) They weren't concerned with any of the things I was ever concerned about, like looks and weight; they just cared about mastering their art. They didn't care that I was a girl or even a model, and that was so refreshing. Don't get me wrong; there was definitely an alpha thing. In a Muay Thai gym, or any male-dominated sport for that matter, there's always going to be an alpha undertone. The guys put me through tests, but they did that with everyone, male or female.

They wanted to see that I was serious about the training and the sport. They pushed me, treating me like any other fighter who was training for a fight. I needed that toughness. Maybe it was because I was a model and I was typically treated like a fragile doll, but I responded to the aggression. I wanted to hit back. I didn't want people to go easy on me. I knew I was ranking at the bottom, and I wanted to work my way up.

Every time I stepped onto the mats, I stepped off a little different. I became a little wiser, gained a little more clarity, felt a little more stillness. It became a form of therapy, but cheaper. When I was hitting the pads or sparring, all I could think about was that moment. My breath. The impact. It was all about the *now*. Giving the shot all I had. If I struggled, it was because of me alone. I felt myself growing as a person. This wasn't just a physical journey anymore.

EVENTUALLY, I chucked my luxury villa on the top of the mountain with an infinity pool and rented a bedroom at the gym. It was a windowless, eight-by-eleven-foot room with a latched wooden door and walls painted in a kaleidoscope of yellow with splatters of pink and blue all over. There was a bed, a TV, a small wardrobe, and a bedside table with a lamp—and an air conditioner, thank God.

Living there just seemed to make sense, since I was there every day, all day.

I had none of my material possessions except for a few sports bras, shorts, a pair of flip-flops, and a pair of running shoes. I also had two dresses—one was a sarong, so that doesn't even really count, and the other was the only thing I had with me that was appropriate to wear out to a restaurant. No makeup, no purses, no high heels . . . That's it. I had nothing else, and I loved it. I was living day by day, in the present.

I didn't know what tomorrow would bring, except for another day of hard but satisfying work. I became completely detached from New York and everything and everyone I had left behind. I forgot about needing and obsessing over that new Gucci bag. I forgot to worry about guys texting me back. I forgot about how I agonized over my reflection in the mirror every morning.

My days were uncomplicated: I'd wake up every day as if I had been hit by a Mack truck, but I would get my ass out of bed, pop

Gaining weight, strength, muscle, and definition while living at Yodyut and training full-time. I was also feeling more and more comfortable with my physical self. Koh Samui, Thailand, 2016.

At the gym, training. Koh Samui, Thailand, 2016.

some supplements, and chug down a Berocca, an electrolyte and vitamin drink.

Then I was out the door for a run. Me. Running. If you had told me several years earlier that I'd be a runner, I would have snickered in disbelief. Being a heavy smoker for more than fifteen years, I never thought running would be an option. My lungs couldn't take it. But with my training, running was a must. The Thais say, "No run, no fight." On one of my early attempts, I had been running uphill in the blazing afternoon sun and one-hundred-degree heat. With each step, I struggled to breathe. My huffing and puffing was so heavy, I heard myself through the music that played in my headphones. I gulped for air, but my lungs wouldn't cooperate. Rather, it felt like bricks were on my chest. It was in that moment that I realized it was either this or smoking. And it was that very day that I quit smoking cold turkey. I never smoked another cigarette again. The more I ran, the better I got, and my lungs eventually forgave me. And I forgave myself for disrespecting my body for so many

Mr. Chit (Thai John Wayne) and me, backstage before he stepped out for a bareknuckle fight at age fortysomething. Koh Samui, Thailand, 2016.

years. I never thought I could run a mile, so running was a *major* achievement.

And running in Thailand, well, there is nothing else like it: Darting through the countryside gets you out of your head, if for no other reason than having to watch where you're going. Dusty, blistering hot roads peppered with palm trees were heavily trafficked by clucking chickens, straggly street dogs, and locals setting up their street stalls for the day's trading. The fragrant smell of chicken grilling on homemade barbecues sat thick in the air.

When I got back, it was time for coffee and Mr. Chit. We'd sit in the lounge, in front of the TV that flickered with an American show that Mr. Chit couldn't understand but would still watch, transfixed, as I helped him roll up the freshly washed hand wraps for the group class.

Then I'd get to work.

Run. Train. Eat. Run. Train some more. Eat. Sleep. Repeat. I was living and breathing Muay Thai.

Life was so simple, and I was happy.

More importantly, I was happy with myself. I watched my body change, and I honestly couldn't remember a time ever in my life when I had looked in a mirror and liked what I saw. What an utterly sad realization. Muscles popped out of my arms, thighs, and calves. I developed a butt, and I didn't freak out about it. I liked how my legs were so sore I could barely walk up or down stairs. I was *so* sore. I was sore in places I never knew existed. I had never felt so worn out before. But I liked the bruises I had on my legs. And I liked that I had a routine—something I hadn't had in a really long time.

I was also hungry. I *wanted* to eat more. I needed to eat more. And for the first time, I *allowed* myself to eat more. No longer was I counting every damn calorie that went into my mouth. And I didn't work out to counteract those incoming calories. Something had switched on inside that stubborn brain of mine, and I saw and felt a new strength in my body. It made me respect it; I wanted to take care of it. I—for the first time in my life—felt ALIVE and WELL. I had energy. I had strength. It was like I had just discovered my own body and what it was really capable of.

Another big revelation: Food is fuel for my body and not, well, the Antichrist. Holy shit, the food that I put into my mouth actually mattered. I saw how I needed to eat for energy, and so, for the first time in umpteen years, I ate. Before Muay Thai, there were two modes for me: eating and not eating. In not-eating mode, I ate nothing, and in eating mode, I ate everything. I was either starving or bingeing; there were no in-betweens. I was either gaining weight or losing it; I had never maintained it. Food was a reward for starvation; exercise was punishment for eating. But now I realized there was another, healthier mode, which is to eat in moderation for both enjoyment and fuel. But I didn't know how to do this. Totally clueless. So I watched and learned: I copied what the other fighters ate before and after training. I learned how to feed myself at twenty-seven years old.

AND I HAD SOME GOOD TEACHERS. Sean Wright, an ex-fighter who frequented the gym for long stints like I did, is a fitness and nutritional expert, and he explained the science behind my body's mysterious aches and pains. I loved learning about my own body and looking at food for its nutritional value for the first time in my life. Because of him, I started using terms like "glycogen," "carb loading," and "amino acids."

Like a curious child, I would ask seemingly simple questions.

"What should I eat, and when?" I asked Son. He had no idea how loaded my question was, as he had no knowledge of my issues with food.

"Eat carbs for breakfast so you have energy, and for dinner try to eat something lighter like vegetables and chicken, with a little bit of rice," he replied. This may sound pretty obvious to you, but it was news to me. Coconut water and bananas for recovery. Nuts for energy. A lot of protein is essential. Got it. And these were things I would eat in between meals. I was fueling my body with what it needed for the first time. I was getting *healthy*.

I made mental notes about other fighters' eating habits, noting when, what, and how much they ate before and after training. And before you knew it, I was eating three solid meals a day, which I hadn't done since I was a kid. And not throwing it up, or following it with ten laxatives. That was a big thing for me. Moderation. Portion size. A balanced meal. Hey, I was eating like other humans, and it was super weird—I had only ever seen that in movies.

I was gaining muscle, and with all that muscle building, my body reacted by wanting protein. You know by now that when I do something, I go big. Almost every day I'd buy an entire rotisserie chicken for two hundred baht from a Halal chicken stall and eat the whole thing with my hands. In one sitting. Easily.

I was trying to feel my way to some sort of normal relationship with food, and it was an extremely emotional journey. I had been living a certain way for fifteen years. And here I was, fighting like a fucking ninja (turtle) and loving it. I was doing things that I never thought I could do. I had a six-pack at one point. I learned how to nourish myself for the first time. I was gaining weight and gaining muscle. Never in my wildest dreams did I ever think that would happen. For the first time, I was working out to see what my body could *do*. I wasn't working out to see how my body could *look*. It was far from easy, and sometimes I would have multiple meltdowns a day. Anxiety attacks. Overwhelming guilt and self-loathing. Occasionally I had to do things for work like send in snapshots of what I looked like because a client was asking for it, and I would have severe meltdowns seeing myself in photographs not looking "how I was supposed to." At first, it was very hard to watch myself get bigger, because for most of my life, I had one very limited definition of beauty. I had been the size 0, thigh-gap girl. That was changing. Big time. It was a complete transformation of both body and mind.

I ALSO HAD PEOPLE LOOKING OUT FOR ME, holding me accountable. Living at the gym, everyone's habits are all out in the open, since we're around each other all the time. So my eating habits were suddenly on display. I ate most of my meals with another Sean—Sean Clancy, who was a European champion and had been living at the gym since it opened its doors. He was practically part of the furniture. He caught on early that I had an unusual relationship with food, and he would often check in on me to make sure that I'd eaten. He'd frequently make me eat when I was regressing into my old habits and didn't want to.

In our downtime, we'd often watch movies, and before we got ourselves comfortable, we'd go to 7-Eleven and get a bunch of snacks (my favorite hobby) and lay them on the coffee table in front of us. During one movie, I ate all the Oreos. The entire package. Old habits die hard.

"What are you doing?! Don't eat all of them. Eat a couple of them and then put them away."

But I couldn't. I didn't know how. So Sean decided he would try to teach me moderation. He'd put a sleeve of Oreos in the fridge, and challenge me to eat one a day. There were so many failed attempts, and I'd end up eating the whole sleeve. Seriously, like a child. Nearly every time, though, Sean would notice the Oreos missing from the fridge and come into my room to a girl sitting on her bed, cheeks bulging with cookies, and black crumbs all over her mouth. Then the guilt would set in. But eventually, I did make that pack last a week. *Hello, my new friend Mr. Moderation, I'm Mia. It's very nice to meet you, finally.* Fueling my body, eating meals, learning about moderation—all new concepts to me. The discipline I was learning in my training helped me create a healthier discipline in my eating habits. My newfound physical strength in the gym was translating to mental and emotional strength, too.

TIME WENT BY. I didn't have a plan about when to go back. All I knew was that I still wanted to do Muay Thai, so I was staying. I just kept living in the moment, day by day. And I loved being one of the guys. It was easy to be around them, and they took me under their collective wing. I liked their outlook and lifestyle. They woke up every morning, happy to have food on their plate and a roof over their head. Happy to move their bodies and feel alive.

The boys, as I affectionately called them, started bringing me to fight nights, which were six nights a week and held at one of the three stadiums in town. It was a great way to unwind after a hard day's training and also to study Muay Thai in action. I observed fighters, their emotions (or lack thereof), their bravery, their personal styles. One night, Sean Clancy had a bare-knuckled fight heavily promoted and televised by Thai Fight (a martial-art entertainment company, much like the UFC) against world champion Saenchai, arguably the greatest fighter on the planet. Everyone from the gym was there to support Sean, and it was the first time I watched someone I knew fight in a professional setting. I was so nervous that I sat completely still—I barely blinked, and I sweated enough for the both of us.

In basic Muay Thai rules, a match has five rounds. Each round is three minutes, with a two-minute rest period in between rounds.

Sean lost in the third round—the fight was stopped because he was so badly cut above the eye—but, holy shit, that didn't matter to me at all. I was so in awe of his courage. He faced the world's greatest fighter in front of a huge stadium audience, broadcast throughout the country on live TV. I was used to performing in front of people on catwalks, and had even done some live TV, but talk about apples and oranges. For Sean, so much emotion, pride, determination, and focus came into play. How did he become so fearless? How did these guys do it?

I wanted to be that fearless.

I was in a training session the next morning when Sean poked his head into the room. I stopped what I was doing and walked right up to him to see the cut up close for myself. I got three inches from his face—with no consideration of personal space—and inspected the gazillion stitches. It was gross, but I was fascinated with the spectacle of a sport that could be so brutal, but also so beautiful.

He was all smiles, laughing as if his face wasn't practically sliced in half. He wasn't fazed by it—he enjoyed it, in fact. To him, it was a battle scar. Seeing him laugh at something an average person would seek pity over, I realized I could toughen up a bit more. In that moment the already immense respect I had for Muay Thai fighters doubled.

This is what they do. What would be a traumatic moment for one person was just another day in the office for them.

Call me crazy, but I thought, *If this is what my life as a Muay Thai fighter is going to look like, sign me up.*

AUGUST. AN EMAIL.

It was Deborah. She had booked a job for me. What was that? A job? New campaign? *Work?* Those words had not been in my vocabulary for several months. I was liking my life, far from New York. I was feeling healthy and happy, and I liked being comfortable with myself. My body changed. I changed. I was living with no judgment, no standards to live up to.

But "reality" was calling. And I needed some money. I needed money so that I could come back to Thailand, to this gym.

Deborah had booked me another Guess campaign. "You shouldn't miss it. You've shot for them before, and you shouldn't do anything to jeopardize this client." She was right, but I felt a jolt of PTSD at reading her words. My mind started flooding with aching self-doubt for the first time since—well, since I had left New York.

My mind raced with a million thoughts at once—thoughts that I hadn't had in months. It was a quick trip, and I would turn around and come back to Thailand, but I was suddenly consumed with how all this would play out. *How will my agent react when she sees me? I am heavier.* I didn't know by how much—I hadn't weighed myself in a long time, and I didn't even care. And hell no, I wasn't going on a diet to get back to that old number on the scale. The thought made me feel sick. It was impossible to go back there.

Come on, Mia, you need the money, I told myself. *It's ONE day.*

And the old me came roaring back.

Old habits.

Old self-destructive thoughts.

And I stopped eating.

12. MY PURPOSE

—

BY THE END OF AUGUST 2016, I had been in Thailand for several months. My body had changed. *I had changed.* All because of Muay Thai. But with that email, I immediately got sucked back into the maelstrom of modeling. I had just five days to prepare for the shoot.

The last time I modeled, my anorexia and my long-standing deep insecurities sent me screaming all the way to Thailand. I thought of that as I went to work whittling down my weight for the shoot. *What the fuck will the client think of me?* I had only gone up to a size six, but that was enormous in the fashion world. *Why would they book me? Why wouldn't they just work with somebody else? Should I just go into retirement?* But I needed to stop questioning everything. Because I had been off the grid for so long, I needed the money. And regardless, I should have been happy that they had asked me back.

Over the next couple of days, all the progress I had made with my eating and confidence took a huge step back as the new, healthy Mia and the old model Mia battled it out in my head. The fight between the two was exhausting. As many of you may know, when your insecurities creep in, they can very quickly consume you and bring you down. Even though I had made enormous steps in my eating disorder recovery, I was still *in* recovery (and I have come to terms with the fact that I will forever be recovering). It's an ongoing process that takes consistent work, as opposed to achieving a particular mindset or reaching a certain number on a scale. So here

I was, on the road to health, but these were still early days. The old anxious Mia easily won out, and I instinctively shifted back to my default mindset, as if autopilot clicked in and those anxieties about having to live up to the expectations the industry placed on me came flooding back. Once I crossed that mental divide, I didn't even want to eat anymore. But since I was still training, I did eat a little bit: stress on "a *little*." At the time there wasn't a kitchen at the gym, outside of a microwave and a plug-in kettle, so I bought a cheap rice cooker. For the next few days, I would use it to steam a chicken breast and a few sprigs of broccoli and sliced carrots and split the food into three micro-portions for breakfast, lunch, and dinner. As strict as this was, this was a drastic improvement from just starving myself. I fancied myself healthy because I was "eating clean," but I was actually doing what a lot of other people with eating disorders do and hiding behind a label. Whether it's gluten-free, keto, Whole 30, or intermittent fasting, any diet can be misappropriated by people who have serious issues with food to mask their disorders, convinced that they are eating healthily because they are following a popular diet. (Some may even use a diet to give them strict rules they "must" follow, deepening their disorder; I know women who are gluten-free even though they do not have a gluten intolerance. Putting a label on it gives their eating habits a whiff of acceptability and takes credibility away from those who need to follow those diets for health purposes.)

In Thailand, my body had been so appreciative of the food I had been giving it (finally); when I stopped, I had little nourishment to energize me in my training sessions. I couldn't keep up the pace or give it my all. I noticed, and my trainers noticed, too.

Mr. Firstt asked me in one morning session, as I hit back at him with a tenth of my usual strength. "Why no power today, Mia?"

"I'm cutting weight for a shoot," I replied, winded.

"Ah, okay, okay," Mr. Firstt acknowledged and backed off. "Cutting weight" was a term Mr. Firstt was very familiar with, because a lot of fighters have to take extreme measures to drop excessive weight to weigh in for a fight. He understood what I was doing and that it could zap my energy.

I kept at it, though. I would supplement the training by doing hundreds of sit-ups after both my morning and evening sessions every day. My default mode of "move more, eat less" was back. After one of the training sessions, I was doing what felt like the millionth sit-up and shifted my eyes toward the gym's floor-to-ceiling mirrors next to me. I wanted to check my form, but I found myself looking at my body. Wow, how my body had changed. I was proud of the healthier, stronger woman who was looking back at me, and woah, look at my abs! For the first time in twenty-seven years, I liked what I saw. It was an incredible feeling. I never achieved such strength and definition before. But at the same time, a vague panic took over. What if I showed up at the shoot only to get sent home because I was too big? Or what if we did the shoot, but they never hired me again? A wave of unease washed over me. It felt like I was about to kamikaze my career.

Another, more logistical issue was that I didn't have any appropriate clothes for the trip. Remember how I came here for a ten-day vacation? Well, it was six months later and I was still living in the same wardrobe. So I took myself to the mall to buy clothes for my foray back into Western civilization.

Once in one of the stores, I headed straight to the jeans section and started looking through the piles of denim. I set aside the 0s and 2s that I used to fit into as I looked for 4s and 6s. *Wow, this is a shock to the system.* I had spent the previous fifteen years trying to fit into the smallest size jeans possible, because that was what I was told was beautiful, ideal. So picking up a size 6 pair of jeans felt like defeat to me.

I had to tell myself it was okay. I had to remind myself that I kicked ass, literally. I was happy. I was healthy. *Progress is a process,* I told myself, and besides, I was stronger than I had ever been or thought I could ever be. *Everything will be fine.* But as I slid on a pair of jeans in a dressing room, there I was staring at the mirror again. The moment hit hard, and that nagging doubt swooped in. I stood there—in that tiny, cold dressing room with that unflattering should-be-illegal fluorescent lighting that every woman across the world has had to endure, and I looked at my body. I really looked at it. I looked at my rounder stomach, my stronger thighs, my bigger arms, and my fuller face. I was making a shift into acceptance, for sure, but it was a shift that went at a snail's pace. The Asian beauty standard had been firmly set in my brain, and I had to slowly break it down. Accepting that I had to buy a bigger pair of jeans was a huge step in my recovery. It meant that I had begun to tear down the standard that I had set for myself. Our insecurities come from us feeling lesser than the beauty standard we set for ourselves. So tearing down the standard that I had set for myself meant letting go of those insecurities.

But I still worried about how people were going to view me at my new size, having only known me as "skinny Mia." I was pretty damn sure they would see me and tell me, "All right, it's been a good run, but it's time for you to move on from modeling. Don't let the door hit you on the way out." And then, poof, it would be over. I would be remembered as just another model, if at all. The last fifteen years of my life wouldn't have amounted to shit, and in the future, I'd be an old lady who would still be holding on to her past, who'd tell anyone and everyone who cared to listen that I used to be a model when I was young. I had been sent home from jobs for being one centimeter too large, so it was hard to imagine pushing through now being two sizes bigger.

No, you're too big, game over played in my head on a loop. I started to prepare myself for the worst and began to imagine what a plan B might look like. It would mean breaking my lease, leaving the United States and moving back to Hong Kong, dusting off my business contacts, and restarting a career in finance. Or maybe I would even move on to a plan C, where I'd move to a shack in Thailand and become a fighter or scuba diving instructor while I grew my own vegetables and raised chickens.

I took my second-guessing and self-doubt on the plane for the twenty-four-hour jaunt to Los Angeles. By the time I arrived at my hotel the evening before the shoot, I was so jet-lagged, hungry, and weak that I made a beeline for the bed. My anxiety had peaked, and I was so on edge that I didn't get much sleep. That morning, I got my groggy ass to the set, and the first thing I did was down a cup of coffee to help wake myself up.

I knew I had to be "on." I had to find that personable, bubbly, and vivacious Mia—and that Mia was not awake. I knocked back one coffee after another, and as I woke up a bit, the coffee also woke up my anxiety. My heart started pounding, and I could feel my hands getting clammy with sweat. I couldn't sit still. Everyone was extremely nice to me, but in my paranoid, self-doubting, anxious thoughts it was because they felt bad for me, even though no one even mentioned my weight. I hadn't felt this way in nearly a year, and I tried not to let my nerves get the better of me.

After lunch, Kim, the shoot's producer, pulled me aside. *This is it. She is going to tell me that I just gained too much weight. They looked through the preliminary photos and nothing is usable. This isn't going to work out.*

"Mia, I just wanted to tell you that you've never looked more beautiful. You seem happier . . . you're glowing."

"Wow, thank you," I managed to say, stunned by her compliment.

The relief! Little did she know how much her words meant to me. In that instant, the wave of anxiety receded. Gone were the little voices telling me that I'd be sent home. I realized they hadn't hired me for being a typical model; they hired me because I was an *atypical* model. I wasn't just a pretty face who took a good photo. It was the personality behind the face they bought into. They hired me for *me. So maybe it's not about my size, and perhaps it is about me.*

It was a validation that I needed to help assuage my self-doubts. The moment also told me that whatever I was doing was working. I should keep up my journey to health and my Muay Thai. Keep being intelligent, outspoken, and feisty, because that's who I am. Just be *myself*. When I peeled away the beauty standards that had been put on me, then stripped away the layer of insecurities, there was this amazing woman who had always been there, but never had a chance to shine. Until now.

Up until this moment, I hadn't been able to wrap my head around the idea that while I was the same woman on paper—the same upbringing, same education, same experiences as a year ago—the thing that had changed was the number on the scale. (The same realization I had when I went from fat to skinny at age thirteen.) I had spent the last year letting go of so much fear, anxiety, angst, and regret. And it wasn't just about weight. As I dealt with those inner demons, I fought with others: the childhood bullying, the sexual abuse, parental abuse, addiction. It was a lifetime of hurt, pain, and toxic thoughts in which I had gone to great lengths to control the chaos with my food and, later, mask the hurt with drugs. The more out of control my life was, the more in control I tried to be, or in the case of drugs, tried to control things by changing who I was. Now it made so much sense to me. I had turned all this into literal blood, sweat, and tears, and I came out on the other side finally able to respect myself, and to ultimately love myself. Surely people would rather see this shiny new version of me that I was becoming, not that fearful, gaunt woman who barely had the energy to smile for the camera. For the first time, I understood that *what really mattered* was the woman I was, and the things I had to say, not my size. And that was a good feeling.

After the shoot, I went straight back home to my gym in Samui. You read that right: home. The gym had become such a fundamental part of me that I thought of it as home, and the people there had become family. My agency knew I needed to be in Thailand and pursue Muay Thai to keep up my mental and emotional strength, so they encouraged me, knowing it was doing a world of good.

It was later that summer when I got a call from Deborah.

"Are you sitting down?" she asked mysteriously.

Oh shit, what did I do now?

"No, nothing's wrong," she said excitedly. "You won the model search!"

"What???" I asked incredulously.

"You won the *Sports Illustrated* model search. You'll be in next year's issue as an official *SI* rookie. Girl, you did it!"

How many times had I looked at Tyra Banks's polka-dot bikini cover and wish that I would one day grace those pages? Now here I was, about to be in the issue for the second time! I. Really. Couldn't. Believe. It. Then again, I had campaigned my heart out, and being the first model from Hong Kong, and half Korean, drew quite a lot of attention from the Asian media. That must have worked in my favor, since I won over other models who had huge followings on Instagram. I was thrilled, humbled, and honored all at the same time.

I was also trepidatious. Thousands of miles away in Thailand, I had been so removed from the fashion world and the stresses that go hand in hand with it. With the shoot not until October, nothing in my immediate orbit changed, so it was hard to see how it would all play out a few months ahead. As September came, I received the call sheet for the shoot.

Here I go, into the great unknown. Would *SI* be as accepting of me and my transformed body? The truth is, *SI* would have accepted, loved, and shot me however I turned up, but I was so deeply damaged by the weight of the industry standards. Several days before the shoot (location: Tulum, Mexico), I tried to close that weight gap between my old weight and new weight as much as possible. I only allowed myself three micro-meals a day, as I had done for Guess. I wanted to have the perfect chiseled *Sports Illustrated* swimsuit body that everyone was used to and, I thought, was the only body people wanted to see. I was happy with how I was changing, but the antiquated beauty industry still abided by their standards, and that was the real test. So whether I liked my new body or not was irrelevant. It didn't help that Deborah reminded me that because of the Internet, for the rest of my life, when people search my name, the *Sports Illustrated* images will show up. So there was a double whammy of needing to look "perfect."

That creeping self-doubt resurfaced and made me lose a couple of steps in my progress away from anorexia's grip. Again, recovery is a fucking long process. I didn't just trade in the old Mia for the new one—it was a long, tough haul. I had broken down the long-festering beauty standard in my head and had decided to be healthier. Still, whenever external pressures got to me—like the upcoming shoot—it brought back those internal pressures that plagued me for years. No one told me that I had to be perfect, exactly, but that was the beauty standard ingrained in me and firmly entrenched in the industry itself. I found myself regressing, maybe a little less each time with each new job, but it was so damn hard not to. The power of such standards, and the resulting expectations and judgment, is so strong it can tear away all the confidence a woman has.

For this second *SI* shoot, I was larger, but I was also healthier and stronger. I still succumbed to pressures of what I had been so conditioned to think I should look like, but the difference between the two shoots in my mental and physical health was drastic—day and night, in fact—even if it wasn't obvious to others. For someone who'd counted every almond eaten, who had made sure not to swallow toothpaste when brushing teeth, who was cautious of a minuscule fluctuation of the scale, I felt like a different person. A person who was no longer obsessed with thigh gaps and protruding collarbones. I focused more on being strong, skilled, and healthy. I had successfully let go of the obvious standard ideals, which demonstrated for me a pretty good and steady-as-she-goes shift in mindset.

WHEN I ARRIVED AT TULUM, I needed to do a quick fitting for the suits to be worn for our shoot the next day. I was more than nervous about how the team would react to my different body. The pressure was on: If having to be "on" for such a high stakes shoot wasn't bad enough, how about adding into the mix having gained a bunch of weight? The pressure I put on myself was 500,000-fold. To make it even more nerve-wracking, while I got in and out of teeny-weeny bikinis in my hotel room, there was an entire team of people (mostly strangers) around me. There was a whole lot of nakedness going on, on my part, so confidence was KEY. You can't be a *SI* swim model and be shy. Part of their beauty is confidence. I hadn't needed to worry, though—the team was nothing but complimentary and supportive. I was again surprised and amazed by people's embrace of me and my body.

Mind you, I look back on those pictures now, and I see how fucking skinny I still was. They were very happy, smiley, upbeat

Behind the scenes, being shot by Ruven Afanador for the 2017 *SI* swimsuit issue. A meatier, healthier Mia who finally ate meals. Tulum, Mexico, 2016.

photos, but I now see the pain in my face. I can see the insecurity still behind the eyes; I was still fighting my body and my dysmorphia. As healthy and strong as I had gotten, and having made that fateful decision to embrace my body and shout it from the rooftops, I still had work to do. (Again, it's a long fucking road, my friends.)

The shoot was in the afternoon, so it was sunset when we wrapped, and the hotel staff brought out margaritas for everyone accompanied, of course, by a mariachi band. *Hell yes, bring on the margaritas!* I was just so beyond excited that it was all over and that I had actually made it through the day.

I again went back to Thailand after this shoot and switched off the model in me to go straight back into training. As supportive as my clients and agents had been, I knew I wasn't ready to go back to modeling day in and day out. It felt good to be back at the gym and to continue working on myself, and Muay Thai was a great tool for helping me do that.

It was sometime in January 2017 when I was ringside at a female fight at the wildly popular Friday night fights at Chaweng Stadium in Koh Samui that it hit me. I was so close, leaning on the canvas, I could feel the spray of sweat as the fighters sent and received punches. At one point, I turned to Mr. Firstt and announced, "I can do that."

"You *want* to do this?" he asked.

"Yes. I want to fight."

"Okay. We fight."

All right then. As I was reentering the modeling arena, I was also entering another arena; I would straddle both worlds as I trained for my first real fight.

But first, duty called. In February 2017, the *Sports Illustrated* issue with me as a rookie would be published, which meant another media blitz. This time, Deborah advised me, I had to stick around in the United States, because I needed to make the most of all the attention. I would be getting a lot of exposure, and potential clients and casting directors would surely be requesting to meet me. I (again) needed to be ready for anything—no matter how long it took me away from Thailand.

This time, when I left the gym, it was very emotional for me because I didn't know when I would be back. This was the place where I had learned how to be myself—I didn't have to wear makeup and high heels to impress anyone. Everything out there was so pure; there was no bullshit. No judgment. No ego. It was just the life of Muay Thai. I was going back into a world where superficiality prevailed—it was a world that revolved around approval, and with the search for approval comes insecurity. I felt I was going from this strong place to a place of stress and self-doubt. I reminded myself that what truly mattered was the woman that I am, and the things that I had to say, not my size. Sure I could just stay in Thailand and do Muay Thai forever and be quite comfortable. There would never be a perfect time to leave, nor is there a time when all of your insecurities and self-doubt are gone. These insecurities, I learned, are what drove me to trust myself, to take that huge leap out of the nest. I may have struggled, but eventually I learned to fly.

Before I left, though, I had to say goodbye to the people who had become my family. This gym was my home, a support system I'd never had before. Mr. Firstt was going to be the hardest to say goodbye to, as we had become super close. We spent so many hours a day, six days a week, just two feet apart, face to face on those mats. He was like a little brother to me. We had our own handshake; we had our own inside jokes; we even had our own song that we would play during every training session—Justin Bieber's "What Do You Mean?" (don't ask). I made him a super-dorky card with a collage of photos of us together and a short note letting him know how much he meant to me.

When I was living in the gym, these guys became my family. Back row, left to right: Eyat, Mr. R, me. Front row, left to right: Mr. Firstt, Owen. Koh Samui, Thailand, 2016.

The guys must have thought I was crazy, because they didn't understand why I was so emotional. They must have been thinking, "Okay, you've got to go back to work, but why are you crying?" I don't think they knew what I had gone through mentally while living there. Several months prior to this, I didn't even know these people, and yet they helped me through something that not even my parents

Squad! After a great morning sparring session. Left to right: Mr. Firstt, me, Owen, Mr. Chit. Koh Samui, Thailand, 2016.

could help me with. They'd seen me at my lowest, and they'd seen me at my best. They'd seen me push myself, but they'd also seen me cry in frustration and pain. And they consoled me. They had seen me starving and fed me. They'd seen me through everything. So, I took that love and encouragement, put it in my pocket for safekeeping, and flew to the United States, knowing I'd be back.

As soon as I was wheels up on that flight, I struggled with a flurry of conflicting thoughts. I was now taking this body and the struggles I'd been through to a world stage. That meant more eyeballs on me—more eyeballs on my body. I knew there would be some judgment to come as I embarked on this journey. Would reporters ask what I thought of my body? Would they ask me why I gained weight? Or how my body had changed? I reminded myself that if worse came to worst, I could always go back to Thailand. If I wasn't ready for it, if I couldn't handle it, I could leave, and it would be fine. Again, plan A was to take this fight to the streets, and if I failed, I had plans B and C.

But you know what? I was eating. I was exercising. I was strong. I'd never been fitter and healthier and happier in my whole life. I thought, *I'm going to go back, and I'm going to stand up for this, because surely this strong, healthy, and confident woman is who we need to in the media.* The Mia before Muay Thai might have fit into all the sample sizes, but she was unhealthy, depressed, and riddled with insecurities. It was like seeing two versions of myself; one was shriveled and gray, and the other was colorful and vibrant. And I needed to stand up for the version of me who was strong and powerful. The version who was finally alive, finally happy. I needed to stand up for her not only for me, but for other women out there, too, because I wish I'd had a woman like me to look up to when I was younger.

But I needed to see how others felt about this newfound purpose. My first stop was my agency in New York. Deborah took one look at me and just smiled. She hadn't seen me in person in several months. I took a deep breath and told her, "Listen, this is who I am. I'm healthy now. I'm happy now. I have a story to tell. I see a problem. I think that we all see a problem, but very few people have dared to stand up and try and change it. I decided that I want to be transparent about my eating disorders and everything that I have been through in my life, because I *know* I'm not alone. Millions of other girls out there are going through exactly the same thing, all the while staring at photos of me in magazines. I don't want to be part of the problem anymore. I want to be part of the solution. They can be healthy and confident. And I want to be the person to show them it's possible."

I surprised myself with how much I had to say. But I knew I wanted to be a voice speaking on behalf of models and all women—to help reshape the beauty standard to one that is both aspirational and attainable. Everything I had felt—the guilt, the self-loathing, the hunger, the anxiety—all in the name of vanity, contributed to that decision. I had been through so fucking much that I couldn't NOT talk about it. Every calorie and drop of sweat expended, every meal skipped, every judgmental glance in the mirror—was because of this brutally unrealistic standard placed on us. Now, at twenty-seven, there was no going back. I was not going to do again what I had done to my body and mind for so many years. I finally realized that it wasn't me who needed to change. The system had to change. The modeling industry is divided between sample size and plus size. Many agencies didn't (and still don't) represent anyone outside a sample size, including my agency at the time. So I was asking them to make space for me and to expand their beauty standard, because change needed to happen on every level. I was also asking them to reconsider their own position in this industry and what they stood for as a company.

I felt my career was teetering in uncertainty, so I figured I had two choices: go out with a fight, or show myself the door. I chose the fight.

I held my breath as I waited for Deborah's reply.

She said, "Let's do this."

Damn, well, look at that. If she could believe in me, maybe I had a chance.

The next few days were a flurry of activity as I got ready for the *SI* press junket. My stylist came to my apartment (I had kept it while I had been in Thailand) to do a fitting with me after pulling a great selection of clothing options. I had gone up two sizes. None of the sample sizes were fitting me. The entire day turned into a crazed rush of trying to get bigger sizes from designer showrooms, and I saw firsthand how hard that was. The PR reps for the brands we were working with didn't have much choice in sizing options. We'd call company after company to only be told, "We don't have it. Sample size is sample size, that's it." And that was pretty indicative of the fashion industry. One has to fit into their sizes, not the other way around. *Why the fuck can't they cater to someone slightly bigger than a sample size—and what does this say about the industry as a whole? Maybe that's the issue that needs to be addressed,* I thought. That was a terrifying moment for me, but we did manage to pull together some outfits that worked. The next day we flew to Houston and did the press tour without a hitch.

Wardrobe mishaps aside, I felt like a new person on this junket. All of a sudden, I had purpose—a clarion call to expand what a "model" looks like and give that image a healthier, more attainable reboot that offers a realistic body ideal for younger women. I wanted to show an industry with deep-seated notions about beauty that it didn't need to be so limited. I wanted to change the modes and norms of the model ideal in the fashion industry and beauty

Me at the press junket for the 2017 *SI* swimsuit issue. Happier, healthier, and on the road to recovery. Houston, Texas, 2016.

standards in societies across the globe. I wanted the industry to throw away all the numbers that measured a woman's success—such as ninety-centimeter (thirty-five-inch) hips or a sample size.

I was ready to take on the industry. With all the *SI* press attention, clients wanted to meet me, especially swimwear and lingerie clients. Magazines wanted to do features on me—I had *Vogue* and various other publications and blogs reach out to me about my story. Yet I got the feeling that while I was getting the attention, I wasn't booking the jobs. My story resonated as a media piece, but it didn't result in work. Yes, the plus-size industry was blowing up, but there is really nothing for sizes 4–12. Enter me—I saw this as an opportunity to bridge this gap, yet clients didn't seem to bite. I went on endless meet and greets with brands, production companies, casting directors, stylists, and photographers, and with every two dozen rejections, I'd get one "yes." But I kept going to the appointments, because just getting in the room meant I had already changed the narrative, even if it was just a little.

Luckily, I had a few clients who aligned with my views and booked me regardless—or because—of my body's changes. If only there were more clients who thought like that, so much damn pressure would be taken off of so many models' shoulders, and ultimately off of all women's shoulders. It was very disheartening because I felt so isolated from the industry. I could feel it taking a toll on me, and I began to feel the familiar pull of depression. I really wanted to go back to my safe space in Thailand. But I couldn't run and hide. I had to be in the States and available in case a job came up or somebody wanted to meet me. I had to stick it out while I felt like I was fighting this insane, losing battle. And this battle was a huge financial strain. It was all for the greater good, but I struggled. *Do I keep going and hope it pays off one day, or do I give up and move on?*

The only thing that made it not seem like a lost cause was social media. Social media has many faults, but one of its biggest pluses is that it's a platform in which there is complete and direct connection to an audience. With Instagram, Twitter, and Facebook I had found a ready audience who wanted to see something different. Something real. When I was in Thailand, I would post content from life at my gym, whether I was taking hits to the stomach during training or mopping up monsoon rains at four A.M. I was sharing what had made me healthy. I wasn't doing it to show off my Muay Thai skills—I'm not the best fighter by any means. I was doing it to promote this active lifestyle—a lifestyle that's about humility and learning, strength and power, and a mindset to match.

I wanted to promote a healthier, attainable lifestyle. I lost things that I was told were the definition of beauty—like the thigh gap, protruding collarbones, and visible hip bones. Instead, I started to see things like shapeliness, a curvy ass, thick thighs—things I had been conditioned to think of as "undesirable." But I was proud of my new muscular build, and I wanted to express that to other women so they could start seeing beauty in a different, more healthy way. I wanted to put a female image out there that I wish I had seen as an impressionable young woman; maybe I would not have developed body dysmorphia and eating disorders. The fact that it was Muay Thai that got me to a healthy place didn't really matter—I was trying to show that there is not a one-size-fits-all diet or workout. Even more importantly, I wanted to speak about being authentic and finding strength within. Most of all, it's not about fitting into someone else's expectations. Especially with the rise of social media, models weren't just *models* anymore. They have voices and are seen and heard—and are followed as role models—so much more than previously. I realized that I could let go of the standards that modeling placed on me when I stepped out of this small, isolated world. I saw what the industry had done to me. I had been a part of the machine as well as a victim of it.

Slowly, between my interactions on social media and growing media coverage, I discovered there were a lot of people who wanted to hear about my story: They wanted to hear what I had gone through as a model and how my body changed with Muay Thai. There were a lot of women who struggled with their insecurities and a lack of representation. And on the reverse side, I heard from people who, through the forum of social media, allowed themselves to open up, perhaps for the first time, about their own issues with current beauty standards. This interaction with people who felt like me—who also felt the sting of the incredible importance society puts on beauty—was what kept me going in those quiet, scary days of my career. Their support and stories were what I needed to keep on going, to continue speaking my truth and telling my story, hoping the industry would catch up. If the rest of the world wanted this change, then brands would need to adjust.

I continued to concentrate on my ongoing journey. I was happy; eating and training, I couldn't believe who I'd transformed into. Life was good. I had a social life. I was going to dinners and normal get-togethers with friends. I found a Muay Thai gym in New York, so I had a little Thai haven in the middle of Manhattan. I kept showing up to castings, kept meeting clients, kept walking into rooms, trying to change their minds with my pitch: "I know you're used to doing it this way, but there's another way that's beautiful, too. It isn't black-and-white. There is a whole spectrum of different colors, shapes, and sizes."

What do I mean? Look at the plus-size world that is thriving, thanks to Ashley Graham and many girls who came up in her wake. The plus-size industry has become a billion-dollar business in its own right. This plus-sized world has its own brand clients, models, and agencies who specialize in this market. I have gone to plus-sized castings to be told, "Well, you need to gain weight." I would go to the more traditional sample-sized castings, and I would be told the opposite: "You need to lose weight."

What they meant was, I needed to pick a lane and gain weight or lose weight so I could fit in somewhere. How ridiculous is that? I was at a normal weight, but in order to get a job, I needed to either lose or gain a lot of weight? Both options were unhealthy for me. It had taken me years to get so strong, and I was not going back. How was an active body not part of this beauty equation? Outside of my few clients, I had trouble finding where I fit in.

I instinctively had a bad reaction from being told this (surprised?). I'd sit at home and think, *How dare you say that, because I am not "too" anything. I am me, and I can be whoever the fuck I want to be, not what you want me to be.* And this applies not only in the modeling world, but the world at large. We should not have to live in a binary world where it's either-or, black and white, good or bad, big or small, beautiful or ugly, merely because that is what people are accustomed to.

I used to think I needed to look a certain way because everyone told me I *had* to look a certain way. Now for the first time in my life, I had respect for my body, and Muay Thai helped me access that. I wanted to show everyone that this body was just as beautiful, if not more beautiful, than the one I had before I left for Thailand. Wouldn't clients love to have that positive energy and body image in their magazine ads and on billboards? Why was this proving to be so darn hard?

Not that long before this, I was sparring with a fighter who had multiple world championship belts. I was depleted because, as much as I tried, I couldn't land a shot. I was getting beaten up, and there was nothing I could do. I would think, *Why am I even sparring this guy? He is levels and levels and levels above me.* So, I gave up. I just let him kick me around and hit me.

"Why aren't you trying? Come on, keep trying! Even if you're losing, keep coming forward, keep walking. Stay strong, and don't show your defeat," he said, egging me on to continue. "Keep going, keep going . . ." In Thailand and in Muay Thai, we call it "having heart." Someone can be the best physically fit fighter in the world, but he needs "heart" to win a fight or be a champion. Others may not be the biggest or strongest, but they will go far because they have heart.

You know what? He was so right. Even when all seems lost, keep going. Keep trying. I took that Muay Thai mentality and kept it tucked away inside myself, applying it not only to my fighting, but to all facets of my life. And eventually jobs did come calling—they gave me a platform where I could do an interview or speak up about what I was about, and I realized, slowly, that people wanted this change just as much as I wanted it. I just needed to keep going, keep pushing.

I needed to keep pushing myself mentally, too. After I had finished the press junket and got settled back into the United States, I was still figuring out new parameters for myself. I suddenly wasn't training six hours a day in the blazing heat; because of that, my metabolism was slower, I didn't need as much food (or the same kinds of food, for that matter) as I had when I was training 24/7. As I continued to work on myself and my recovery, it was challenging to be back in my old environment where I used to starve myself and chain-smoke, never leaving the house. So, to keep me from the grips of that previous life, I spent a lot of time at my local Muay Thai gym, which helped to cure my homesickness and keep me sane while I tried to figure shit out. When I put those gloves on, I was a different version of myself (still am). *I'm Killa Kang!* I took all that confidence that came soaring back in the ring into the offices of clients and fought that fight every day. But I also wanted to go back to Thailand to have that fight I boldly announced to Mr. Firstt a few months back.

As if to dare me to keep my word, Son set a date for my fight: My debut was to take place on May 7, 2017, in Thailand, at the Samui International Stadium, against Thai fighter Nong B. There is a common phrase in my gym: "Train hard, fight easy." Its meaning is pretty self-evident: Train as hard as you possibly can, so you're more than prepared for what comes in the ring. So, I trained HARD.

I pushed to my absolute physical limit. I trained and trained until I felt like I had nothing left.

It was a very different level of training leading up to a fight. My determination and strength were tested in more ways than one, and they'd push me to the edge of giving up. At first the guys were more perplexed as to why I wanted to fight in the first place. Early on, they said, "Don't fight, you're pretty. Why would you do that?" I told them that I wanted to fight because I wanted to be strong like them.

An understanding based on trust. There was always three-way trust from the get-go: I trusted my trainer—whatever he said, I did. I trusted he knew what I needed and what was best for me. In turn, he had to trust me, that I would show up every day and do what he told me to do. And finally, I had to trust myself that I could do it. With that trust, my trainer would try to break me, and I would allow it. Just when I thought the session was over, I'd get an order of two hundred kicks, one hundred knees, or shark-tank clinching. This was all for the sole purpose of mining for the potential he knew I had. He brought that heart out in me so I could walk into the fight hungry and confident.

COME FIGHT DAY, I FELT PREPARED. I was a wad of nerves, and my mind raced, so much so that what came next was a blur. Suddenly I was in the ring, with Mr. Firstt and the whole Yodyut gang surrounding me in my corner. Mr. Firstt yelled, "Gloves on!" And my gloves were laced up and taped, and I remember thinking, *Wow, I could have chosen any hobby, and this is what I chose to do.*

I looked at Sean Wright, who said, "All you need to think about is going out there and viciously assaulting her."

Mr. Firstt removed my mongkol (a traditional headband that is blessed for good luck) and assured me, "It's okay. You do this every day, today is the same."

He turned me around and I started walking to the center of the ring. I looked back at him, and a rush of emotion swept over me; surprisingly, I felt angry and abandoned. *How could they just let me walk in here alone?* Then it hit me. *I am alone. It's just me in this ring. (Well, and my opponent.) But I alone can win this fight. All the responsibility is on me.*

DING! Mr. Firstt and I had gone over this moment a million times—when the bell rang, I would come out hard with a jab and a front kick. But I guess Mike Tyson was right: Everyone has a plan till you get punched in the face. There was so much adrenaline rushing through me that the next thing I knew, I was hit in the face. In an instant, she was coming at me and she wasn't stopping. It was disorienting. I walked backward as she came forward, hitting me with so much force, I was literally and figuratively stunned. I was in shock. And then again, BOOM. The adrenaline coursing throughout my body was so strong. I felt an insane pain in my face. She'd caught me with an elbow in my left eye. In the corner after round one, Son told me that I need to keep my hands up as Mr. Firstt slathered Vaseline on my eye.

"Am I cut?" I asked him.

"No," he answered. I looked in his face and knew he was lying. He probably thought if he told me the truth, it would get in my head and distract me, but really it would have just lit a fire under me. *If I take more hits to the face, this cut is going to open up. I need to knock her out.*

Okay, let's go. In the corner they told me I won the second round. "Just keep going, she's getting hurt," someone said. All of a sudden it was round three. I went heavy on the hands. Punch, punch, punch. I thought, *Keep punching her. She's gonna go down. You're tired, but she's more tired.* Her head jolted back. I remember seeing her eyes roll back. I kept punching. The ref came between us and stopped the fight. I didn't understand what happened, but he was holding her head while her corner came over to her. I immediately went to her and gave her a hug, and she hugged me back. The ref then dragged me back to the center of the ring and raised my arm. I realized, *Holy shit, it was a technical knockout. I won.*

I was flush with adrenaline, but all I remember was feeling an overwhelming disappointment. *Why don't I feel happy?* Winning was irrelevant; I felt I could have done better. I could have knocked her out in round one. I paid my respects to my opponent and went back to my corner. Mr. Firstt congratulated me as he took out my mouth guard and started shaking me in excitement.

As soon as my mouthguard was taken out, I looked in Mr. Firstt's eyes and said, "I want to do it again."

It was the scariest, most amazing thing I had ever done.

13. TRAIN HARD, FIGHT EASY: HOW I LIVE NOW

—

THAT FIGHT CAPPED OFF MY BATTLE with my inner demons.

I still face inner demons every day, but I have rewired my thinking and have developed a few techniques to channel my insecurities and negative emotions in more positive ways. It all started with the *decision* to recover. It's not all rainbows, hearts, and unicorns, believe me. Some days I win, some days I lose. But now I know how to handle them, and if I hadn't decided to make a change for myself, I don't know where I would be today.

I'm now based in New York (for the time being, at least) and, to my surprise, still modeling full-time, among other things. I still do Muay Thai (and hopefully will be able to do it until the day I die), and I'm trying my hand at different types of martial arts as well. For me, practicing martial arts is an incredible tool for self-improvement. It forces you into a humbling position of self-reflection and accountability.

And I am sober. I have been for years. I don't do drugs, but I will always have addictive tendencies. I am still cigarette-free. I have recovered from my eating disorders for the most part, but I still have moments of vulnerability. I have worked hard to change my thought patterns, which has helped change my actions. It's like the Oreos I ate living at my gym. At first, I couldn't help but eat the entire sleeve.

But I learned to change my action. Just have a few and put the packet back. Or when I ate a meal. I'd have to sit through the guilt and self-hatred afterward, faced with the temptation to take a laxative or make myself throw up. Over time, it got easier. The more I practiced it, the better and more successful I was at it.

I am not going to lie—it's a struggle. But with each day, the voice of that purple monster sounds farther and farther away, although he still creeps up on me during moments of weakness. In fact, I had an intense relapse in January 2020, while preparing for the season premiere of my TV show *Spy Games*. I had just landed in Austin, Texas, and I was on my way to the connecting flight to New York City, having come in from a shoot in Mexico. I shouldn't have done it, but I did: I took out my phone and checked my emails as I hustled through the terminal. The show's producers had sent me a file with a selection of publicity photos and videos that were about to be released to the media. I opened it and stopped in my tracks. Scanning through a few pictures, all I could think of was, "I look *so fat*." I hated what I saw. I was flooded with a deep wave of overwhelming emotions and self-loathing that I hadn't felt in a long time. It didn't help that these images would be seen by millions as I made my TV debut. I dropped my bag and just starting crying. Wait, I thought, *I thought looked good that day—did I not even look into a fucking mirror? I look terrible.*

I need to lose weight.

I need to lose weight.

I need to lose weight.

It didn't matter that I didn't; in fact, I had lost weight for the show. The purple monster came in like a storm, telling me, "Wow, you do look fat, you should get control over this and starve yourself." I shook my head as if physically trying to shake him out of me.

I had been planning to eat before my connection, but after seeing those photos, eating was the last thing I wanted to do. I forced myself to sit at a restaurant and order a couple of healthy options. I ate, slowly—hating every mouthful, but I ate. Afterward, I sat with the guilt and the self-loathing. I used the hard-won techniques to talk myself down. I told myself that what I was seeing was not real. It was the monster talking. I told myself I was having a moment of weakness where my insecurities were overriding rational thinking. And most importantly, I reminded myself that **my weight may fluctuate, but** *my value* **doesn't.** I sat through them, and my emotions eventually settled. Once I felt that the episode had passed, I took to my phone, started writing, and posted the whole episode on social media. I find that sharing these moments publicly helps my insecurities fade away. It's as if writing them down transfers the pain and worry onto the page (or post); now they're "there" and not in my head anymore. Besides, *everyone* has insecurities, especially today, and being more open about what scares us can benefit all of us. If I can share my vulnerabilities and make one woman—or man—feel better, then it was worth it.

This is not to say I look at myself in the mirror and don't see room for improvement. That's real. Loving yourself includes wanting to be the best version of yourself. That's self-respect. I wake up every day and look in the mirror and see a woman with an excellent education, who runs her own business, and who lives life abiding by a code of ethics. The size of my jeans is irrelevant. What I ate today doesn't matter. Tomorrow, I want to be a better woman than I was today—stronger, smarter, tougher. And that kind of thinking quiets the monster.

By rewiring my thinking and changing my actions, I have gained back my self-love. Everyone was born with self-love, and without judgment, self-doubt, or insecurities. And as we go through life, we are taught to judge ourselves, to hate our bodies, to question our worthiness. I read somewhere recently that perfectionism is the fear of rejection and abandonment, and that rang so true for me.

I realized after writing this book that perfectionism was the root of all my disorders. And perfectionism was a reaction to the abuse and abandonment I dealt with as a child. Maybe the struggles I had with eating disorders and drugs were always in the cards for me. I am (slowly) getting over them by finally addressing perfectionism head-on. That in itself is a slow process, but every day it gets better. How? By understanding that perfection doesn't exist. There is another saying about perfectionism, that it's the enemy of the good. So I stand to reason that if that is the case, the first step of self-love is understanding you are not perfect.

I also still work on my self-esteem, and I will forever, just like everyone else. I even get those days when I feel so hideous and unworthy, and all I want to do is stay in bed in my fat pants, eat, cry, and see no one. And it's okay to have those days. I want you to know we all struggle with that. But it is a struggle I am proud to take on every day. I have decided that I am worthy, I am enough, and I am great as I am. I have spent my whole life beating myself up for, ultimately, no reason. How do we change that? With a decision to stop. I have learned to love my insecurities and flaws—they are what make me *me*. They are humbling. They drive me to improve myself, to be the best version of myself I can possibly be.

When I came back to New York, in recovery, I made it my mission to walk into as many rooms as I can and try to broaden the concept of beauty. Most of the time, it's disheartening, but the fact that people are letting me in the room is half the battle, and getting them to hear me out is a victory. While I am a tell-it-like-it-is type of person, for so much of my life, I did not speak up for myself. But now I decided to be proud of my voice and use it—maybe someone would listen. If not, it's still a noble purpose. Even today, after every shoot, I tell myself that if I don't ever work again as a model, at least I tried to make a difference. For every win you have, people don't see the number of losses you took to get to that win.

As you now know, I learned all this the hard way. But I have also become adept at ignoring all the judgment around us. The pressure to conform. When I tell people I have two degrees, they don't believe it. I've heard, "She is a model, so she must be stupid." When I told people I model, I heard that I don't look like a model—either I'm too fat, too short, too this, too that. When I fought, I heard that, as a woman, I was too "fragile" to fight. I decided to throw these perceptions out the window. Because if you are waiting for approval from someone, you'll always be doubting yourself, and you'll never get anywhere in life: Did you know that Steven Spielberg was rejected by the University of Southern California three times? That thirty publishers passed on Stephen King's Carrie before Doubleday picked it up? That Jay-Z was passed over by every record label, so he decided to become his own producer? They didn't give up when they were rejected; they just pushed through because they believed in themselves.

Find out who you are and who you want to be without conforming to your mom's or your dad's or your best friends' expectations. Life is not about finding yourself—it's a journey based on decisions, making yourself into who you want to become. You'll never be able to forge a path for yourself by trying to fit in.

Along the way, remind yourself of how far you've come. Track your progress. It's not about reaching a final point. You won't wake up one day and be cured, recovered, or finished. Keep moving on your journey. And when you stumble, remind yourself not to stop. Get up and put one foot in front of the other.

I encourage women to access their strength. I never thought I would be able to do a push-up or even run a mile. We are so strong, and it's such a shame for us not to see what we are capable of, especially because we are so busy trying to be skinny or whatever else the media is trying to tell us we need to be. I want to help other women access their inner badass so they can become the best version of themselves. There is no better feeling than being a strong and confident woman, at any size. And funnily enough, I realize now that the reason I was so obsessed with the Ninja Turtles all those years ago is that they taught me that strength and bravery sometimes come from the most unlikely of places, like a gang of turtles who save the world, or a model who had to travel to a gym in Thailand to finally understand what beauty actually is.

With this book, I hope I've shown that if I can do it, anyone can.

Mr. Firstt and me. Koh Samui, Thailand, 2020.

Mr. Firstt and me, training. Koh Samui, Thailand, 2020.

Mr. Firstt and me, training. Koh Samui, Thailand, 2020.

Mr. Firstt and me. Koh Samui,
Thailand, 2020.

EPILOGUE

—

DEAR EIGHTEEN-YEAR-OLD-MIA,

I'm writing to give you some advice. I know you're stubborn, and you probably don't want it, but hopefully, I can provide you with insight that will take some pressure off you. Because right now, although everything looks "perfect" from the outside, I know you're struggling. Really struggling.

You're a successful international model, and you've accomplished more at your young age than you ever thought you would. Well done. You're signed with top global agencies and working with some of the most exceptionally creative fashion minds in the world. You're in demand, independent, and self-sufficient. Life seems good; you "have it all."

But I know you're still not happy. In fact, you're more miserable now than you've ever been, and it's only going to get worse.

What I know that no one else knows is that your insecurities are at an all-time high. You hate yourself. You wake up every morning, look in the mirror, and detest what you see. You fall asleep every night thinking about what you can do to improve your imperfections. You don't eat, and no, that square of chocolate or a bite of a protein bar here and there doesn't count. And those laxatives you take because you can't live with the guilt when you do eat will wreak havoc on your body.

You don't want to be like this. You've tried eating—remember, you love food!—but when you eat you bloat because your body can't digest anymore. You've been living like this for years, since you were thirteen. You even passed out on the tram on the way to that photo shoot the other day—we both know that this happens regularly. Hiding this is consuming you. You thought if you could lose weight, then you'd be happy and could resume life as normal, looking skinny—looking like what a woman "should look like"—but now you're trapped in a vicious cycle. The frustrations of this endless nightmare have led you to suicidal thoughts—you've never admitted this to anyone. If you have to live with this burdening guilt every time you eat for the rest of your life, you would rather tap out. But let me tell you that there is a way out of this. Recovery is not only possible, but it's coming your way.

You're a smart young woman who's debating whether to go to university. You told your parents you would go, but I know you don't want to lose momentum with your career. GO! Develop your mind. When was the last time you even picked up a book? Your appearance will fade, but learning and experience expand your universe. Develop your intelligence, work toward your potential. Develop yourself as a person—your values, experiences, integrity, what you contribute to the world. Become the woman that you always dreamed of being as a little girl, because right now, this isn't her.

As long as you can remember, you have been told how you should look, from growing up with a mother who was always conscious of her looks, to living in a culture where being thin was the only way to be beautiful, to working in an industry where you have to conform to an unrealistic size. The pressure not only has been felt but has now consumed your mind and body. You feel like there is a mold you need to fit into to be deemed as "beautiful," and if you are "beautiful," you will be happy. It is time for you to stop believing this crap, as well as all the societal pressures you have ever felt.

Let me tell you now: Stop trying to fit in. Be secure with yourself. Confidence comes from nowhere else but inside you. You will get better only when you want to get better; no one can force you to start recovering, not even thirtysomething me. But the first step is to respect yourself. Begin that process of getting to know yourself and learning to love yourself. When that happens, everything will fall into place.

All my love,
Mia Kang

ACKNOWLEDGMENTS

—

Thank you to my parents for raising me and shaping me to be the person that I am. Thank you, Daddy, for my life; I'm grateful for everything you've done for me.

Thank you to my siblings, Malcolm, Alistair, Alex, Anouk, and Gaby, for always protecting me.

My friends: thank you for loving me; I don't deserve you.

Thank you to Tania Quintanilla, Clarissa Luna, and Dana Cash—the powerhouse women behind the cover image of this book.

Thank you to the incredible team of intelligent women who helped create this book. My agent, Meg Thompson; my editor, Sam Weiner at Abrams; and my writer, Kathy Huck. It's not easy trying to capture a voice like mine, and you've all done so with astounding care. It's been a dream of mine to be an author; thank you for making that come true.

Thank you for picking up this book.

This is for our daughters and their daughters.